www.wadsworth.com

wadsworth.com is the World Wide Web site for Wadsworth and is your direct source to dozens of online resources.

At *wadsworth.com* you can find out about supplements, demonstration software, and student resources. You can also send email to many of our authors and preview new publications and exciting new technologies.

wadsworth.com
Changing the way the world learns®

The Wadsworth College Success Series

Clason and Beck, *On the Edge of Success* (2003). ISBN: 0-534-56973-0

Gordon and Minnick, *Foundations: A Reader for New College Students*, 2nd Ed. (2002). ISBN: 0-534-52431-1

Hallberg, Hallberg and Rochieris, *Making the Dean's List: A Workbook to Accompany the College Success Factors Index* (2004). ISBN: 0-534-24862-4

Holkeboer and Walker, *Right from the Start: Taking Charge of Your College Success*, 4th Ed. (2004). ISBN: 0-534-59967-2

Petrie and Denson, *A Student Athlete's Guide to College Success: Peak Performance in Class and in Life*, 2nd Ed. (2003). ISBN: 0-534-57000-3

Santrock and Halonen, *Your Guide to College Success: Strategies for Achieving Your Goals*, Media Edition, 3rd Ed. (2004). ISBN: 0-534-60804-3

Steltenpohl, Shipton and Villines, *Orientation to College: A Reader on Becoming an Educated Person*, 2nd Ed. (2004). ISBN: 0-534-59958-3

Van Blerkom, *Orientation to College Learning*, 4th Ed. (2004). ISBN: 0-534-60813-2

Wahlstrom and Williams, *Learning Success: Being Your Best at College & Life*, Media Edition, 3rd Ed. (2002). ISBN: 0-534-57314-2

✎ THE FIRST-YEAR EXPERIENCE™ SERIES

Gardner and Jewler, *Your College Experience: Strategies for Success*, Media Edition, 5th Ed. (2003). ISBN: 0-534-59382-8

Gardner and Jewler, *Your College Experience: Strategies for Success*, Concise Media Edition, 5th Ed. (2004). ISBN: 0-534-60759-4

Gardner and Jewler, *Your College Experience: Strategies for Success*, Expanded Reader, 5th Ed. (2003). ISBN: 0-534-59985-0

✎ STUDY SKILLS/CRITICAL THINKING

Longman and Atkinson, *CLASS: College Learning and Study Skills*, 6th Ed. (2002). ISBN: 0-534-56962-5

Longman and Atkinson, *SMART: Study Methods and Reading Techniques*, 2nd Ed. (1999). ISBN: 0-534-54981-0

Smith, Knudsvig, and Walter, *Critical Thinking: Building the Basics*, 2nd Ed. (2003). ISBN: 0-534-59976-1

Sotiriou, *Integrating College Study Skills: Reasoning in Reading, Listening, and Writing*, 6th Ed. (2002). ISBN: 0-534-57297-9

Van Blerkom, *College Study Skills: Becoming a Strategic Learner*, 4th Ed. (2003). ISBN: 0-534-57467-X

Watson, *Learning Skills for College and Life* (2001). ISBN: 0-534-56161-6

✎ STUDENT ASSESSMENT TOOL

Hallberg, *College Success Factors Index*, http://success.wadsworth.com

ORIENTATION TO COLLEGE

A Reader on Becoming an Educated Person

SECOND EDITION

Elizabeth Steltenpohl

Jane Shipton

Sharon Villines

Empire State College
State University of New York

THOMSON

™

WADSWORTH

Australia • Canada • Mexico • Singapore • Spain
United Kingdom • United States

THOMSON

—★—™

WADSWORTH

Editor-in-Chief: Marcus Boggs
Manager, College Success: Annie Mitchell
Assistant Editor: Kirsten Markson
Technology Project Manager: Barry Connolly
Advertising Project Manager: Stacey Purviance
Project Manager, Editorial Production:
    Catherine Morris
Print/Media Buyer: Karen Hunt

Permissions Editor: Elizabeth Zuber
Production Service: Forbes Mill Press
Text Designer: Robin Gold
Copy Editor: Robin Gold
Cover Designer: Lisa Langhoff
Cover Image: Dominic Rouse/Getty Images
Compositor: Forbes Mill Press
Text and Cover Printer: Webcom

Printed in Canada
1 2 3 4 5 6 7 07 06 05 04 03

For more information about our products,
contact us at:
Thomson Learning Academic Resource Center
1-800-423-0563

For permission to use material from this text,
contact us by:
Phone: 1-800-730-2214
Fax: 1-800-730-2215
Web: http://www.thomsonrights.com

Library of Congress Control Number: 2003101525

ISBN 0-534-59958-3

Wadsworth/Thomson Learning
10 Davis Drive
Belmont, CA 94002-3098
USA

Asia
Thomson Learning
5 Shenton Way #01-01
UIC Building
Singapore 068808

Australia/New Zealand
Nelson Thomson Learning
102 Dodds Street
Southbank, Victoria 3006
Australia

Canada
Nelson Thomson Learning
1120 Birchmount Road
Toronto, Ontario M1K 5G4
Canada

Europe/Middle East/Africa
Thomson Learning
High Holborn House
50/51 Bedford Row
London WC1R 4LR
United Kingdom

Latin America
Thomson Learning
Seneca, 53
Colonia Polanco
11560 Mexico D.F.
Mexico

Spain
Paraninfo
Calle/Magallanes, 25
28015 Madrid, Spain

Contents

Preface: To the Instructor

Orientation to College: A Reader on Becoming an Educated Person is designed to help college students understand how to engage with their college education and especially to appreciate what they can learn from study of the liberal arts. The readings present learning as a life-long, developmental process that requires introspection, reflection, dialogue, and a spirit of discovery. Some readings are classic selections; others represent the most recent research and thinking about learning and the challenges of the future workplace. Liberal arts studies are presented as fundamental to becoming informed, productive, and successful adults, workers, and citizens.

This selection of readings, commentaries, and activities evolved from the experiences of Elizabeth Steltenpohl and the late Jane Shipton during 15 years of teaching seminars for entering and returning college students at Empire State College, State University of New York. Although most of these students possessed adequate academic skills, many had enrolled in college only to get a degree and a job, or a better job. Their narrow focus on grades, credits, and "getting through" inhibited and circumscribed not only their ability to learn but ultimately defeated their purpose for attending college. Many were not only failing to learn what their future employers expected college graduates to know but making themselves unnecessarily miserable in the process.

The authors began searching for learning activities, especially readings, that would introduce these students to broader concepts of learning and knowledge. When they presented these to their students, they witnessed a major transformation. Most students became eager, purposeful learners who began to understand that learning is a developmental, participatory process; acquisition of knowledge is a mindful dialogue between the learner and the world; and success in their jobs would be dependent on this same process of analysis and understanding. They also began to understand that learning is, or can be, an intriguing, exciting adventure.

During this same period, I was working with a large number of arts students who were resisting doing any study involving books, particularly those related to history, languages, literature, and philosophy. They just wanted to "make art." My future painters, actors, and dancers alike had little awareness that making art would be a complex process that involved understanding and interacting with the world around them. Being an artist would require being a full member of their culture, with the ability to analyze and interpret and inspire. It would require an understanding of life as lived by generations past in order to comprehend the life they would soon be interpreting.

I was very relieved to find the collection of readings that my colleagues were using with their students. They helped my students understand the importance not only of liberal arts studies but also the learning process and what it could help them accomplish. I soon started hearing comments like "These readings should be required for all students" and "I'm saving this book for my son so he will enjoy school."

On the strength of my students' experience with the photocopied text, I encouraged the authors to seek a publisher and they succeeded. Wadsworth had begun their College Success series and understood the need for a reader of college-level materials that helped beginning students understand important concepts relating to learning and education.

The first edition was formally adopted as a text at a number of community colleges, private liberal arts colleges, and state universities. It was gratifying to see this work finally being shared widely.

This second, revised edition of *Orientation to College* was prepared in consultation with Elizabeth Steltenpohl. Unfortunately, Jane Shipton died in late 1998 and is greatly missed.

Many professors took the time to suggest some new or updated readings for this revision and to share their students' experiences with the text. These affirmed our belief in the worth of orientation to college courses based principally on academic content rather than study skills. On one campus, the proposal for a credit-bearing college orientation course was accepted because the professors of advanced-level courses were very impressed with the high academic quality of the readings. On another campus, the writing instructors asked for copies of the text because their beginning students were now writing much more interesting papers than in previous years. Professors also reported that in subsequent studies, students were choosing more challenging subjects for research papers because they had been intrigued by ideas they discovered in this text.

The text consists of short readings from the works of a broad range of scholars, educators, historians, psychologists, social theorists, and government and business leaders. The readings are arranged to lead students to an understanding of how people develop and change as persons and as learners in college, what being an educated person means, and what they will need in order to function in the dramatically changing workplace. In each chapter, introductions establish a context for the readings and summaries emphasize relationships among readings. Each reading is followed by activities and questions designed to develop the level of critical and reflective thinking required in college courses. Activities requiring use of the Internet are included at the end of each chapter along with questions requiring students to reflect on the similarities and differences between the views of various authors.

The readings also introduce students to college-level material, and some are more challenging than those often found in beginning college texts. This was done purposely to expose students to the range of difficulty they will be confronting in college. On completing the readings, students will have a greater sense of confidence that they can handle the challenges their college studies will present.

The chapters, designed as discrete units, can be used in whatever order is appropriate for a given group of students. Two activities span the text: a personal definition of an educated person and a statement of educational goals. Students will be asked to write these in the introduction and then to reflect and revise them at the end of each chapter. A journal of notes on the readings, activities, and questions is suggested as a learning tool that is not only helpful but is a time-honored academic exercise, one that explorers, scientists, and philosophers have been using for centuries. The concept and purposes of the academic journal are discussed in the Introduction in "How to Use This Book."

STRUCTURE OF THE TEXT

The introduction, On Becoming an Educated Person, presents a reading that explains why the question "What is an educated person?" is important, introduces the first questions and activities, and explains how to use the text, including the traditional function and importance of the academic journal.

- Chapter 1: The Purposes of College gives a brief explanation of the vocabulary and methods colleges use in structuring their programs and

certifying learning. Then the chapter focuses on what society expects
from colleges and their graduates, how the concept of the educated person has changed throughout history, and the unique function of colleges
and universities as communities of learning.

- Chapter 2: The Role of the Liberal Arts in a College Education explains
  the concept and history of the liberal arts, the nature of liberal inquiry,
  the place of liberal studies in a college education, and their importance
  in becoming employable.

- Chapter 3: Education and the Idea of Culture explains the concept of culture, the importance of cultural literacy, education as affirming one's cultural identity, the role of college in preserving cultures, and the importance
  of multicultural knowledge and understanding in a global society.

- Chapter 4: Education and Personal Development presents a college education as a foundation for personal growth, explores theories of psychologists
  and educators on how we grow and develop throughout life, and how this
  affects not only learning but happiness and personal satisfaction in life.

- Chapter 5: Thinking and Learning considers learning as a developmental process that requires engagement, reflection, and critical thinking,
  and further, that learning is vital in developing the brain and thus increasing one's ability to learn. Learning is presented as a natural, positive experience resulting in optimum functioning.

- Chapter 6: Learning How to Learn develops the idea that individuals
  learn differently, explores ways of organizing learning, describes the role
  of self-directed learning, and treats collaborative learning as fundamental to the learning team and to team functioning commonly expected in
  the new workplace.

- Chapter 7: Education and Work examines the nature of work in the
  twenty-first century, the new skills that will be required, the importance
  of lifelong learning, the liberal arts as essential to the kind of learning
  that will be expected, and the importance of self-knowledge in relating
  to the new workplace.

NEW IN THE SECOND EDITION

A number of changes have been made in this edition. While the themes of the text
remain the same: Developing as a Person, Developing as a Learner, Becoming an

Educated Person, and Becoming Employable, the previous arrangement of the chapters into four parts has been dropped with each chapter now being independent.

The chapters have been rearranged to move The Purposes of College to the beginning, followed by The Role of the Liberal Arts in a College Education and Education, and the Idea of Culture. These are followed by the chapters on development and learning: Education and Personal Development, Thinking and Learning, and Learning How to Learn. Education and Work remains the final chapter.

In each of the first six chapters a new reading has been added or substituted for a reading in the first edition of the text and three new readings have been substituted to update Chapter 7: Education and Work. Chapters have been standardized to approximately the same length with five to six readings in each plus an introduction and summary. Questions and Activities for Reflection have been limited to three or four questions per reading and most have been revised for clarity and to reflect new material.

The chapter summaries now include new activities: "Using the Internet," that requires use of InfoTrac® College Edition, testing sites, or Web searches; and "Summarizing Activities and Questions for Reflection" that require reflection on questions that refer to several readings in the chapter.

ACKNOWLEDGMENTS

First Edition

We want to acknowledge the educators and scholars who consented to the inclusion of their writings and the hundreds of students who participated in our college-entry seminars that led to the development of this book. We also want to acknowledge the contributions of colleagues within and outside Empire State College whose thinking helped us shape our ideas including Harriet N. Cabell, The University of Alabama, New College; John R. Kelbley, Ohio University, Zanesville; Saundra King, Chattanooga State Technical Community College; Barry McArdle, Brescia College; Jacquelyn H. Scott, Morehead State University; and Edna F. Wilson, La Salle University. We would further like to thank our editor, Angela Gantner Wrahtz, for her interest in the freshman-year experience that enabled us to share our approach and materials with others.

Elizabeth Steltenpohl
Jane Shipton
Sharon Villines

Second Edition

I want to express my continuing appreciation for the pioneering work of Elizabeth Steltenpohl and Jane Shipton in the area of the freshman-year experience. This book would not exist without them. I further want to thank those who contributed to the second edition: Alan Mandell, Director of the Mentoring Institute at Empire State College and my other colleagues there who contributed ideas, readings, and unending challenges; Shannah Albert, Price-WaterhouseCoopers Consulting, who helped shape many of the ideas relating to learning and work and gave me an understanding of the "work hard, play hard" culture of corporate life; and to Franklin "Spike" Mendelsohn and Isaac and Gretchen Hoff who shared hours of observations about personality differences, brain development, and related cognitive functions.

And to Annie Mitchell and Kirsten Markson of the College Success Series and Robin Gold of Forbes Mill Press for their wonderful work in producing this edition. It was thankfully a team effort.

I would also like to thank the reviewers for this edition whose comments greatly enriched the scope and reorganization of the readings: Kristine S. Bruss, Bethany Lutheran College; Colleen M. Courtney, Lynn University; Herbert C. Herbert, University of Louisiana, Lafayette; Jori Psencik, University of Texas, Dallas; Jamie J. Shepherd, Whittier College; Sarah Spreda, University of Texas, Dallas; Vicki Elaine Rhodes White, Emmanuel College; and John Douglas Winborn, Middle Tennessee State University

Many, many thanks to the students who made teaching worthwhile by learning to be curious and to enjoy becoming educated.

Sharon Villines

On Becoming an Educated Person

For many students, choosing to attend college is an act of faith based on the belief that college will provide whatever is needed to achieve success in life. If you are one of these students, you may have only a vague concept of what you will be expected to learn in college or expected to know as a college graduate. You probably have even less understanding of how to go about learning it. You are not alone.

In this introductory reading, Thomas Jones, as a professor at Metropolitan State University in Minnesota, explains how he was sitting at his own graduation ceremony listening to the commencement speaker when he was first asked to think about why he had gone to college or what he was supposed to have learned there.

As you read, picture yourself in a cap and gown sitting beside the future Professor Jones and think about how you can avoid the consequences that he faced regarding the "educated person question."

THE EDUCATED PERSON

Thomas B. Jones

My interest in the educated person question goes back a long way. Just how far back was confirmed the other day when I found a tattered, twenty-year-old file containing my diploma, my transcripts, and a list of graduation requirements. These documents took me back to a hot June day in 1964. The day I graduated from college. . . .

At 11 A.M., several thousand black-cloaked comrades and I gathered outside the football stadium for the graduation ceremony. Soon we trooped into the stadium and spread over row upon row of folding chairs parked between the 20- and 50-yard lines. Once seated, I started daydreaming, imagining myself quarterbacking a dazzling, length-of-the-field touchdown drive. Unfortunately, the droning of innumerable deans and dignitaries bogged down my football fantasy well short of the goal line.

Frustrated in my make-believe athletic glory, I tried to forget the sweaty heat and tried even harder to focus on the major commencement speaker. Only his final words caught my attention.

He spoke earnestly about the need for students to reflect on the question: "What is an educated person?" He said that answers to that question should be the preface, substance, and measure of an undergraduate education. For those of us planning to continue on in academic life as college faculty, the speaker emphasized that the educated person question should be at the center of our professional lives.

"What the hell is he babbling about," asked one of my friends, still suffering the after effects of the previous night's party. I laughed and said, "I have absolutely no idea."

But that wasn't quite true. I understood much of what the commencement speaker had said, and I took him seriously at that moment because I planned a career in college teaching.

I didn't, however, remember that the university had ever discussed the educated person question with me or any of my classmates. And it seemed odd that the last formal activity of undergraduate study would be the first mention of this consequential question. If, as the commencement speaker had so strongly suggested, the question had such importance for higher education, my classmates and I should have discussed it at some point before we graduated. But we never had.

Excerpt from "The Educated Person" in *The Educated Person: A Collection of Contemporary American Essays* edited by Thomas B. Jones (St. Paul, MN: Metropolitan State University). Revised edition, 1989, pp. 101–105. Reprinted with permission from Thomas B. Jones, Professor, Metropolitan State University.

We had completed our college education without discussing the educated person question, without questioning the rationale behind graduation requirements, without any process by which to plan out four years of undergraduate study, and without any standards we understood by which to judge our educational progress. We just drifted from one classroom to another, followed the required paths toward graduation, and never took responsibility for making our own academic decisions. Speaking for myself, only by chance did I acquire some of the essential perspectives I identify now, many years after the fact, as essential for becoming an educated person.

Of course, the transcript of my college education—a curious jumble of numbers, course abbreviations, and As, Bs, and Cs—gives the impression that I gained the depth and breadth of learning so honored by college presidents in their graduation speeches and fund-raising pitches. But I know better. That transcript merely charts my stumbling, unwitting progress toward graduation.

I know today that I didn't master a number of important subjects and skills during my undergraduate years. I certainly had but little exposure to interdisciplinary thinking and teaching. I didn't appreciate the values and abilities that survive the memory of specific course content and give college study its strongest hold on life. And finally, I couldn't explain to anyone with any measure of confidence and sophistication exactly why my college education gave me any special claim to being an educated person.

What if I had confronted the educated person question as an undergraduate student? Why would it have made a difference?

The process of posing the educated person question and searching for legitimate answers to it would have been invaluable for me as I started and as I progressed through college. Digging out the answers would have made it possible for me to plan my college study with some larger vision—even within the structured system of graduation requirements I faced. I could have understood better why certain subjects had to be included in my education. I could have looked for the understandings and skills in each learning experience that would serve me in study across the curriculum and in the contexts of life outside the college classroom. I could have tried a wider range of study with my elective choices rather than building a specialized major and minor. I could have seen more clearly the relationship between various disciplines and how they can strengthen and enliven each other. I could have judged the value of my overall college education as well as the academic reasoning that stood behind it. Most important, I could have known that becoming an educated person is part of a lifelong process of learning, study, reflection, experience, and action—not just four years of classes.

ACTIVITIES AND QUESTIONS FOR REFLECTION

The central purpose of this text is to consider the "educated person question." The readings and activities are designed to help you understand the various expectations of the educated person in our society and to develop your own personal expectations so you will be able to fully participate in your education and avoid drifting from one course to another as Jones did.

The following questions and activities will help you explore and apply insights gained from this reading and to reflect on the issues raised.

1. *Did you have difficulty imagining yourself sitting next to the young Professor Jones in a cap and gown? Why or why not?*

2. *Select a few people you admire and consider to be educated. Ask them how they would describe an educated person. (You may do this in person, by email, or by telephone.)*

   After reviewing your interview responses and considering your own ideas about what being educated might mean to yourself and others, write several paragraphs describing your ideal of an educated person. You may use someone you know or have read about as a model.

3. *What would you need to learn to reach your ideal?*

ABOUT THIS BOOK AND THINKING
ABOUT HOW TO USE IT

Like many of the questions you will confront in college and in life, there is no one right answer to the question, "What is an educated person?" There are, however, *educated responses*. An educated, or informed, response is one based on the best knowledge available, and these responses are the kind you will be expected to make in college and as a college graduate. Your answer will be informed by what you have learned from the readings and how you applied them in thinking about your personal goals, those of the community in which you live, and the occupations you are considering. Not only will your answer be informed, but it will be *your* answer for yourself, and the quality or appropriateness of your answer will be yours to judge.

The comments at the beginning of each chapter and each reading place the readings in context and explain why they are considered important. The chapter summaries emphasize and synthesize the major points in the readings and present further activities that allow you to contrast and compare the ideas in the readings.

You will frequently encounter new words or familiar words used in new ways. We have chosen not to include a glossary in the text because it is important as a college student that you develop the habit of keeping a dictionary nearby when you study. A good dictionary will provide much greater understanding of new words or new meanings than would be possible to include in the text. Using a dictionary regularly will not only enable you to understand more completely what you are reading but will increase your vocabulary, allowing you to express yourself more clearly and specifically.

Throughout the text, you will be exploring new ideas. You will need to reflect on these ideas and relate them to your own understanding and experience so you can fully incorporate them into your fund of knowledge. If you allow time to read each reading twice, you will achieve fuller understanding. Writing down your thoughts about the readings will further help you remember them.

The Readings

The readings in *Orientation to College* are divided into chapters that will introduce you to various dimensions of college, the learning process, ways of enriching your college experience, and the skills needed to participate in to-day's rapidly changing world. They are representative of the reading and application of ideas that you will be expected to master in college. Some are more difficult than others. The more difficult readings are included not to discourage you but to introduce you to the full range of reading difficulty that you will encounter in college. When you complete this text you will have greater confidence in your ability to handle college studies and know the areas in which you will need more preparation.

Activities and Questions for Reflection

The activities and questions at the end of each reading, as appeared at the end of the Jones reading, are designed to encourage you to reflect on your own experience and ideas as well as on those of others. These questions are intended to help you understand that college is more than a place where you become certified to work in certain jobs; it is a place where you can broaden your perspectives, develop both personally and intellectually, and prepare yourself to achieve your full potential. A well-educated person not only has knowledge but knows how to use that knowledge to make significant contributions in society.

The Activities and Questions for Reflection are also intended to help you think critically, to connect new ideas with what you already know, and to discover any deeper meaning they may have for you. As you progress through this study, your own ideas about yourself and your education will become clearer and will also change. Some activities are specifically designed to help you compare earlier responses with later ones.

Using the Internet

The most invigorating innovation in the field of education in many years is the development of the Internet. The ability to search for information anywhere in the world is an unprecedented level of access. Extensive information on every conceivable subject is now available to anyone who has access to a computer connected to the Internet. An important part of your education will be developing the skills to use these resources.

At the end of each chapter, we have suggested activities to help introduce you to the Internet. These exercises are far from exhaustive. Virtually every reading includes a topic, a person, or a set of facts that you could learn more about by doing online research. Internet resources are not only extensive; many are current to the day or the hour. These are the same sources professional scholars and researchers are using to collect and report their findings.

The range of information available to you and the guides to finding it are so extensive it will take you some time to learn to use them, but this will be a vital part of your education and preparation for work.

Keeping an Academic Journal

> Reading maketh a full person, conference a ready person, writing an exact person.
>
> *Francis Bacon*

Often we think we know what we mean but just can't explain it. This is generally not true. We "sort of" know what we mean. Writing forces us to be clear and specific, and to think through our feelings or impressions about a subject. Difficulties expressing ourselves are often not writing problems but evidence of our unformed ideas and incomplete thinking. The academic journal is the traditional place to record and work through these often potent but undeveloped thoughts. This Introduction has been rewritten at least 20 times, and the ideas within it much more than that.

Journals have been kept by many of our most important leaders in all areas of thought. They are considered essential in many professional fields, and historically journal-keeping has been a standard practice for explorers, naturalists, anthropologists, inventors, chemists, medical researchers, and of course, writers. Journals take many forms, but generally they serve two basic functions:

1. As a place to save thoughts and ideas that are still unformed until there is time to develop them
2. As a place to record notes, thoughts, and activities in chronological order so they can be reviewed, be reflected upon, and serve as a resource for later work or studies

It is not uncommon—in fact, it is probably the norm—that understanding develops over time and what we think today, we won't understand until tomorrow. If we lose those thoughts, we have nothing to build on. A journal is both a convenient secure place to store ideas and a foundation for future thinking.

The Importance of Goal Setting

Why are you attending college? What do you hope to achieve? How can your college help you achieve your goals? With clear answers to these questions, your college experience will be much more satisfying and productive. Rather than aimlessly trying to do your best, as Professor Jones reported was his experience in "The Educated Person," you can focus your efforts on achieving your goals and understanding where your studies fit into your overall plan.

Success depends on understanding what success means for you. Winning a baseball championship will have little meaning if what you really wanted was to understand the feeding patterns of sharks. Just doing well with what is presented to you may not be the best way to get where you want to go.

How do your life goals relate to your goals for your college education? Unless you know where you want to go, you won't know what you need to help you get there. Defining your goals allows you to be clearer about what you need from college. Knowing what you need maximizes your ability to achieve your goals.

This text is designed to help you examine, re-examine, and define your goals as you begin your college education. The goals of the text are to

1. Expand your understanding of the many concepts and purposes of a college education

2. Increase your appreciation of the richness of your own experience as you draw on it to enhance your development as a learner

3. Heighten your awareness of becoming an adult and the ways in which education can contribute to your personal development

4. Explore the potential of your role in the world of work and the future of the culture in which you choose to live

Considering your education in this broad context will help you expand your perspectives and maximize the opportunities provided by attending college and completing a degree.

Throughout the text, at the end of each chapter you will be asked to review your goals for college. For the purposes of the text we will refer to these goals as statements of

1. Your goals for college

2. Your definition of an educated person

You may add other statements to these, and your instructor may have additional suggestions. The purpose of these statements is to focus your studies around developing a clearer understanding of what you hope to accomplish in college and in life.

As you read, ideas and information will be presented that are intended to broaden your thinking about what a college education can mean for you. You will probably want to revise these statements many times. A journal is the best place to record them so you can review and revise your thinking as appropriate for you.

Before you begin reading, take time to write the first draft of your goals statements.

~~ CHAPTER 1

The Purposes of College

INTRODUCTION: WHAT IS *COLLEGE?*

We often refer to college as if all colleges and college experiences were the same. We say "going to college" as if it were the same as spending a year in Paris or buying season tickets to the symphony. Going to college is not only a much more demanding experience, but there are many different kinds of colleges and college studies. This variety, and the complexity in the terms used to describe them, exists because the colleges and their programs are designed for different purposes and have different expectations of their students. Society also expects many services from educational institutions that you have probably not considered at all.

The following introduction will explain some of the technical terms that relate to "going to college" and provide an overview of college degree programs and their requirements. This will create a context for the readings in this chapter that explore the purposes of college more deeply and help you understand your college better. Specific information about the programs your college offers and the terms it uses to measure requirements are in your college catalog.

Colleges, Universities, and Professional Schools

The term *college* is used to refer to a variety of institutions that provide *higher education,* studies beyond secondary, preparatory, or high school. These institutions include community colleges, four-year colleges, professional schools, and universities.

Historically, a college was a residential institution on a *campus,* a cluster of buildings enclosing a *green,* or a yard. It offered four years of study leading to a *baccalaureate* or bachelor's degree. Four-year colleges were and often still are *liberal arts* colleges that offer a traditional program of history, philosophy, languages, mathematics, and sciences. Some liberal arts colleges offer more specialized five-year degrees in professional areas such as music and engineering. Based on the English boarding school model, these colleges traditionally served only full-time students who were required to live on campus. Admission was restricted to unmarried students 18 to 22 years of age and all parts of college life were subject to school regulations.

Some four-year colleges still follow this model, but most schools now have programs for students who attend part time or who do not live on campus. Today, less than a quarter of all students attending college are in the traditional 18- to 22-year-old age group, and a good many more kinds of institutions offer a much wider range of degrees and certifications.

The fastest growing colleges today are community colleges. They offer two-year degree programs in the liberal arts in preparation for transferring to a four-year college, certificate programs and two-year degrees for specific licensed occupations, such as police officers, and a wide range of studies in continuing education programs that are not part of degree or certification programs. Increasingly, community colleges are offering four-year programs in highly skilled technical areas.

Professional schools, often called institutes of technology, prepare students for work in specific industries such as the arts, business, textiles, engineering, or film and television. They offer highly skilled, concentrated educations. Not all offer degrees, but if they do, they will include a base of liberal arts studies, often taken at a college nearby. Professional schools may be residential or nonresidential or a combination.

Universities are large institutions that include liberal arts colleges, professional schools, and research facilities like laboratories, hospitals, and agricultural centers. Universities are based on the German model of higher education that is more concerned with the intellectual life of scholars and research than is the English model, which focuses on creating an ideal community to shape the lives of students. Within the university, a school of arts and humanities will typically award liberal arts degrees like a traditional four-year college, and other schools will emphasize advanced or graduate degrees for students who have completed their four-year degrees. Each school within a university may have its own admissions program and function very much like an independent institution.

Degrees, Accreditation, and Professional Standards

A *degree* is a certificate of achievement indicating completion of a program of studies. Requirements or standards for degrees are established by state education departments, by associations of colleges, and by professional associations. Colleges whose programs meet minimum standards in each of the fields in which they offer programs, certifications, or degrees are granted *accreditation*. Students who have taken courses at accredited schools are guaranteed that other accredited schools will accept their coursework and degrees. These studies are considered *transferable*.

In addition to general degree requirements, sometimes professional requirements must be met before you can enter some fields of work. Accounting, public school teaching, medicine, and psychology are examples of fields in which certain studies are required before college graduates can be admitted to accredited graduate programs or licensed for professional practice.

The traditional college degree is the Bachelor of Arts (BA) degree that requires a broad preparation in history, theory, and languages. A newer degree that is quite common is the Bachelor of Science (BS) degree that may include a slightly larger proportion of technical, applied, or laboratory studies. The words *arts* and s*ciences* as used in these degree designations do not refer to the fine arts or to the sciences specifically. One may have a Bachelor of Arts degree in biology or a Bachelor of Science degree in arts education, for example.

There are also many specialized degrees, much more contemporary, that indicate professional preparation including the Bachelor of Music (BMus), Bachelor of Architecture (BArch), Bachelor of Fine Arts (BFA), and the Bachelor of Professional Studies (BPS). Rather than creating more professional degree designations, many schools now award the Bachelor of Professional Studies in a wide variety of *applied* or professional studies.

The parallel two-year degrees, which may or may not be preparation for four-year degrees, include the Associate of Arts (AA), the Associate of Science (AS), and the Associate of Applied Science (AAS) degrees.

Most degrees, particularly four-year degrees, will have minimum requirements for *general learning* that specify a number of studies in a broad range of subjects and for a *major* or a concentration of focused studies. General learning requirements are often mistakenly confused with *liberal studies* or *liberal arts studies*. General learning may include liberal studies, but what distinguishes it is the breadth of subjects studied, rather than the kind of studies. The major, on the other hand, is a series of studies designed to provide depth of study and a level of mastery in a subject area or a topic. The major normally consists of a structured program of increasingly focused studies that lead to and require more challenging study.

Advanced Degrees and Post Graduate Study

Some fields require study beyond the four-year degree. The Master of Arts (MA) and the Master of Science (MS) degrees require one or two years of study beyond a bachelor's degree. There are also professional degrees that require three years of study, for example, the Master of Fine Arts (MFA) degree, which is awarded in all areas of the arts. Master's degrees may be preparation for a specific licensed occupation like teaching, or a preparatory program for admission to a Doctor of Philosophy degree program.

The Doctor of Philosophy (PhD) degree is the traditional degree expected of university professors in the humanities and sciences including Literature, History, Philosophy, Psychology, Chemistry, Biology, Physics, and Mathematics. The PhD normally requires a year of course work beyond the Master's degree, extensive written and oral exams, and a scholarly research work. Although a doctorate can technically be completed in three years, five years is closer to the norm.

Credits, Hours, Units, and Study Requirements

Over time, a terminology has developed that colleges use to record the studies students are required to complete before receiving a degree. These studies are measured in *credits, hours,* or *units* over periods of time, usually months, measured in *semesters, trimesters,* or *quarters* depending on the college's yearly calendar. The requirements for degrees are stated in terms of a number of *credits,* or courses in particular subjects. Thus, you might be required to complete 3 hours of psychology each semester of your first year, or 1 unit during each of three quarters. These systems of measurement were developed as course offerings became more complex, and they vary from institution to institution. There are, however, some accepted standards for each system as well as means of translating them.

Along with credit hours and units, a numbering system is often used. One- and two-hundred level course numbers usually indicate introductory or lower division courses to be completed in the first two years of college and three-hundred level and above indicate upper-division or advanced level courses.

For each hour in a lecture class, a college student is usually expected to spend two to three hours reading and studying. For technical or laboratory courses like chemistry or dance that require use of equipment available only in the classroom, the standard is reversed. Not all colleges, courses, or professors follow the same standards, but the general trend is that in college you should expect to spend twice to three times as many hours in independent study as in class. For many students, this requires a big adjustment.

The Meaning of a College Education

The readings in this chapter address the central questions about the meaning of a college education—not only what your college education could mean to you but also what you as a college graduate will mean to your community. Societies need educated people, and this chapter will discuss some of those needs as well as the possibilities a college education can offer to you.

Many students, when asked about their purposes or goals for attending college, will say their families expect them to attend, or they want a college degree, or they want to get a good job—or all three. To plan your college program well, it is important to be more specific about your purposes. Having clear purposes provides a strong motivation and is a good predictor of success.

The readings in this chapter are intended to help you reflect on your own purposes or goals for attending college and to begin examining your assumptions about what becoming educated may require of you.

↤

IN THIS FIRST READING IN THIS CHAPTER, Ernest Boyer, as president of a research institution, the Carnegie Foundation for the Advancement of Teaching, discusses the history and changing expectations of the American college. Boyer was one of the most influential voices in the calls for educational reform in the 1980s and continues after his death to have a major impact on education policies around the world. This reading is from a Carnegie Foundation study, College: The Undergraduate Experience in America, *that examined colleges and their goals. Boyer discusses two goals that he and the other authors of the report on the study believed are essential.*

AS YOU READ, note how the goals of American colleges have changed and look for the two goals Boyer thinks are essential today.

↤

TWO ESSENTIAL GOALS

Ernest L. Boyer

An effective college has a clear and vital mission. Administrators, faculty, and students share a vision of what the institution is seeking to accomplish. The goals at such an institution flow from the needs of society and also from the needs of the persons seeking education.

But can the modern college, with all its separations and divisions, be guided by a common vision? And can the search for goals be something more than a diversion?

America's first colleges were guided by a vision of coherence. The goal was to train not only the clergy, but a new civic leadership as well. These struggling institutions sought "to develop a sense of unity where, in a society created from many of the nations of Europe, there might otherwise be aimlessness and uncontrolled diversity" [Frederick Rudolph stated in his groundbreaking study, *The American College and University*].

The confidence of professors and their students in this era "owed much to their membership in an established middle class, a commitment to European learning, and a Christian conception of character and culture." Within that framework, bitter disputes sometimes did rage, but from today's perspective the colonial college seems stiflingly monolithic.

The first students at tiny Harvard College advanced in lockstep fashion, studied a common curriculum, one subject a day, from 8:00 A.M. until 5:00 P.M., Monday through Friday, and a half day on Saturday. In the first year, there was logic, Greek and Hebrew, rhetoric, divinity catechetical, history, and the nature of plants. The second year included ethics and politics, Aramaic, and further studies in rhetoric and divinity catechetical. The final year of college was capped by arithmetic, astronomy, Syriac, more Greek, rhetoric, and, of course, divinity catechetical.

This academic core was considered absolute and immutable, to be accepted, not criticized or questioned. The goal was to discipline the mind and, through such training, graduates were to move comfortably into prestigious professions—the clergy, business, medicine, law, and civic leadership.

Our present academic world would be unrecognizable to the men who founded Harvard College in 1636. The fixed curriculum of the colonial era is as much an anachronism today as the stocks in the village square. Separations and divisions, not unity, mark the undergraduate program. Narrow departmentalization divides the campus. So distinctive are the different disciplines in method and content, the argument goes, that there is no way to connect them in the minds of students. Knowledge is so vast and specialization so persistent that shared goals cannot be defined.

There is, we believe, a way out of our dilemma. While preparing this report we repeatedly were reminded that two powerful traditions—*individuality and community*—

have been at the heart of the undergraduate experiences. These two priorities have defined throughout the years the boundaries of the collegiate debate about purposes and goals and within these traditions there is, perhaps, sufficient common ground on which a vital academic program can be built.

The focus on individuality, on the personal benefits and the utility of education, has a rich tradition in American higher education. Throughout the years, students have come to college to pursue their own goals, to follow their own aptitudes; to become productive, self-reliant human beings; and, with new knowledge, to continue learning after college days are over. Serving individual interests has been a top priority in higher education.

But amidst diversity, the claims of community must be vigorously affirmed. By community we mean an undergraduate experience that helps students go beyond their own private interests, learn about the world around them, develop a sense of civic and social responsibility, and discover how they, as individuals, can contribute to the larger society of which they are a part.

Robert Bellah, [American sociologist and] co-author of *Habits of the Heart,* observes that "since World War II, the traditions of atomistic individualism have grown stronger, while the traditions of the individual in society have grown weaker. The sense of cohesive community is lost." In an era when an emphasis on narrow vocationalism dominates many campuses, the challenge is to help students relate what they have learned to concerns beyond themselves.

Individuals should become empowered to live productive, independent lives. They also should be helped to go beyond private interests and place their own lives in larger context. When the observant Frenchman [and author of *Democracy in America*] Alexis de Tocqueville visited the United States in the 1830s, he warned that "as individualism grows, people forget their ancestors and form the habit of thinking of themselves in isolation and imagine their whole destiny is in their hands." To counter this cultural disintegration, Tocqueville argued, "Citizens must turn from the private inlets and occasionally take a look at something other than themselves."

We suggest, then, that within the traditions of individuality and community, educational and social purposes for the undergraduate experience can be defined. The individual preferences of each student must be served. But beyond diversity, the college has an obligation to give students a sense of passage toward a more coherent view of knowledge and a more integrated life.

Individualism is necessary for a free and creative society, and the historic strength of our democracy lies in its commitment to personal improvement and fulfillment. We need individualism but, at the same time, we must be mindful of the consequences of selfishness. It is appropriate, therefore, for educational institutions that are preparing students to be citizens in a participatory democracy to understand the dilemmas and paradoxes of individualistic culture.

Just as we search culturally to maintain the necessary balance between private and public obligations, in education we seek the same end. The college, at its best, recognizes that, although we live alone, we also are deeply dependent on each other. Through an effective college education, students should become personally empowered and also committed to the common good.

ACTIVITIES AND QUESTIONS FOR REFLECTION

1. *What are the goals of your college? These may be stated in the college catalog as a mission statement or statement of purpose. What do these goals mean for your education? Do they support or align with your personal goals?*

2. *You would probably agree with Boyer's view that one important goal for a college education is the opportunity for students to pursue their own educational interests, but Boyer proposes a second goal for undergraduate education, "the common good." Do you agree? Why?*

3. *Boyer cites a need for colleges to provide students with "a more coherent view of knowledge and a more integrated life." Do you consider this to be an important goal for your college education? Why or why not?*

THE BACCALAUREATE DEGREE, the traditional or historical name for the bachelor's degree, originally consisted of a set curriculum of liberal arts studies that included history, religion, and ancient languages. Today, specific subject requirements vary widely from college to college, and the requirement to study ancient languages is not at all common.

In the following reading, author Howard Bowen, as professor of economics and higher education at Claremont Graduate Center, University of California, described what he viewed as the studies that would lead a student to become a well-educated person. Bowen uses the terms personal *education and* practical *education to identify the two major parts of his proposed program.*

AS YOU READ, look for the differences between a personal education and a practical education and for the significance of each in a bachelor's degree program.

THE BACCALAUREATE DEGREE: WHAT DOES IT MEAN? WHAT SHOULD IT MEAN?

Howard R. Bowen

The baccalaureate degree signifies many things. It usually refers to four academic years of time served or 120 semester credits earned. For some students, it means a broad liberal education without any training for a specific vocation; for others, specialized vocational training with minimal liberal learning. For some students, it means admission at about age 18, immediately after high school graduation; for others it means admission before completion of high school work or many years beyond the age of 18. For some, it means almost exclusive attention to required studies; for others, unrestricted electives.

For some it means full-time studies combined with residence on a campus and participation in a rich extracurricular and social life; for others, part-time study with residence

Excerpt from *American Association for Higher Education Bulletin,* Vol. 34, No. 3, November 1981, pp. 11–15. Reprinted by permission.

off campus, and no extracurricular participation. For some it represents the tutelage of renowned professors and access to richly appointed libraries, laboratories, and museums and with commodious recreational and social facilities; for others it represents staff and facilities reeking with poverty.

Despite the wide range of requirements and conditions under which baccalaureate degrees are earned, there is a certain modal concept of that degree. The concept is deeply embedded in the traditions of American higher education. In general, the degree is conceived as representing completion of a four-year program following upon a high school "preparatory" program. It involves some breadth of learning among the traditional academic subjects including the sciences, social studies, and humanities, and some modest specialization in a single field or areas. The specialization may be in an academic field having no career potential other than teaching the same subject, or it may be in fields such as nursing, engineering, business, or an allied health profession. Even those vocational fields that demand most of the students' time, engineering being the prime example, make obeisance to breadth of learning by requiring students to take a few courses in fields such as English and economics. The course requirements and the guidance afforded students, however, usually steer them toward a diversified program intended to help them become well-educated and cultivated human beings.

The concept of the baccalaureate degree includes not only [the students'] learning of certain subjects, but also their broad emotional and moral development and their prac-

tical competence as citizens and as members of families and organizations. Much emphasis is placed on sound values, aesthetic sensibility, religious interest, human understanding, physical development, and fruitful leisure. It is expected that these characteristics will be nurtured partly through the curriculum and partly through extracurricular facilities, programs, and experiences.

The modal concept of the baccalaureate degree cannot be defined in terms of a list of courses taken, a major field selected, the amount of time served, the physical facilities available, or the residential arrangement. In the end, it must be defined in terms of characteristics imparted to students, that is to say, by the change in them that occurs from entrance upon a course of study and related experiences and completion of that course of study. The course of study and related experiences need not involve attendance at high school or college. They may be derived from the educational activities of churches, businesses, the armed services, labor unions, libraries, the mass media, etc., or may be achieved through experiential learning and independent study. The object is the well-educated person, not a particular educational regimen.

These ideas bring us to two of the most difficult questions in educational theory and practice: What are the characteristics of a well-educated person? How can one tell whether a particular person or group of people is well educated?

Characteristics of the Well-Educated Person

I would define a well-educated person as one who had achieved a balanced combination of personal and practical learning. This level of education could be achieved through study and other experiences in the traditional educational system of the United States including the equivalent of the two final years of high school and four years of college. I do not imply, however, that going to school and college would be the only means of achieving it. The level of learning I am suggesting would qualify for a baccalaureate degree regardless of the process by which it was attained.

The education to achieve this learning would be of two types: personal education by which I mean broad development and fulfillment of the whole person, and practical education by which I mean training for work, family life, politics, consumer choices, health, leisure activities, and other practical affairs. The words *personal* and *practical* are akin to but not the same as *liberal* and *vocational*. I have deliberately avoided the latter two words because they are hackneyed, ambiguous, and charged with emotion.

The distinction between personal and practical education is not clean-cut. The overlap is great. Personal education, though primarily designed to enhance each individual as a person, can have important consequences for work and other practical affairs. Practical education, though primarily designed to enhance specific skills of use in work and other practical affairs, may be influential in the development of the individual personality. Yet the distinction is worth making because of the tendency of the two types of education to get out of balance.

In recent times, for example, practical education, especially that related to future careers, has tended to overwhelm personal

education. I do not suggest, however, that practical education is in some sense illegitimate or unnecessary. People understandably want to, and should, prepare themselves, in one way or another, for work and other practical affairs. Each person should find a vocation (in the sense of "calling") through which he or she would be able to contribute to society something of value. The ideal is a reasonable balance between personal and practical education such that the general development of the person is not unduly sacrificed to self-centered pecuniary ends.

Much of practical education is derived from experiences throughout life, and it should not overwhelm personal education during the school years. In achieving the ideal balance, it is necessary to consider the whole of education—from kindergarten through graduate school and beyond, including not only school and college but other educational media as well. Some stages or places of education may be more suited to practical education and some more congenial to personal education. It is a balance over a lifetime, not necessarily within each semester of a school or college career, that should be sought.

With these preliminary remarks, let me describe an education that might produce "well-educated people"—of whom I hope there might someday be a great many. Ideally, such an education would be defined in terms of educational achievements or outcomes, rather than specific subjects or operations performed. However, provisionally, one can be more specific by casting the definition in terms of subjects, though not necessarily courses. These subjects would constitute a six-year program, two years in high school and four years in college, but building upon a suitable elementary education.

I. Personal education

  A. The common core

    1. Language skills including reading, writing, speaking, and, in an era of electronic communication, listening —all in English.

    2. Logic, mathematics, and computer science.

    3. History of western civilization with special emphasis on the development of democratic institutions.

    4. Philosophy.

    5. Religious studies.

    6. National and world geography with special reference to peoples, cultures, economics, ecology, and relationships. Perhaps cosmology could be fitted in here.

    7. Foreign languages: not required but with incentives or encouragement such that a substantial minority of persons would elect to study them *in some depth* so that the nation could have contact with many foreign cultures.

    8. Educational opportunities: training and guidance related to opportunities and techniques for lifelong educational use of formal adult education, radio, TV, books, magazines, newspapers, libraries, churches, museums, musical organizations, armed forces, workplaces, unions, clubs, experiential learning, and independent study. ("Education is the acquisition of the art of the utilization of knowledge."—A. N. Whitehead.)

    9. Career opportunities: the concept of vocation, the world of work, and choice of vocation.

  B. Required fields within each of which rather limited choices of specific courses would be permitted. In each field, emphasis would be on fundamental principles, methods, and great issues.

    1. Natural sciences

    2. The humanities

    3. The arts

    4. Social studies

II. Practical education

  A. Meeting the requirement of a major field of study in the sciences and arts which might provide the basis for a vocation or for graduate or professional study leading eventually to a vocation, or preparing for a vocation through undergraduate study, apprenticeship, on-the-job experience and training, etc.

  B. Preparing for other practical affairs such as interpersonal relations, management of personal business, child development, health, consumer choice, and use of leisure.

In general, the requirements for the portion of the program related to *personal* education would be at a level of rigor such that it could be completed by an average student in four years of full-time study—two years in high school and two years in college. And the portion relating to practical education could be completed in two years of full-time study in college. However, I am not necessarily implying that all personal education would be completed before any practical education was begun. Practical and personal education might for many students be carried on simultaneously. Moreover, some of each might be worked into the extracurricular program.

Traditionally, it has been expected that the formal curriculum would be enhanced and reinforced by an environment rich in discussion, interpersonal relationships, cultural amenities, and democratic values. Some of the education would occur by partaking of a suitable environment as well as by attending relatively small institutions; it was easy—though not cheap—to create the appropriate educational environment.

But in a day of part-time commuters and huge institutions, it is not so easy to create environments to complement the curriculum. One of the most urgent needs of contemporary higher education is to find ways of creating complementary environments, or to make use of suitable environments that already exist in the wider community. I have the impression that many European countries have done better than we Americans in providing extracurricular opportunities for nonresident students.

In defining the kind of education I have in mind in terms of a list of subjects and a specified duration of study, I emphatically do not imply that all learning would take place in schools and colleges. Some of it (or for some students, all of it) might occur elsewhere. Moreover, I do not imply that the various parts of the program would occur in a particular sequence. Personal and practical education might occur at different ages for different individuals. The subjects might be combined or integrated in different ways. A wide range of instructional methods and facilities might be employed.

Experimentation with new curricula and modes of learning would be possible. Indeed, diversity would be desirable and essential to fit the education to students of varying backgrounds and interests and to avoid the risk of placing all the educational eggs in one basket. The listing of subjects is intended not to lay down a fixed regimen, but to be specific about the basic ingredients of the education that would be calculated to produce "well-educated people."

Defining education by means of a list of subjects has the merit of specificity but the drawback of not coming to grips with the underlying spirit and purpose of the education. A given set of subjects can be taught and learned with quite different outcomes depending on the basic qualities of mind, character, and temperament that are sought and on the spirit in which the education is conducted. These are reflected especially in the relative emphasis given to positive knowledge and to matters of values and in the kinds of persons serving as exemplars.

The Educational Ideal

The education I have described is in a sense traditional in spirit, if not in detail. This kind of education has been advocated by leading educational philosophers for centuries though the recommended means for achieving it have evolved steadily over the centuries. It is also quite close to some contemporary educational practice—for example, in those high schools that adhere to basic studies in their college preparatory programs and in those colleges and universities that offer genuine liberal education to undergraduates. In general, the institutions that are held in highest esteem are devoted to this kind of education.

However, as one compares the proposed education to that offered currently in the rank and file of American high schools and colleges, glaring differences appear. The proposed program would place relatively greater emphasis on values, would give relatively greater attention to the affective development of students, and would demand considerably greater rigor than does the education offered in most contemporary institutions.

ACTIVITIES AND QUESTIONS FOR REFLECTION

1. *What is the basis for the author's claim that the program he proposes leads to becoming a well-educated person?*

2. *Do your ideas for your degree, whether it is a two- or four-year degree, differ from those suggested by Bowen? How? Why?*

3. *How do Bowen's concepts of personal and practical education relate to Boyer's two essential goals in the previous reading?*

IN THIS READING, David Pierce, as president and CEO of the American Association of Community Colleges, identifies the needs of society that he believes higher education should meet and that community colleges have a unique role in providing. Pierce presents the argument that not only do workers need skills to get good jobs and businesses need highly skilled workers to maintain their productivity, but in a democracy, the government needs informed citizens.

AS YOU READ, try to understand what Pierce means by each of the six social needs he describes and how they might be important in sustaining a democracy.

WHAT DOES SOCIETY NEED FROM HIGHER EDUCATION?

David R. Pierce

Although higher education cannot solve all of society's problems, it can act as a resource. Higher education performs certain functions that cannot be done by any other segment of our society. It also supports other institutions, such as government, business, museums, etc. in vital ways.

Society requires the following from higher education:

To train a skilled, intelligent, creative, and responsible workforce;

To transmit, sustain, and extend the arts and humanities, the scientific tradition, the historical record, and other aspects of our living culture;

To support a citizenry that participates responsibly in community affairs including public governance and cares about our country and the world;

To provide a forum for integrating a multitude of peoples and synthesizing a wealth of ideologies;

To be a resource for people searching for ideas and information on solving social, economic, political, and scientific problems;

To give individuals access to lifelong learning in a changing world.

Excerpt from "What Does Society Need from Higher Education?" in a Wingspread Group on Higher Education. *An American Imperative: Higher Expectations in Higher Education* (Racine, WI: The Johnson Foundation, 1993), pp. 122–124. Reprinted by permission of the Johnson Foundation, Racine, WI.

Training a Skilled Workforce

As society increases in complexity, its need for skilled, autonomous workers increases. The pace of change—social, technological, political, and economic—is accelerating, and with it the demand for highly skilled workers. As society moves from a manufacturing and industrial economy to a service and information economy, new skills are required. The information explosion has created a demand for people who have not only knowledge, but the resources to gather, analyze, and synthesize information, and technological advances require workers with advanced training in science, mathematics, engineering, technology, and other fields. Our economy will continue to evolve, and higher education must evolve with it, preparing workers for jobs that may not even exist yet. Society, workers, and businesses must be prepared for the unexpected—because that is what will face us in the future. Without workers who have the skills to adapt to new situations, businesses will fail. In addition, workers who lack skills for the future face a cycle of unemployment and despair. Society owes its members more, and it looks to higher education to provide citizens with the tools they require to improve their life situation.

Sustaining a Living Culture

Society does not live by bread alone—it also needs poetry. Preparing people for work gives them the means to live; the traditions and values of our culture give them a reason to live. The visual and performing arts, literature, philosophical and religious traditions, history, and the social, physical, and life sciences all have merit aside from their "usefulness" in providing people with work and solving concrete problems. Knowledge, ideas, and creativity are ends in themselves; higher education must help strengthen them. There has been a storm of controversy surrounding this aspect of higher education; at times the battle over the curriculum threatens to turn into a bonfire of the humanities. Although higher education has often been criticized during these turbulent times, in a sense the controversy shows that colleges and universities are doing their job. Sustaining a living culture means preserving some old ideas while abandoning others, and selecting and incorporating some new ideas while rejecting others. This process cannot and should not be easy, tidy, or painless. But it is necessary.

Supporting Participatory Democracy

If we lived in an authoritarian nation ruled by a small group, society would have much less need for universal education. However, our society requires of citizens that they participate in their own governance. Under a democratic system, the government is only as good as the people who elect it—sometimes worse. If we want a government based upon intelligence, compassion, ethics, and excellence, we must inculcate those values in our future leaders and citizens. Citizens must be aware of the needs and problems of the community so that the political process will be energized to confront the problems. Community colleges can address these issues through programs to inform and educate the citizens, through activities that provide a forum and a voice for the diverse concerns and interests within a community, and through work with other institutions in the community to ensure the interests of all are represented and heard. As Thomas Jefferson said, "If a nation expects to be ignorant and free, in a state of civilization, it expects what never was and never will be."

Integrating Diverse People and Ideologies

As our nation becomes more diverse and our world becomes smaller, society has an ever-greater need to expose all of its members to other cultures and ideologies. To maintain a coherent and peaceful society—both national and global—requires that our people understand and accept one another—even if they do not always agree. The goal is not a homogeneous society, but a tolerant one.

Providing Resources for Solving Problems

Like museums and libraries, which often maintain close ties to institutions of higher education, colleges and universities are a resource for businesses, government agencies, organizations, and individuals doing research into a wide variety of questions. While our society's technological and scientific progress boggles the mind, our intellectual and spiritual progress has not kept pace with the multitude of social problems that now plague us. Society is in desperate need of assistance in combating poverty, pollution, social unrest, racism, sexism, crime, and many other problems. Higher education, as other segments of society, must do whatever it can to help over-come the many obstacles we face. While higher education cannot take sole responsibility for solving global problems, it can provide valuable resources—such as information, research, and facilities. Even more mundane, local problems faced by small businesses—such as how industrial processes work—and by individuals—such as one person's research into his or her own genealogy—may benefit from the resources available at the average institution of higher education.

Providing Access to Lifelong Learning in a Changing World

This would be a better society if everyone continued to learn. So goes the conventional wisdom. Simply encourage people who want to learn and the battle is nearly won. Well, that just isn't so. For one thing, it's a lot tougher to find access to learning than one might think. Barriers to access such as financial constraints, fear, complacency, age, sex or race discrimination are roadblocks to learning. The open door of the community college is the access point to postsecondary education for all members of the community. This is often the most meaningful expression of equality in a community. This access must be supported by appropriate financial aid policies. It must be made real by the provision of remediation programs, occupational programs, and transfer programs. Ernest Boyer said that the purpose of education is to "empower individuals to live competently in their communities." That is an appropriate role for higher education; it is an appropriate role for the community college.

ACTIVITIES AND QUESTIONS FOR REFLECTION

1. *Do you understand what Pierce means by a move from a "manufacturing and industrial economy" to a "service and information economy"? How would this affect the planning of a college education intended to prepare you for the future?*

2. *Pierce believes that sustaining "a living culture" is one of the goals of higher education. Why does he believe that this produces controversy?*

3. *What did Thomas Jefferson mean when he said that a nation could not be both ignorant and free?*

4. *What relationship do you see between this reading and the two previous readings in this chapter relative to our society's expectations of colleges?*

IN THE SECOND READING addressing the question, "What does society need from higher education?" Robert Atwell, as president of the American Council on Education, objects to the emphasis on what society wants from colleges and stresses instead what it needs. Further, he believes that meeting these needs is essential in sustaining a free society.

AS YOU READ, think about the meaning for our society of each of the needs Atwell identifies.

WHAT DOES SOCIETY NEED FROM HIGHER EDUCATION?
Robert H. Atwell

Most contemporary discussions of society's requirements of higher education begin with economic considerations—most often, the need for colleges and universities to prepare students to work and compete in the global economy of the twenty-first century. We often hear a similarly instrumental approach advocated for university research, that it should be the source of scientific advances and technological developments that improve the nation's health and contribute to the strength of its economy.

I take no exception to either of these views, and to one degree or another, have argued them myself. However, for purposes of this brief paper, I want to distinguish between what society *wants* from higher educa-tion—a list that seems to expand daily and one that includes many legitimate expecta-tions—and what at base society *needs*. In the latter category I place a set of interrelated roles and functions: the teaching of citizen-ship and values; the academy as an indepen-dent critic of society; and higher education as an agent of social change.

As valuable as these roles and functions are, many members of society would not view them as self-evidently desirable, and some might actively oppose them. Nonethe-less, I would maintain that if higher educa-tion fails to fulfill these roles and functions, it will undermine both our democratic society and the support on which it depends for its continued vitality.

Excerpt from "What Does Society Need from Higher Education?" in a Wingspread Group on Higher Ed-ucation. *An American Imperative: Higher Expectations in Higher Education* (Racine, WI: The Johnson Foundation, 1993), pp. 51–53. Reprinted by permission of the Johnson Foundation, Racine, WI.

Teaching Citizenship and Values

Higher education is not value neutral. The essence of liberal learning—what distinguishes higher education from vocational training—is the communication of a basic set of values, including tolerance, understanding, a love of learning, and a devotion to free inquiry and free expression. Debates over the core curriculum or canon often miss the point that liberal learning is fundamentally expansive and inclusive. Much as we might like to reach agreement on a set of facts, ideas, and works, familiarity with which would define an individual as educated, accomplishing such a goal is a hopeless—and perhaps pointless—task. Insistence on its realization often springs from the spirit of ideology rather than inquiry, and runs the risk of establishing a totalitarian academic regime with little tolerance for new ideas.

Indeed, in an age when the quantity of information is expanding exponentially and coming at us in ever more forms, the importance of inculcating the values named above is greater than ever. Without them, it is impossible for society to sort through its political, economic, and social dilemmas effectively, or humanely. The apportionment of health care, the application of technology, the complexities of international relations—these are but some of the challenges we face now, and will for the foreseeable future, that will test our capacity for rigorous analysis, informed judgment, moral rectitude, and devotion to democratic principles. As daunting and divisive as these challenges are, unless we approach them in this fashion our society risks Yugoslavia of the soul.

The job of colleges and universities, then, is to prepare students to be citizens who can make wise choices and exercise leadership in all spheres of society. Citizenship is not identical to patriotism—at least not the narrow notion of it that we hear expressed too often, and that makes it "the last refuge of scoundrels." Citizenship requires active participation in society, in the solution of its problems, what we often now call "service." This concept of citizenship is the basis of President Clinton's call for a national service program; it should be no surprise that it has drawn an enthusiastic response from the nation's youth, as well as many of their elders. It also is behind the explosion of community service activities at colleges and universities through such programs as Campus Compact. These programs are valuable for the benefits they provide to society and to the student's understanding of society. They form an important base on which any national effort should build.

Higher Education as an Independent Critic of Society

Colleges and universities often are at their best when they are most annoying, when they stand a little apart from the daily life of society and point out its flaws.

Universities can be catalytic in bringing about positive change. In Eastern Europe, the universities and their students were important engines of the fall of communism in 1989. In our own country, whatever else one might want to say about the 1960s on college campuses, I would argue that universities and their students played a fundamental role in exposing the flaws of American foreign policy and certainly helped to bring about the end of our involvement in Vietnam.

In a larger sense, however, it seems to me that universities have failed in their roles as critics of society. Derek Bok has pointed out that in teaching and research, universities are responsive to what society chooses to pay for, not what it needs the most. Obviously, our institutions do and will serve society. But I believe more must be done to encourage faculty members and students to assume a critical stance, to use the knowledge and resources assembled on the campus—and the time available to them—to perform this function. Criticism may not be what most citizens and officeholders want to hear, but it is essential to social progress and the functioning of a democratic society.

Higher Education as an Agent of Social Change

Transmitting values and taking a critical stance together constitute a formula for social change. There is no avoiding the fact that colleges and universities have assumed a central position in our society; the positions taken and activities engaged in by academic leaders, faculty members, and students have an impact far beyond the boundaries of the campus. I believe all these actors should recognize this fact and act on it for the betterment of society and their own institutions.

Colleges and universities become agents of social change through both their internal and their external activities. Let me cite two ex-

amples: diversity and internationalization. By making our campuses—and that includes the curriculum—more inclusive and welcoming to minorities, women, and others who historically have been excluded or neglected, we foster change both within the institution and outside it. Similarly, emphasizing the study of foreign languages and cultures, promotion of increased student exchange, and developing stronger international ties among institutions changes both the campus and the broader society. Again, this is a tricky process and difficulties along the way are inevitable, especially with regard to diversity. But when those difficulties occur, we must resist the rush to regulation, the temptation to believe we can solve all problems by drafting codes and imposing punishments. At the same time, we must be prepared to argue that requiring students to learn about things, ideas, places, and people with which they are unfamiliar is not penalty but an essential part of a liberal education.

Perhaps John Masefield [an English author] said it best: "there are few earthly things more splendid than a University. In these days of broken frontiers and collapsing values, when the dams are down and the floods are making misery, when every future looks somewhat grim and every ancient foothold has become something of a quagmire, wherever a University stands, it stands and shines; wherever it exists, the free minds of men [and I would add women], urged on to full and fair inquiry, may still bring wisdom into human affairs."

ACTIVITIES AND QUESTIONS FOR REFLECTION

1. *Would you agree that the needs Atwell identifies as college purposes are important in a democratic society? Why or why not?*

2. *How are Atwell's goals for a college education different from the previous two readings in relation to the experience of various cultural and ethnic groups in our society?*

3. *Do the goals you have identified so far for your college education include any related to your role as a member of society? If so, what are they? If not, think about whether you want to add such a goal and how you might state it.*

IN THE PRECEDING READINGS on the purposes of a college education, the authors addressed the need for higher education to provide our society with responsible citizens who have the resources and knowledge to address social issues and sustain a strong community. This relationship between education and community is not a new one. In the following reading, Henry Perkinson, as a professor at New York University, describes the kind of educated person society has needed at different periods of history, going back to the fourth century B.C. He describes four major changes in the idea of the educated person and its relation to society over the years.

AS YOU READ, notice the changes in the studies required of the ideally educated person in each era.

THE EDUCATED PERSON: A CHANGING IDEAL

Henry J. Perkinson

"Whom then do I call educated?" Socrates [who developed the now-accepted theory that the earth and other planets revolve around the sun] asked. He was not the first to try to describe the ideal educated person, nor the last. The educational theorists of each age have created their own ideals of the educated person.

In most cases, these educational theorists have constructed the ideal educated person as the ideal leader. Plato, a contemporary of Socrates, dreamed up an ideal state, the Republic, where the rulers were philosophers. These philosopher-kings received an education that developed their intellects to grasp the essence of things. Where ordinary people had mere opinion about the nature of things, philosophers were supposed to have certain knowledge. They alone understood the true nature of justice, equality, freedom, goodness. Their education rendered them ideal rulers, capable of making the best decisions for the state and society.

Socrates ridiculed Plato's ideal state as a utopian dream and denounced Plato's educational program as a fantastic fiction: Knowledge of the essence of things simply was not possible. Lacking such omniscience, we must, Socrates admitted, rely on opinion. But that opinion should be the best opinion available: It

Excerpt from "The Educated Person: A Changing Ideal," *New York University Education Quarterly,* Vol. 10, No. 2, Winter 1979, pp. 17–21. Reprinted by permission.

should be "right opinion." And "right opinion" is traditional opinion. Thus, those decisions are best which best cohere with the traditions of one's own culture. Good decisions will never contradict or contravene the best that has been thought and said and done in the past.

Humanism vs. Philosophy

Socrates and Plato established the categories that have continued to dominate the debate about the ideal of the educated person. This debate has centered on how to prepare leaders to make the best decisions possible. On the one side, we have the followers of Socrates, who argue in favor of the humanities. The study of the history and literature of one's culture is the proper study for future leaders. Those who are steeped in their own culture will have right opinions, so they will make the best decisions possible.

On the other side, we have the followers of Plato, who declare that the study of philosophy (and, in later times, the study of science) will best prepare future decision-makers by developing the skills and the methods needed to obtain certain knowledge about the nature of things. Those leaders who have true understanding will make the best decisions possible.

Originally intended for the proper education of the clergy, the humanities came to be regarded as the proper education for the civil leaders in the newly emerging nation-states of Europe. The economic expansion in Europe enabled civil leaders to hire troops and administrators to recover, protect, and maintain their states. These kings and princes required loyal, honest, and trustworthy governors to assist in nation-building. The humanistic edu-

cators, the followers of Socrates, promised that the study of the humanities—both the sacred and the secular works of Latin and Greek antiquity—would train future governors to love virtue and abhor vice. The study of the humanities would insure right opinion and develop the right moral character.

The Protestant Reformation and the Catholic Counter-Reformation later institutionalized humanism as the educational model of Europe, and each country developed its own humanistic schools for the training of future leaders. In Latin grammar schools in England, in gymnasia in Germany, and in Jesuit colleges in France, Italy, and Spain, the future leaders of the state and of the Church prepared themselves by studying the classical works of antiquity.

The Scientific Method

The triumph of the humanistic ideal of the educated person began to be undermined as early as the seventeenth century when men of genius—Newton, Galileo, Bacon, and Descartes, to name a few—demonstrated that whatever wisdom the classics of antiquity did possess, they did not contain an accurate reading of the nature of things. The rise of modern science and the birth of modern philosophy once again raised high the expectations that mankind finally would fulfill Plato's dream of certain knowledge of the essence of things. All that was needed was the correct method. Francis Bacon, the father of modern empiricism, and René Descartes, the father of modern rationalism, each claimed to have developed the method whereby one could finally discover the true nature of things.

Schools began to install a scientific-philosophical program of studies in addition to their classical humanistic program. By the mid-nineteenth century, most agreed that the study of the ancient classics had failed to produce ideal educated persons. Throughout the Western world, people had begun to view the ideal educated person as an expert, as one who had certain, or scientific, knowledge: a specialist. Only someone who had been educated in the scientific method—trained to observe, reason, and experiment within some domain of knowledge—could make the best decisions within that domain.

The demise of classical humanistic education can also be linked to the birth of Romanticism. The classical humanistic education had always been conservative. It had sought to educate future leaders through initiation into the traditional wisdom. But Romanticism introduced quite a different conception of the function of the humanities: as arts that nourished human or humane sentiments and emotions. Construed in this way, a humanist education in literature and history was no longer antagonistic to science and philosophy. An education in the humanities now complemented an education in the sciences. An education in the sciences gave future leaders true knowledge and the method for obtaining new knowledge, while the humanities, especially modern literature and history, developed the proper sentiments so that future leaders would apply their scientific knowledge in humane and sensitive ways.

Socialization

Perhaps an even more profound influence was the growing democratization of Western civilization. From the time of Plato, the ideal educated person in the West had been someone who was a leader and a decision-maker. And from the time of Plato, these had been few in number. Education in the West was reserved for an elite: those likely to become the future leaders and decision-makers. As Western civilization became more democratized, many persons began to challenge the notion of reserving education for an elite. A democracy had to educate so that all citizens could wisely select and reject their decision-makers. By the early twentieth century, "progressive" theorists were envisioning a democracy where all people would participate as decision-makers. According to educational theorists like John Dewey, the schools of a democracy had to teach all people, not just an elite, how to think.

To appreciate the enormity of the task decreed by Dewey and others we have to realize that throughout the Western world ever since the sixteenth century, schools for the common people—first under the aegis of the churches, later under the aegis of the state—had always functioned to make the masses loyal and obedient followers, not decision-makers. Few even regarded these schools as real educational institutions in the manner of the grammar school, or the gymnasium, or the college. Real educational institutions prepared future leaders and decision-makers, whereas schools for the common people socialized the masses, accommodating them to existing arrangements and accustoming them to accept the decisions made by their civic and religious leaders.

It is true that this dual school arrangement, with one kind of school for the elite, another kind for the common people, never flourished in America. America never had an aristocracy like that of Europe; here, just about everyone had to work or take up some profession. Right from the start, the common schools were agencies of socialization. They prepared the young for the world they inhabited by helping them to understand, accept, and fit into the existing political, social, and economic arrangements.

Not surprisingly, the proposals put forward by Dewey and others to use the common or public schools to prepare all people to be decision-makers never got off the ground. America did not have a participant democracy, and all attempts to use the schools to create one were irrelevant since the schools were supposed to socialize the young to the existing arrangements. The schools continued to socialize, turning out not leaders, but functionaries. Schools churned out loyal citizens who patriotically supported the American system of government. They imbued each new generation with the common values, beliefs, and attitudes that sustained the arrangements in American society. As to their economic function, the schools not only prepared each child to take his or her place as a unit in the production system, they also secured commitment to the continuous expansion and prosperity of the American people.

Disenchantment

In the waning years of the twentieth century, Americans have become more and more confused about education and schooling. There is a frantic casting about for an appropriate ideal of the educated person. From the follow-

ers of Plato and the followers of Socrates we hear complaints that the truly educated person must know philosophy, or science or literature, or history. But whatever else it might have done, that traditional ideal of the educated person as a leader has served to legitimize elitism and authoritarianism in Western civilization. No educational program can prepare people to make the best decisions possible. All leaders are fallible human beings. They will always make mistakes, no matter how—or how long—we educate them. They will continue to make decisions that bring about pain, discomfort, and adversity. Quite obviously, the traditional ideal of the educated person was a fraud, although not a deliberate fraud. The educational theorists really believed they knew how to prepare people to make the best decisions possible.

The emergence of democracy in the West over two hundred years ago was the signal that people were no longer going to accept the educational theorists' promises that they could train leaders who would make the best decisions possible. In a democracy leaders are accountable for the decisions—accountable to those affected by their decisions.

Educating Concerned Critics

Since leaders are held accountable in a democracy, it matters not so much who they are or how we educate them. In a democracy, it is the education of the entire people that is of paramount importance. The educational institutions must prepare people to be critical. For if leaders and decision makers are to be held accountable, then the people must be eternally vigilant.

No one better understood what American democracy was all about than Thomas Jefferson; and no one more clearly perceived that the ideal educated person demanded by democratic civilization. In a bill for the "Diffusion of Knowledge" in Virginia in 1789, Jefferson proposed that all citizens should go to school for three years at public expense, to be taught reading, writing, arithmetic, and history. Jefferson thought that three years spent pursuing this simple curriculum would be sufficient to help people hold their leaders accountable. If all people knew how to read and write so that they could use newspapers, and if all studied history so that they could spot tyranny in all its guises—then, he reasoned, people would be able to guard their own liberty. It is true that Jefferson's plan included a project to select and train future leaders, the "natural aristocracy," but his main concern, he declared, was with the universal education of all future citizens.

To reject the traditional Western ideal of the educated person is not to reject the study of philosophy, or history, or science, or literature. It is only to point out that these studies will not produce the best decision-makers possible. Yet, these studies will, I believe, make all people better able to hold those leaders accountable for their decisions. There is probably no particular program of studies essential to the education of a concerned critic, for the concerned critic, I believe, is less a product of what is taught than of how he or she is taught. However we go about producing them, such educated persons will, by holding all their leaders accountable, make better decisions possible.

ACTIVITIES AND QUESTIONS FOR REFLECTION

1. *What kind of education was prescribed as being ideal in the first three eras discussed by Perkinson? Try drawing a diagram to illustrate your answer.*

2. *What brought about the collapse of the traditional ideal of the educated person as leader and decision maker?*

3. *What does Perkinson suggest should be the goal of the educated person today? How are these similar to previous recommendations in this chapter?*

THE CONCLUDING READING in this chapter on the purposes of college is by one of the most influential English philosophers, Alfred North Whitehead, who thought deeply about education. In one essay in his classic work, The Aims of Education, *Whitehead argues that the university has only one function.*

AS YOU READ, look for Whitehead's purpose of the university—it may surprise you.

Universities and Their Function
Alfred North Whitehead

The universities are schools of education, and schools of research. But the primary reason for their existence is not to be found either in the mere knowledge conveyed to the students or in the mere opportunities for research afforded to the members of the faculty.

Both these functions could be performed at a cheaper rate, apart from these very expensive institutions. Books are cheap, and the system of apprenticeship is well understood. So far as the mere imparting of information is concerned, no university has had any justification for existence since the popularization of printing in the fifteenth century. Yet the chief impetus to the foundation of universities comes after that date, and in more recent times has even increased.

The justification for a university is that it preserves the connection between knowledge and the zest of life, by uniting the young and the old in the imaginative consideration of learning. The university imparts information, but it imparts it imaginatively. At least, this is the function which it should perform for society. A university which fails in this respect has no reason for existence. This atmosphere of excitement, arising from imaginative consideration, transforms knowledge. A fact is no longer a bare fact: it is invested with all its possibilities. It is no longer a burden on the memory: it is energizing as the poet of our dreams, and as the architect of our purposes.

Imagination is not to be divorced from the facts: it is a way of illuminating the facts.

It works by eliciting the general principles which apply to the facts, as they exist, and then by an intellectual survey of alternative possibilities which are consistent with those principles. It enables them to construct an intellectual vision of a new world, and it preserves the zest of life by the suggestion of satisfying purposes.

Youth is imaginative, and if the imagination be strengthened by discipline, this energy of imagination can in great measure be preserved through life. The tragedy of the world is that those who are imaginative have but slight experience, and those who are experienced have feeble imaginations. Fools act on imagination without knowledge; pedants act on knowledge without imagination. The task of the university is to weld together imagination and experience.

The way in which a university should function in the preparation for an intellectual career, such as modern business or one of the older professions, is by promoting the imaginative consideration of the various general principles underlying that career. Its students thus pass into their period of technical apprenticeship with which their imaginations already practiced in connecting details with general principles. The routine then receives its meaning, and also illuminates the principles with give it that meaning. Hence, instead of a drudgery issuing in a blind rule of thumb, the properly trained person has some hope of obtaining an imagination disciplined by detailed facts and by necessary habits.

Thus the proper function of a university is the imaginative acquisition of knowledge. Apart from this importance of the imagination, there is no reason why business people, and other professionals, should not pick up their facts bit by bit as they want them for particular occasions. A university is imaginative or it is nothing—at least nothing useful.

⊢⇀

ACTIVITIES AND QUESTIONS FOR REFLECTION

1. *What does Whitehead mean when he says a university imparts information "imaginatively"? And, what does "the imaginative acquisition of knowledge" mean? Had you ever thought of the university in these terms before?*

2. *How do Whitehead's concepts of the university compare with those of previous authors in this chapter? Does society need a place for the imagination?*

3. *Do you find education to be "drudgery"? How does or could Whitehead's suggestion of imaginative acquisition of knowledge make education more (or even more) interesting to you?*

CHAPTER 1

⌐ The Purposes of College

SUMMARY

The readings in this chapter have raised many questions about the purposes and goals of college: how your education can help you reach your personal goals, how it should meet the needs of the larger community, how education is necessary in a democratic society, and how the college campus should nurture the free exchange of ideas. Your responses to these questions will reflect your own assumptions about what a college education is intended to accomplish. Not all students, teachers, or colleges will agree.

Just as it is important to understand your personal goals, it is important to understand the goals of those around you. When people give advice, they are making assumptions based on their own goals. Questioning their assumptions will help you determine if the advice agrees with your own goals.

You may not be very clear about your own goals at this point, but the questions raised in this chapter are ones you will want to continue to ask yourself as you pursue your college studies.

Using the Internet

Colleges, universities, and professional schools now have Web sites where they describe their programs and their goals or mission statements. These are usually found on the homepage or in a section on the history of the college.

A good resource on colleges is *Peterson's Guide to Colleges and Universities* Web site, www.petersons.com/, where you can find information about colleges and universities, graduate programs, distance learning, summer opportunities, study abroad, financial aid, test preparation, and career exploration. Using their search function you can find the Web sites of a wide variety of colleges that offer specific programs, are located in specific geographic areas, or are of various sizes.

1. Look at the goals or mission statements of at least five colleges. How do they differ?

2. How do you feel about the schools that have clear, easy-to-find statements compared with those that do not? How might this reflect their effectiveness in working with students?

3. What does this investigation suggest to you about the importance of your own goals?

SUMMARIZING ACTIVITIES AND QUESTIONS FOR REFLECTION

1. *Are the goals of your college as stated in the catalog or online complementary to your goals? Will the course of study recommended help you reach your goals? Do you know yet?*

2. *The readings in this chapter have raised ideas that you had probably not considered. What meaning do these ideas have for you? Have they led you to raise questions about any of your previous assumptions about the purposes of college?*

3. *What changes in your goals for college do these readings suggest? As suggested in the "Introduction: On Becoming an Educated Person," revise your statements of goals for attending college and of an educated person to reflect what you have learned from the readings and activities in this chapter.*

The Role of the Liberal Arts in a College Education

INTRODUCTION: JOINING THE ACADEMIC CONVERSATION

College degree requirements normally include a number of courses in the liberal arts and sciences or, in short, the "liberal arts." These are studies in the history and theory of the arts, humanities, mathematics, and the natural, physical, and social sciences. These requirements may be stated in terms of a set core of introductory courses or as a certain number of credits in specific subjects. Beginning students feel most burdened with these studies and often resent them as irrelevant to their career goals or personal interests.

Simply put, the liberal arts and sciences provide the theoretical basis for all practical or "applied" studies. Proficiency in science and mathematics, for example, is necessary to the understanding of technology, engineering, business, and other professionally oriented studies. Liberal arts and sciences also provide a broad understanding of ourselves as persons and citizens and of our culture and social relations. They provide the foundation for becoming educated.

Lee Knefelkamp, now a professor at Columbia University, reminisced in writing about her own introduction to college at Macalaster in St. Paul, Minnesota, a small, traditional liberal arts college:

> A young woman is on her way to a faculty member's home for a book discussion at the end of freshman orientation. Like her first-year student peers, she feels awkward, fearful, and unsure of her ability to meet the academic

demands of college. She enters the house, is greeted by Professor Patricia Kane, and is ushered into a small room lined with books. She sits in front of a fireplace with ten other first-year students and begins to talk about ideas.

The experience was transforming for that student because it gave her a vision of what academic life could be when professors took students seriously and cared about what students thought. This was the conversation that began my own seasons of academic life.

Eudora Welty [, the acclaimed author of autobiographical fiction,] has written about the kind of transforming event my peers and I were privileged to experience: "As we discover, we remember. Remembering, we discover. And most intensely do we experience this when our separate journeys converge." From that evening on, Pat Kane's past and present were linked with my future. Her vision of the academy and the role of the faculty changed my understanding of the academy and challenged me to reconceptualize the role of the student. Learning was not about passive receptivity to the wisdom of the faculty; it was about joining the academic conversation.

To join the "academic conversation" and for college to become a transforming experience, you will need to understand more about the history and nature of the academic community and the nature of the liberal arts. The readings in this chapter were selected to help you more fully understand the liberal arts and the value of a liberal arts education.

IN THE FOLLOWING READING, A. Bartlett Giamatti, as President of Yale University, addresses a freshman class in Yale College, the university's undergraduate program, as they begin their study toward a "liberal education" in a classic liberal arts program. He explains that a liberal education is unrelated to the content of a study but, rather, is concerned with the attitude taken toward the study of that content.

AS YOU READ, look for the characteristics of the attitude of mind that Giamatti contends the student must develop and assume to obtain a liberal education.

THE EARTHLY USE OF A LIBERAL EDUCATION
A. Bartlett Giamatti

Each of us experiences college differently. I can assure you that soon your normal anxieties will recede and a genuine excitement will begin, a rousing motion of the spirit unlike anything you have experienced before. And that will mark the beginning of it, the grand adventure that you now undertake, never alone but on your own, the voyage of exploration in freedom that is the development of your own mind. Generations have preceded you in this splendid opening out of the self as you use the mind to explore the mind, and, if the human race is rational, generations will come after you. But each of you will experience your education uniquely—charting and ordering and dwelling in the land of your own intellect and sensibility, discovering powers you had only dreamed of and mysteries you had not imagined and reaches you had not thought that thought could reach. There will be pain and some considerable loneliness at times, and not all the terrain will be green and refreshing. There will be awesome wastes and depths as well as heights. The adventure of discovery is, however, thrilling because you will sharpen and focus your powers of analysis, of creativity, of rationality, of feeling—of thinking with your whole being. If at Yale you can experience the joy that the acquisition and creation of knowledge for its own sake brings, the adventure will last your whole life and you will have discovered the distinction between living as a full human being and merely existing.

If there is a single term to describe the education that can spark a lifelong love of learning, it is the term *liberal education*. A liberal education has nothing to do with those political designer labels *liberal* and *conservative* that some so lovingly stitch on to every idea they pull off, or put on, the rack. A liberal education is not one that seeks to implant the precepts of a specific religious or political orthodoxy. Nor is it an education intending to prepare for immediate immersion in a profession. . . .

At Yale College education is "liberal" in Cardinal Newman's sense of the word. As he says in the fifth discourse of *The Idea of a University,*

> That alone is liberal knowledge which stands on its own pretensions, which is independent of sequel, expects no complement, refuses to be informed (as it is called) by any end, or absorbed in any art, in order duly to present itself to our contemplation. The most ordinary pursuits have this specific character, if they are self-sufficient and complete; the highest lose it, when they minister to something beyond them.

As Newman emphasizes, a liberal education is not defined by the content or by the subject matter of a course of study. It is a common error, for instance, to equate a liberal education with the so-called liberal arts or *studia humanitatis*. To study the liberal arts or the humanities is not necessarily to acquire a liberal education unless one studies these and allied subjects in a spirit that, as Newman has it, seeks no immediate sequel, that is independent of a profession's advantage. If you pursue the study of anything not for the intrinsic rewards of exercising and developing the power of the mind but because you press toward a professional goal, then you are pursuing not a liberal education but rather something else.

A liberal education is defined by the attitude of the mind toward the knowledge the mind explores and creates. Such education occurs when you pursue knowledge because you are motivated to experience and absorb what comes of thinking—thinking about the traditions of our common human heritage in all its forms, thinking about new patterns or designs in what the world proffers today— whether in philosophic texts or financial markets or chemical combinations—thinking in order to create new knowledge that others will then explore. A liberal education . . . embraces physics as well as French, lasers as well as literature, social science and physical and biological sciences as well as the arts and humanities. A liberal education rests on the supposition that our humanity is enriched by the pursuit of learning for its own sake; it is dedicated to the proposition that growth in thought, and in the power to think, increases the pleasure, breadth, and value of life.

"That is very touching," I will be told, "that is all very well, but how does someone make a living with this joy of learning and pleasure in the pursuit of learning? What is the earthly use of all this kind of education later on, in the practical, real world?" These are not trivial questions, though the presuppositions behind them puzzle me somewhat. I am puzzled, for instance, by the unexamined assumption that the "real world" is always thought to lie outside or beyond the realm of education. I am puzzled by the confident assumption that only in certain parts of daily life do people make "real" decisions and do "real" acts lead to "real" consequences. I am puzzled by those who think that ideas do not have reality or that knowledge is irrelevant to the workings of daily life.

To invert Plato and to believe that ideas are unreal and that their pursuit has no power for practical or useful good is to shrink reality and define ignorance. To speak directly to the questions posed by the skeptic of the idea of a liberal education, I can say only this: ideas and their pursuit define our humanity and make us human. Ideas, embodied in data and values, beliefs, principles, and original insights, must be pursued because they are valuable in themselves and because they are the stuff of life. There is nothing more necessary to the full, free, and decent life of a person or of a people or of the human race than to free the mind by passionately and rationally exercising the mind's power to inquire freely. There can be no more practical education, in my opinion, than one that launches you on the course of fulfilling your human capacities to reason and to imagine freely and that hones your abilities to express the results of your thinking in speech and in writing with logic, clarity, and grace.

While such an education may be deemed impractical by those wedded to the notion that nothing in life is more important than one's career, nevertheless I welcome you to a liberal education's rigorous and demanding pleasures. Fear not, you will not be impeded from making a living because you have learned to think for yourself and because you take pleasure in the operation of the mind and in the pursuit of new ideas. And you will need to make a living. The world will not provide you with sustenance or employment. You will have to work for it. I am instead speaking of another dimension of your lives, the dimension of your spirit that will last longer than a job, that will outlast a profession, that will represent by the end of your time on earth the sum of your human significance. That is the dimension represented by the mind unfettered, "freely ranging onley within the Zodiack of his owne wit," as the old poet said. There is no greater power a human being can develop for the individual's or for the public's good.

And I believe that the good, for individuals and for communities, is the end to which education must tend. I affirm Newman's vision that a liberal education is one seeking no sequel or complement. I take him to be writing of the motive or tendency of the mind operating initially within the educational process. But I believe there is also a larger tendency or motive, which is animated by the pursuit of ideas for their own sake. I believe that the pleasure in the pursuit of knowledge joins and is finally at one with our general human desire for a life elevated by dignity, decency, and moral progress. That larger hope does not come later; it exists inextricably intertwined with a liberal education. The joy of intellectual pursuit and the pursuit of the good and decent life are no more separable than on a fair spring day the sweet breeze is separable from the sunlight.

In the common pursuit of ideas for themselves and of the larger or common good, the freedom that the individual mind wishes for itself, it also seeks for others. How could it be otherwise? In the pursuit of knowledge leading to the good, you cannot wish for others less than you wish for yourself. Thus, in the pursuit of freedom, the individual finds it necessary to order or to limit the surge to freedom so that others in the community are not denied the very condition each of us seeks. A liberal education desires to foster a freedom of the mind that will also contribute, in its measure, to the freedom of others.

We learn, therefore, that there is no true freedom without order; we learn that there are limits to our freedom, limits we learn to choose freely in order not to undermine what we seek. After all, if there were, on the one hand, no restraints at all, only anarchy of intellect and chaos of community would result. On the other hand, if all were restraint, and release of inquiry and thought were stifled, only a death of the spirit and a denial of any freedom could result. There must be an interplay of restraint and release, of order and freedom, in our individual lives and in our life together. Without such interplay within each of us, there can be no good life for any of us. If there is no striving for the good life for all of us, however, there cannot be a good life for any one of us. We must learn how freedom depends for its existence upon freely chosen (because rationally understood) forms of order.

ACTIVITIES AND QUESTIONS FOR REFLECTION

1. *In your own words, how would you explain the attitude of mind the author believes is necessary to become liberally educated?*

2. *Do you agree with the limits he suggests on "freedom of the mind"? What limits do you believe might be necessary?*

3. *What "earthly use" of a liberal education can you imagine for yourself?*

An important aim of colleges is to provide learning experiences that lead students to develop their ability to think. Theodore Hesburgh, the former president of Notre Dame University, describes it as " . . . the ability to think clearly, logically, deeply, and widely about a variety of human questions. This includes the meaning and purpose of human life."

In the following article, Wayne Booth, of the University of Chicago, provides an example of the differences between our everyday approach to thinking and using words, and the approach you will encounter in college. This kind of thinking and use of words is required for clear expression of thoughts and feelings in the kind of serious discussion that society expects of a college graduate. To introduce this kind of thinking, he examines the many meanings attached to the word idea. *Ideas are the foundation of studies in the liberal arts.*

As you read, look for the main characteristics Booth identifies as the attributes of an idea, the difference between an opinion and an idea, and the relationship between ideas and education.

What Is an Idea?

Wayne C. Booth

"I've got an idea; let's go get a hamburger."

"All right, now, as sales representatives we must brainstorm for ideas to increase profits."

"The way Ray flatters the boss gives you the idea he's bucking for a promotion, doesn't it?"

"Hey, listen to this; I've just had an idea for attaching the boat to the top of the car without having to buy a carrier."

"The idea of good defense is to keep pressure on the other team without committing errors ourselves."

Excerpt from *The Harper & Row Reader: Liberal Education Through Reading and Writing,* Third Edition, by Marshall W. Gregory and Wayne C. Booth (New York: HarperCollins, 1992), pp. 15–18.

"What did you say that set of books was called? *The Great Ideas?* What does that mean?"

The word *idea,* as you can see, is used in a great many ways. In most of the examples above it means something like "intention," "opinion," or "mental image." The "idea" of going for a hamburger is really a mental picture of a possible action, just as the "idea" of a boat carrier is a mental image of a mechanical device. The "ideas" of good defense and Ray the flatterer are really opinions held by the speakers, while the appeal for "ideas" about how to increase profits is really an appeal for opinions (which may also involve mental images) from fellow workers. None of these examples, however, encompasses the meaning of "idea" as it has always been used by those who engage in serious discussions of politics, history, intellectual movements, and social affairs. Even the last example, an allusion to the famous set of books edited by Robert Maynard Hutchins and Mortimer Adler at the University of Chicago, does not yet express an idea; it only directs us toward a source where ideas may be encountered.

These uses of "idea" are entirely appropriate in their contexts. Words play different roles at different times. One can "fish" for either trout or compliments, and a scalp, an executive, and a toilet (in the Navy) are all "heads." Usually, these different uses have overlapping, not opposed, meanings. For example, we wouldn't know what fishing for compliments meant unless we already knew what fishing for trout meant; and the "heads" we just referred to are all indications of position or place. In the same way, the different uses of the word *idea* overlap. Even the most enduring ideas may appear to some as "mere opinion." What, then, does *idea* mean in the context of serious talk, and what keeps some mental images from being ideas in our sense?

Three central features distinguish an idea from other kinds of mental products:

1. An idea is always connected to other ideas that lead to it, follow from it, or somehow support it.

Like a family member, an idea always exists amid a network of ancestors, parents, brothers, sisters, and cousins. An idea could no more spring into existence by itself than a plant could grow without a seed, soil, and a suitable environment. For example, the idea that acts of racial discrimination are immoral grows out of and is surrounded by a complex of other, related ideas about the nature of human beings and the nature of moral conduct:

a. Racial differences are irrelevant to human nature.

b. The sort of respect that is due to any human being as a human being is due equally to *all* human beings.

c. It is immoral to deny to any human being the rights and privileges due to every human being.

And so on. You can see that a great many other ideas surround, support, and follow from the leading idea.

2. An idea always has the capacity to generate other ideas.

Ideas not only have ancestors and parents, but they make their own offspring. The idea that *racial* discrimination is immoral, for example, is the offspring of the idea that *any* sort of bigotry is wrong.

3. An idea is always capable of yielding more than one argument or position.

An idea never has a fixed, once-and-for-all meaning, and it always requires interpretation and discussion. Whenever interpretation is required and discussion permitted, disagreements will exist. Ideas are always to some degree controversial, but the kind of controversy produced by the clash of ideas—unlike the kind of controversy produced by a clash of prejudices—is one in which *reasons* are offered and tested by both sides in the debate. As reasons are considered, positions that seemed fixed turn into ideas that move with argument.

In recent years, for example, the idea that racial discrimination is immoral, combined with the idea that past discriminations should be compensated for, has led to the follow-up idea that minority groups should, in some cases, receive preferred treatment, such as being granted admission to medical school with lower scores than those of competing applicants from majority groups. Some people have charged that this is "reverse discrimination," while others advance arguments for and against such positions with great intellectual and moral vigor. Regardless of where you stand on this issue, you can see that interpretations of ideas yield a multiplicity of positions.

There are obviously many kinds of mental products that do not qualify as ideas according to these criteria. "Two plus two equals four," for example, is not an idea. Without reference to the ideas that lie behind it, it can neither be interpreted nor used. In and of itself, "two plus two equals four" is simply a brute fact, not an idea. However, as a statement it is clearly the product of ideas: the idea of quantity, the idea that the world can be understood and manipulated in terms of systems of numbers, and so on.

Many of our everyday notions, opinions, and pictures of things also fail to qualify as ideas. "I hate John" may be an intelligible utterance—it indicates the feelings of the speaker—but it is not an idea. The "parents" of this utterance lie in the psychology or biography of the speaker, not in other ideas, and it can neither yield its own offspring nor support an argument. "Catholics are sheep," "All communists in government are traitors," "Christianity is the only true religion," "Republicans stink," "Most people on welfare are cheaters," and "Premarital sex is OK if you know what you're doing" are all such non-ideas. With appropriate development or modification, some of these opinions could be turned into ideas, but what keeps them from qualifying as ideas in their present form is that they are only minimally related (and in some instances totally unrelated) to other ideas. One sign that you are being offered mindless, bigoted, or fanatical opinions, not ideas, is the presence of emotion-charged generalizations, unsupported by evidence or argument. Catch words, clichés, and code phrases ("welfare cheaters," "dumb jocks," "a typical woman," "crazy, atheistical scientists") are a sure sign that emotions have shoved ideas out of the picture.

A liberal education is an education in ideas—not merely memorizing them, but learning to move among them, balancing one against the other, negotiating relationships, accommodating new arguments, and returning for a closer look.

ACTIVITIES AND QUESTIONS FOR REFLECTION

1. *Had you thought about "ideas" in the way Booth discusses them before reading this article? How would you have described you own thought processes before this reading?*

2. *To test your understanding of the difference between an* idea *and an* opinion *as described by Booth, select a short article, feature, or news report from your local newspaper and analyze its content for opinions and ideas. What parts are opinions? Why? What parts are ideas? Why? You could analyze a news story or interview from television or radio instead.*

3. *Did Booth's explanations of ideas and opinions suggest any qualities you would like to have as an educated person?*

IN THIS READING, Carey Brush, as vice president for Academic Affairs at the State University of New York at Oneonta, provides a brief overview of the history and the changing role of particular liberal arts subjects in higher education. You will see that the concept of what is important in education has changed significantly but a principle remains even as the subjects change.

AS YOU READ, look for the principal goal of liberal studies in education throughout history.

THE LIBERAL STUDIES

Carey W. Brush

What, you may ask, are the liberal studies, or, if you prefer, the liberal arts? In ancient Greece, the liberal arts were those studies necessary to prepare free men for political life. In an attempt to balance physical with mental culture, letters with mathematics, and aesthetic with moral training, Greek education included, on the elementary level, grammar, drawing, music, and gymnastics, and, on the advanced level, mathematics, astronomy, rhetoric, philosophy, and dialectic, or, as we know it today, logic. In outlining his concept of the ideal education for future leaders of the state, Plato stressed arithmetic, geometry, and astronomy, but reserved the preeminent position for dialectic.

Although Plato said very little about education for the masses, his famous pupil, Aristotle, distinguished between liberal education designed to prepare the aristocracy for citizenship, and vocational education designed to fit the lower classes for an occupation. Shorn of the reference of class structure, this distinction continues to be descriptive of our system of higher education.

With some modifications, the Romans adopted and transmitted Greek ideas on liberal education. In the first century B.C., Marcus Varro defined the liberal arts as grammar, rhetoric, logic, arithmetic, geometry, astronomy, music, architecture, and medicine; but most Roman scholars spoke of the liberal arts as indefinite in number until the late fourth century A.D. At that time, Martianus Capella wrote an allegorical story entitled *The Marriage of Mercury and Philology* in which the seven bridesmaids represented the liberal arts of Varro minus medicine and architecture. Thus the knowledge which was basic to a liberal education had been systematized and condensed into seven disciplines largely literary and mathematical in content.

In the sixth century, Cassiodorus, a retired Roman statesman and founder of a monastic order, discovered, in the scriptures, justification for the seven liberal arts as the basis of theological study. Shortly thereafter, Isidore, Bishop of Seville, used the terms *trivium* for the three elementary disciplines of grammar, rhetoric, and logic, and *quadrivium* for the higher disciplines of arithmetic, geometry, astronomy, and music.

After the fall of Rome, the liberal arts survived mainly in the monastic orders, but with an orientation quite different from their Greek origins. One authority writes:

> The spirit of Christian asceticism opposed four central features of Greek thought in liberal education: the cult of the body, intellectual and aesthetic culture, the political concept of education for service to the state, and the disparagement of manual labor.

By the time of the Renaissance, the old liberal education had become so exclusively the province of the clergy, that it was largely professional in nature. When liberal learning revived, it did so within the social milieu of the nobles and burghers of the free cities of Europe. Instead of other-worldly concerns, the new education concentrated on the study of man and his society, and the term "citizen" returned to honored usage.

With the humanists of the renaissance believing that the Latin and Greek classics were

the best sources for the study of human nature, grammar, which is actually language and literature in their broadest sense, became the queen of the liberal arts. In the ensuing centuries, the vernacular languages challenged the dominant position of Latin and Greek; the natural sciences contended for a place in the curriculum; and the social sciences offered new approaches to the study of man and his institutions. Thus by the end of the nineteenth century, the old concept of the liberal studies as consisting mainly of letters and mathematics had been broadened to include the natural and the social sciences. Now, instead of referring to the seven liberal arts, we speak of four major divisions of learning—humanities, mathematics, natural sciences, and social sciences.

While the content of the liberal studies has expanded, the purpose of a liberal education remains relatively unchanged—to prepare individuals to live the good life and to be responsible citizens. As Aristotle separated liberal education from vocational or professional studies, so the faculty of the University of Pennsylvania in 1829 agreed that liberal education "is not designed . . . to qualify the student in a special manner for any particular profession or pursuit . . . but to aid in the development of all his faculties in their just proportions; and by discipline and instruction, to furnish him with those general qualifications, which are useful and ornamental in every profession. . . ."

A few years later, John Stuart Mill in his inaugural address as Rector of St. Andrews University in Scotland affirmed the necessity for a good liberal education before beginning professional studies. He said:

Men are men before they are lawyers or physicians or manufacturers; and if you make them capable and sensible men they will make themselves capable and sensible lawyers or physicians.

More recently A. Whitney Griswold in his inaugural address as President of Yale University declared that the fundamental purpose of the liberal studies "lies not in their specific content, but in their stimulus to the individual student's powers of reason, judgment, and imagination."

Although there is no consensus today on the specific content which should be included in a college undergraduate program of liberal education, most educators recognize that any subject can be taught liberally or *illiberally*— a truth recognized by Aristotle. A former Dean of Yale College, William DeVane, contends that a subject is taught liberally in direct proportion to the historical perspectives and philosophical implications introduced. Alfred North Whitehead in his famous essay "The Aims of Education" warned that it is important to teach a few studies thoroughly and imaginatively, and eliminate that "fatal disconnection of subjects" which is the antithesis of liberal education.

Since a liberal education traditionally connotes a breadth of experience, there is general agreement among educators that a student should have some formal course work in each of the four major divisions of learning. It is for this reason that we often require undergraduates to study some subjects in which they seemingly have little interest or aptitude, and not because we agree with Mr. Dooley, the famous American humorist of a half century ago, who said, "It makes no difference what you teach a boy so long as he don't like it."

ACTIVITIES AND QUESTIONS FOR REFLECTION

1. *In this reading, what does the word* liberal *in "liberal arts" mean?*

2. *Have the* purposes *of the liberal arts changed over time? How? Or why not?*

3. *Can you see a connection between the origin of the liberal arts in Greece and the educational needs of a democratic society today? What is it?*

4. *Within the four major divisions of the liberal arts identified by the author, can you name specific fields of study in each? For example, a field of study in the humanities would be English. Try constructing a diagram to illustrate your classification of the liberal arts fields.*

IN THE FOLLOWING READING, Henry Rosovsky, a former dean of Harvard College, the undergraduate liberal arts college within Harvard University, goes beyond the earlier definitions of a liberal arts education as proficiency in certain fields. He analyzes the abilities that characterize the liberally educated person and proposes five standards or criteria that can be used to determine whether or not a person is liberally educated.

AS YOU READ, look for the essential elements of the author's five standards.

THE PURPOSES OF LIBERAL EDUCATION
Henry Rosovsky

Some years ago I attempted to formulate a standard for liberal education in our time:

1. An educated person must be able to think and write clearly and effectively. By this I mean that students, when they receive bachelor's degrees, must be able to communicate with precision, cogency, and force. To put it in yet another way: students should be trained to think critically.

2. An educated person should have a *critical appreciation* of the ways in which we gain knowledge and understanding of the universe, of society, and of ourselves. Thus, he or she should have an *informed acquaintance* with the mathematical and experimental methods of the physical and biological sciences; with the main forms of analysis and the historical and quantitative techniques needed for investigating the workings and development of modern society; with some of the important scholarly, literary, and artistic achievements of the past; and with the major religious and philosophical conceptions of mankind.

This ambitious definition may appear to be impractical. Most members of university faculties would have to confess their own difficulty in measuring up to such a standard. But that is a shortsighted view. First, to have a stated ideal is valuable in itself. Second, the general formulation that I have used does translate into standard areas, for example, physics, history, or English literature. I am not suggesting that each of these areas can be mastered by every educated person. But we are not in search of mastery; the goal is informed acquaintance and that can be adequately achieved—at any historical moment—by a set of requirements that has a sufficiently broad conception.

The leap from informed acquaintance to critical appreciation is more important and more difficult. To achieve that quality, we have to move beyond content to the general applicability of what is taught and how it is taught. The growth of knowledge is very rapid, and we should encourage our students to be lifetime learners. Time constraints are great and only certain subjects can be selected. We can expect a non-scientist to take science courses, but we cannot expect all of these students to study physics, biology, chemistry, geology, and mathematics. Therefore, the general utility of required subjects has to be especially great. Ideally, they should combine significant content with an emphasis on the larger methodology of a specific subject. For example, studying economics is all right from the point of view of liberal education, but considering that field in the general context of the social sciences is of much higher value.

3. An educated American, in the last quarter of this century, cannot be provincial in the sense of being ignorant of other cultures and other times. It is no longer possible to conduct our lives without reference to the wider world or to the historical forces that have shaped the present and will shape the future. Perhaps few educated people will ever possess a sufficiently broad perspective. But it seems clear to me that a crucial difference

between the educated and the uneducated is the extent to which one's life experience is viewed in wider contexts.

4. An educated person is expected to have some understanding of, and experience in thinking about, moral and ethical problems. While these issues change very little over the centuries, they acquire a new urgency for each generation when it is personally confronted with the dilemmas of choice. It may well be that the most significant quality in educated persons is the informed judgment that enables them to make discriminating moral choices.

5. Finally, an educated individual should have achieved depth in some field of knowledge. Here I have in mind something that lies between the levels of professional competence and informed acquaintance. In American college terminology, it is called a "major" or "concentration." The theory is straightforward: cumulative learning is an effective way to develop powers of reasoning and analysis because it requires the consideration of increasingly complex phenomena, techniques, and analytical constructs. It is expected that in every major, students will gain sufficient control of the data, theory, and methods to define the issues in a given problem, develop the evidence and arguments that may reasonably be advanced on the various sides of each issue, and reach conclusions based on a convincing evaluation of the evidence. . . .

William Johnson Cory, a master at Eton, said it very well over a hundred years ago. Addressing a group of young men in 1861, he told them that:

You are not engaged so much in acquiring knowledge as in making mental efforts under criticism. A certain amount of knowledge you can indeed with average faculties acquire so as to retain; nor need you regret the hours that you have spent on much that is forgotten, for the shadow of lost knowledge at least protects you from many illusions.

But you go to a great school, not for knowledge so much as for arts and habits; for the habit of attention, for the art of expression, for the art of assuming at a moment's notice a new intellectual posture, for the art of entering quickly into another person's thoughts, for the habit of submitting to censure and refutation, for the art of indicating assent or dissent in graduated terms, for the habit of regarding minute points of accuracy, for the habit of working out what is possible in a given time, for taste, for discrimination, for mental courage and mental soberness.

Above all, you go to a great school for self-knowledge.

In my view, these remarks describe some of the central principles for undergraduate education today. Students will forget many of the facts that they are taught and new developments will make much of what is imparted today invalid in years hence. I think we might all agree that an understanding of the value and uses of intellect is essential for an educated person.

ACTIVITIES AND QUESTIONS FOR REFLECTION

1. *What challenges to education does the current knowledge explosion pose?*

2. *Describe the balance between new knowledge and old knowledge proposed by the author.*

3. *What does the author mean when he uses the term "informed acquaintance" concerning an area of learning outside a student's major or concentration?*

4. *Would your educational goals meet the author's five standards? If not, what changes would you need to make?*

⟺

ARE THE LIBERAL ARTS RELEVANT to the technological age and the information society in which we are increasingly living today? Bruce Strasser, a corporate consultant, discusses in this reading the place of science and the arts in contemporary education. He further illustrates the usefulness of liberal studies for various occupations.

AS YOU READ, look for the reasons Strasser gives for the value of the liberal arts and sciences in an information society, in general and in specific occupations.

⟺

BEYOND THE MACHINE: LIBERAL EDUCATION FOR AN INFORMATION SOCIETY
Bruce E. Strasser

Students today are graduating into a vastly different society than in the past—one which is technologically advanced and increasingly engaged in the production, processing, and distribution of information.

This evolution into an Information Society is having social and economic impacts as profound and far reaching as the industrial revolution. Already more than half the United States work force is engaged in information-related activities, or in developing and operating the vast infrastructure of telecommunications networks and computers that makes them possible.

This Information Society needs people who are knowledgeable about science and technology and who have new kinds of skills and intellectual abilities that will enable them to cope with and make the most of recent advances in information technologies. These technologies are transforming not only the way we live and work but our relationships with other people and the basic aspirations and values of our society.

[Architectural historian] Lewis Mumford pointed out, "Our capacity to go beyond the machine rests upon our power to assimilate the machine. Until we have absorbed the lessons of the mechanical realm, we cannot go further in our development towards the richly organic, the more profoundly human."

Excerpt from *The Necessary Learning* edited by Robert Moynihan (Lanham, MD: University Press of America, 1989), pp. 46–53. Copyright 1989 by University Press of America. Reprinted by permission.

Understanding these new technologies is a prerequisite to controlling them, to make them our servants instead of our masters, to use them to enhance our lives and strengthen human values.

In short, in any technologically advanced society, a liberal education without science is a contradiction in terms. And in a post-industrial information society, the mastery of information machines—computers and telecommunications—is essential and should be as much a part of a liberal education as books, pencils, and blackboards were in previous ages.

The idea of science as part of a liberal education is not new. Early medieval universities included medicine along with art, law, and theology as major areas of study. After Copernicus [who developed the theory that the earth revolves around the sun], . . . astronomy became part of the curriculum.

Early seventeenth century universities offered arithmetic, geometry, and astronomy along with grammar, logic, and rhetoric. The educated gentleman could aspire to learning virtually all that was known. And while the nobility educated its children in languages, literature, music, and art, it did not neglect engineering for warfare and defense. Mathematics and astronomy were studied for purposes of navigation in an increasing mercantile world.

Francis Bacon considered all knowledge, including the sciences, to be the province of the educated man. He promulgated in *Novum Organum* the idea that learning should have a purpose beyond knowledge for its own sake. Knowledge provided power that could be used to enhance the quality of life.

Yale University's charter, written in 1701, was a little ahead of its time in stating explicitly that students should "be educated that they might be fitted for public employment both in church and civil state."

During the industrial revolution, although education in the arts and humanities was always available, colleges and universities increasingly offered professional training in specific fields such as engineering, science, medicine, business administration, and law. As the specific knowledge required for professional careers increased, there simply wasn't time (or the inclination) to provide more than a cursory look at the arts and the humanities.

C. P. Snow [an English cultural analyst] in 1956 lamented this specialization and warned of the consequences of the diverging cultures of science and literature.

Since then, the two cultures have further divided into many more. As more and more information is generated in all fields—sciences, engineering, law, medicine, history, art, etc.—it is impossible for a person to be fully knowledgeable in more than one or two subjects. Scholars and practitioners have had to narrow their focus. People knowledgeable in one subject have difficulty understanding people expert in other areas. Our society has become inundated with knowledge and fragmented with specialization.

This isolation within and between the arts and the sciences has generated cries to do something about it. Reintegrate education! Teach science in humanities courses and include the arts in engineering courses! Teach physicians about the law and lawyers about humanity! And at the same time remedy deficient secondary school education and teach everyone how to read and write!

What about the liberal arts? Are there no places in the Information Age for the traditional arts and humanities major?—yes, of course, in the traditional fields of education and the arts, and in the burgeoning information age industries of journalism, publishing, television, and entertainment. Also, as in the past, some liberal arts majors will find their way into business and government, probably at starting salaries half that of engineering, law or business administration majors.

The difference will be that in all occupations new generations of computers, faster, smarter, and less costly than before, will play a greater role.

Knowledge of computers and computer networks, what they can do, and how to use them, will be keys to success in the business and professional world.

One of the tasks of a liberal arts education is to enhance a student's ability to think critically rather than act routinely and to make decisions based on good value judgments. A liberal education should produce citizens who can determine what *should* be done humanistically, in contrast to what engineers say *can* be done technically. This requires analytic ability, the willingness to observe and question, and to integrate and synthesize disparate knowledge in several fields into coherent wholes. With new technologies continually altering the spectrum of choices and problems that our society faces, and any decision likely to generate more problems and choices and the need for more decisions, this process has become very complicated.

However, with the help of computers, instantly accessible databases and expert computer programs, liberal arts graduates with only a basic knowledge of technology can be prepared for active citizenship in the information age.

Therefore, in their role of producing an educated citizenry, liberal arts colleges should be giving their students an appreciation of, and perspective on, the technologies underlying our society.

With such knowledge they will be better able to assess new technologies and proposed projects: to ask penetrating questions and challenge dubious statements, to examine facts and conventional values critically, and to anticipate a broader range of future consequences and alternatives in using or misusing the technologies.

Science and technology pervade our culture. They are among mankind's greatest intellectual achievements. Therefore, science literacy should be a legitimate aim of a liberal arts education. That means, as Jacques Barzun said, knowing enough about science and technology to appreciate what they have to offer the world. One needs not be a scientist to appreciate the beauty and significance of its accomplishments any more than one needs be a musician to appreciate music, an artist to appreciate painting, or an author to appreciate literature.

Science literacy is a hallmark of an educated person and will, it is hoped, encourage citizens to be *agents of social change*; that is, not only to contribute towards the continuity of our culture, but also to participate intelligently in shaping its future.

ACTIVITIES AND QUESTIONS FOR REFLECTION

1. *According to Strasser, how are today's technological developments affecting the nature of our society?*

2. *What does he believe is the contribution of science and of the arts in higher education today?*

3. *How do Strasser's recommendations on the content of a liberal education compare with those you noted in earlier readings in this chapter?*

4. *How is your overall understanding of liberal education affected by this reading?*

⌐⟍

*THE LAST READING IN THIS CHAPTER is by Edmund Pellegrino, a medical doc-
tor and professor at Georgetown University in Washington, D.C., where he
is director of the Center for Clinical Bioethics. Bioethics is a good example of
a field of study that did not exist 100 years ago. Biotechnology has made it
necessary to reconsider our definitions of life and the purposes of medical
care and raised questions that only studies in philosophy and ethics can
address. Pellegrino's comments were made in an address to a graduating class
at Wilkes College in Wilkes-Barre, Pennsylvania.*

AS YOU READ, look for Pellegrino's true tests of the educated mind.

⌐⟍

HAVING A DEGREE AND BEING EDUCATED
Edmund D. Pellegrino

Few humans live completely free of illusions.
Reality is sometimes just too harsh to bear
without them. But comforting as they can be,
some illusions are too dangerous to be har-
bored for very long. Eventually they must
meet the test of reality—or we slip into psy-
chosis.

I want to examine a prevalent illusion
with you today—one to which you are most
susceptible at this moment, namely, that *having* a degree is the same as *being* educated. It
is a bit *gauche,* I admit, to ask embarrassing
questions at a time of celebration. But your
personal happiness and the world you create
depend on how well your illusion is brought

into focus. And this *emboldens* me to intrude
briefly on the satisfaction you justly feel with
your academic accomplishment.

The degree you receive today is only a
certificate of exposure, not a guarantee of in-
fection. Some may have caught the virus of
education, others only a mild case, and still
others may be totally immune. To which category do you belong? Should you care? How
can you tell?

The illusion of an education has always
plagued the honest person. It is particularly
seductive in a technological society like ours.
We intermingle education with training, and
liberal with professional studies, so intimately

Reprinted from *Foundations: A Reader for New College Students,* Second Edition, edited by Virginia N.
Gordon and Thomas L. Minnick (Belmont, CA: Wadsworth, 2002), pp. 277–280. Copyright © 2002
Wadsworth Group.

that they are hard to disentangle. We reward specific skills in politics, sports, business, and academia. We exalt those who can *do* something—those who are experts.

It becomes easy to forget that free and civilized societies are not built on information alone. Primitive and despotic societies have their experts too! Computers and animals can be trained to store and retrieve information, to learn, and even to out-perform us. What they can never do is direct the wise use of their information. They are imprisoned by their programmers and their own expertise. The more intensive that expertise, the more it cages them; the less they can function outside its restricted perimeter.

In a technological society experts proliferate like toadstools on a damp lawn. Some are genuine. Others are quick studies specializing in the predigestion of other people's thoughts. They crowd the TV screens, the radio waves, the printed page, eager to tell us what to believe and how to live—from sex and politics to religion and international affairs. They manufacture our culture, give us our opinions and our conversational *gambits*.

Now that you have a degree in something, you are in danger of stepping quietly into the cage of your own expertise—leaving everything else to the other experts. Whether they are genuine or phony makes little difference. If you do, you sacrifice the most precious endowment of an education—the freedom to make up your own mind—to be an authentic person. Knowledge, as Santayana said, is recognition of something absent. It is a salutation—not an embrace—a beginning, not an end.

You cannot predict when you will be brutally confronted by the falsity of your illusion like the juror who was interviewed following a recent murder trial. He was responding to one of those puerile how-does-it-feel questions that is the trademark of the telecaster's *vacuity*. "Being a juror was a terrible thing," he said. "I had to think like I never thought before. . . . I had to understand words like justice and truth. . . . Why do they make people like us judges?"

This is the pathetic lament of a sincere, sympathetic, but uneducated man. He was surely an expert in something but he could not grapple with the kind of question that separates humans from animals and computers. Justice and truth are awesome questions indeed. But who should answer those questions? Is being a juror another specialty? Do we need a degree in justice and truth? Does not a civilized and democratic society depend upon some common comprehension of what these words mean?

These same questions underlie every important public and private decision—from genetic engineering to nuclear proliferation, from prolonging human life to industrial pollution. They determine *how* we should use our expert knowledge, *whether* we should use it, and *for what* purposes. The welfare of the nation and the world depend on our capacity to think straight and act rightly—not on the amount of information we have amassed.

To be a juror, to be a person, to live with satisfaction, requires more than a trained mind—it requires an educated one, a mind that does not parrot other men's opinions or values but frames its own, a mind that can resist the potential tyranny of experts, one that can read, write, speak, manipulate symbols, argue, and judge, and whose imagination is as free as its reason.

These attributes are not synonymous with simple exposure to what is *euphemistically* called an education in the humanities or liberal arts, even when these are genuine—as often they are not. That belief only piles one illusion upon another. Rather than courses taken, or degrees conferred, the true tests of an educated mind are in its operations. Let me suggest some questions that indicate whether your mind operates like an educated one—no matter what your major may have been.

First, have you learned how to learn without your teacher? Can you work up a new subject, find the information, separate the relevant from the trivial, and express it in your own language? Can you discern which are your teacher's thoughts and which are your own? Your first freedom must be form the subtle despotism of even a great teacher's ideas.

Second, can you ask critical questions, no matter what subject is before you—those questions that expose a line of argument, evaluate the claims being made upon you, the evidence adduced, the logic employed? Can you sift fact from opinion, the plausible from the proven, the rhetorical from the logical? Can you use skepticism as a constructive tool and not as a refuge for intellectual sloth? Do you apply the same critical rigor to your own thoughts and actions? Or are you merely rearranging your prejudices when you think you are thinking?

Third, do you really understand what you are reading, what people are saying, what words they are using? Is your own language clear, concrete, and concise? Are you acquainted with the literature of your own language—with its structure and nuance?

Fourth, are your actions your own—based in an understanding and commitment to values you can defend? Can you discern the value conflicts underlying personal and public choices and distinguish what is a compromise to principle and what is not? Is your approach to moral judgments reasoned or emotional? When all the facts are in, when the facts are doubtful and action must be taken, can you choose wisely, prudently, and reasonably?

Fifth, can you form your own reasoned judgments about works of art—whether a novel, sonata, sculpture, or painting? Or are you enslaved by the critic, the book reviewer, and the "opinion makers" vacillating with their fads and pretentiousness? Artists try to evoke experiences in us, to transform us as humans. Is your imagination free enough to respond sensitively, or are you among the multitude of those who demand the explicitness of violence, pornography, dialogue—that is the sure sign of a dead imagination and an impoverished creativity?

Sixth, are your political opinions of the same order as your school and athletic loyalties—rooting for your side and ignoring the issues and ideas your side propounds? Free societies need independent voters who look at issues and not labels, who will be loyal to their ideals, not just to parties and factions. Do you make your insight as an expert the measure of social need? There is no illusion more fatal to good government!

If you can answer yes to some of these indicators, then you have imbibed the essence of a liberal education, one which assures that your actions are under the direction of your thought, that you are your own person, no matter what courses you took and what degree you receive today. You will also have achieved what is hoped for you:

> Education is thought of as not just imparting the knowledge of a professional discipline, but also as demonstrating a certain way of life—a way of life which is humane and thoughtful, yet also critical and above all rational.

If your answers are mostly negative (and I hope they are not), then you are in danger of harboring an illusion—one that is dangerous to you and society. The paradox is that the expert too has need of an educated mind. Professional and technical people make value decisions daily. To protect those whose values they affect, to counter the distorted pride of mere information, to use their capabilities for humane ends, experts too must reflect critically on what they do. The liberal arts, precisely because they are not specialties, are the indispensable accoutrements of any mind that claims to be human.

There are two kinds of freedom without which we cannot lead truly human lives. One kind is political and it is guaranteed by the Bill of Rights. The other is intellectual and is spiritual and is guaranteed by an education that liberates the mind. Political freedom assures that we can express our opinions freely; a liberal education assures that the opinions we express are free. Each depends so much on the other that to threaten one is to threaten the other.

This is why I vex you with such a serious topic on this very happy occasion. The matter is too important for indifference or comfortable illusions. My hope is that by nettling you a bit I can prevent what is now a harmless illusion from becoming a delusion—firm, fixed belief, impervious either to experience or reason.

May I remind you in closing that the people who made our nation, who endowed it with the practical wisdom that distinguished its history, were people without formal degrees. One of the best among them, Abraham Lincoln, went so far as to say: "No policy that does not rest upon philosophical public opinion can be permanently maintained." Philosophical public opinion is not the work of information or expertise but of an educated mind, one that matches the aim of Wilkes to impart a way of life that is ". . . humane and thoughtful, yet also critical and above all rational."

T. S. Eliot, in his poem "The Dry Salvages," said: "We have had the experience of an education—I hope you have not missed the meaning." You have had the experience of an education—I hope you have not missed the meaning.

ACTIVITIES AND QUESTIONS FOR REFLECTION

1. *How is the illusion of being educated affected by technology?*

2 *What is the difference between Pellegrino's "information" and Booth's "ideas"?*

3. *Which of the author's indicators of a truly educated person seem most important to you in forming your concept of an educated person?*

4. *The author cites two kinds of freedom. One is guaranteed to American citizens by the Bill of Rights. How do we achieve the other? How can it be limited by what the author calls "the tyranny of experts"?*

CHAPTER 2

⟶ *The Role of the Liberal Arts in a College Education*

SUMMARY

John Henry Cardinal Newman, who was quoted in this chapter and will be quoted in other readings, gave a famous series of lectures in 1852 and 1854 on the founding of the Catholic University of Dublin. In these lectures, published as *The Idea of a University,* Newman defined the university as "a place of teaching universal knowledge . . . the place to which a thousand schools make contributions; in which the intellect may safely range and speculate. . . . It is a place where inquiry is pushed forward, discoveries verified and perfected, and rashness rendered innocuous, and error exposed, by the collision of mind with mind, and knowledge with knowledge. . . . It is a seat of wisdom, a light of the world, a minister of the faith, an Alma Mater of the rising generation."

Although many times the first year dorm will not resemble a seat of wisdom and your classroom will feel less like a seat of knowledge than a seat of confusion, these seemingly lofty ideas are at the heart of the idea of college and of the educated person. That is the dream of most of your professors and certainly of the founders of your college. Even though the practice is often not perfect, this is the dream that underlies liberal arts education.

Using the Internet

Using InfoTrac College Edition, online libraries, or other Web sites, find biographies of at least two of the authors of readings or scholars mentioned in this chapter along with another article each has written.

1. What kinds of educations did the authors pursue?

2. How did their interest in a liberal arts education affect their careers? What are their interests outside the university?

3. Why did you choose these particular authors to research? What did you learn that you expected to learn? What was unexpected?

SUMMARIZING ACTIVITIES AND QUESTIONS FOR REFLECTION

1. *How has your understanding of the liberal arts been affected by these readings? Which reading was most provocative for you? Why?*

2. *What similarities and differences did you find between the articles?*

3. *Which of the liberal arts and sciences would you like to include in your college program? Why?*

4. *How did these readings change your ideas about the educated person? Your goals for your college education? Make appropriate revisions to your statement of goals for your college education and your conception of an educated person.*

Education and the Idea of Culture

INTRODUCTION: THE MEANINGS OF CULTURE

As human beings we live in social systems—families, religious communities, and workplaces, all of which develop their own cultures, their own standards for living and making judgments. There is much debate about how much a human culture is determined by the physical environment or by genetics, but most agree that from the day we are born, culture is learned.

Social classes are in effect cultures. From birth we learn the values and expectations of our socioeconomic class. Colleges develop cultures. Engineers will share certain attitudes and expectations about life and musicians will share others. These cultures determine what is acceptable and how to behave. They govern what we think about ourselves and others. They determine how to get things done within that system or group.

At one point in American history, it was thought to be desirable for all Americans to assimilate into one culture, "the melting pot," and it is still common for Americans to deny that there are differences between us. Until very late in the twentieth century, for example, our textbooks and children's books portrayed all Americans with one skin color and as favoring Western European foods.

The readings in this chapter examine the nature and value of our American cultures and explore the value of assimilation. These authors explain why it is important for you to understand your culture and subcultures, how this "cultural literacy" will make you stronger as an individual, how it will enable you to communicate with members of other cultures, and finally, how it will help you learn to identify and understand "how things get done" in your culture and in other cultures. This skill will be increasingly required of you in your work and social life in this age of globalization.

IN THE FIRST READING IN THIS CHAPTER, Laurent Daloz, professor at Lesley College in Cambridge, Massachusetts, tells a story about the lives of two women—one living in a primitive society in New Guinea and one living in rural Vermont. Their views of themselves and their worlds were formed as children living in homogeneous family systems. They were adults before they were exposed to different ways of seeing the world. This unanticipated exposure causes them to question their personal values and those of their families and friends. They now reach personal crises as they are presented with broadened and transformed frames of reference for thinking about themselves and their world.

AS YOU READ, consider the relationship between "tribal thinking," or cultural norms, and education. What challenges does this present for personal identity?

BEYOND TRIBALISM

Laurent A. Daloz

A central task of human development involves learning how to care for oneself in ways that increasingly incorporate the needs and concerns of others. . . . Thus is born the culture of adolescence, a world characterized by conformity to the expectations of others, by membership in the tribe. Many people live out their lives struggling to meet the expectations of their spouses, children, or friends, finding a kind of equilibrium as loyal tribal members. But not all. For some, the world shifts again, and they lose their balance once more. Consider Lale and Susan.

Lale

A woman in her late twenties, Lale is one of a small group of people in the Southern Highlands of New Guinea known as the Kutubu, a name meaning "the people." As a girl, Lale was closely watched by her family; it would not do to have her taken without bride payment or worse, kidnapped by the enemy. When Lale came of age, she was married to a man in a neighboring village and in time became the mother of three children. Lale's husband, Beni, spends much of his time with the other men of the tribe hunting

Excerpt from "Beyond Tribalism: Renaming the Good, the True, and the Beautiful," *Adult Education Quarterly*, Vol. 38, No. 4, Summer, 1988, pp. 234–241. Reprinted by permission of Laurent A. Daloz.

in the surrounding jungle or strengthening the village's defensive perimeter against the omnipresent danger of attack from the enemy in the North. He accepts without question his duty to join with the other men in protection of the tribe's women and children. For her part, Lale is glad to be protected. She is proud to be a Kutubu and cannot imagine any other kind of life. She accepts without question the laws and customs of her tribe, and her highest wish is to be a good wife and mother. It is a good life. To Lale, this is the way it has always been and always should be.

One day, she accompanies her friend to a regional market established by the government to foster trade and communication among the various local tribes. There she discovers women from other tribes. It is a whole new world.

Susan

Susan grew up in a small farming community in the northeastern corner of Vermont. Her parents watched her closely as a child for it would have been deeply humiliating for them had she become pregnant and been forced to marry. They were relieved when she graduated from high school and settled down to marry Armand, a young man from a neighboring village. While she raised their three children, he spent most of his time on the road driving a truck and serving his time as a member of the National Guard. Armand is a staunch patriot and is proud of the American flag on his truck he has named, "Miss Liberty." Susan shares her husband's patriotism and accepts without question his view, an echo of her father's, that America is the

greatest country in the world. She is proud to be an American. She cannot understand why some people she sees on TV seem so critical and nods approvingly when her husband snorts, "if they don't like it here, they can [leave]." This is a good life, and people should be thankful, not critical.

Then one day, going over family finances together, they come to the conclusion that Susan will need to get a job to supplement their income. Armand doesn't like the idea, but it seems they have no choice. Relieved that the children are all at school, Susan begins taking typing classes at the local community college. To meet a degree requirement, she takes a course in the Humanities where she discovers that her teacher, whom she greatly admires, does not share her husband's views. Nor do several of her classmates whom she respects. It is a whole new world.

Sustaining Ignorance

It would be a mistake, of course, to deny the differences between Lale and Susan. They live literally worlds and continents apart, in societies which, in many ways, are dramatically different. Yet the similarities are compelling. Each has encountered a new world which threatens her former balance. Let's look more closely.

Both Lale and Susan consider themselves normal people. They are well cared for, reasonably happy, and, above all, want to keep it that way. Each was carefully nurtured and protected by her family as she moved from childhood into adolescence. The delicate bridge between the first home and the second was crossed without incident, and each woman remains protected: first by her father, then by her husband. Within the circle of his arms she is safe. Their men, moreover, accept those responsibilities as given: to protect and provide for their families. Things as they are are things as they should be.

Each woman is held, as well, by her community. Each has learned right and wrong from her parents and, with little slippage, finds the same rules in her husband's home. Each takes it as her duty to pass on those same values to her children so that they, too, may be held as firmly by their community as she has been. Since they have come to see themselves as surrounded by a dangerous world, the circle of protection around their villages is doubly important, and each holds with special intensity to the beliefs with which she was reared. And although she may not express those beliefs often, when she does, it is with a sense of the obvious: Isn't it common sense to believe as we do? Rarely does either woman reflect upon or criticize the given truths of her culture, and she views with suspicion those who do. To be critical, she believes, is, at best, the province of men, and at worst, of traitors.

But there is one problem. Because Lale's and Susan's worlds have been born of communal, given traditions rather than constructed from an individual confrontation with doubt and uncertainty, those worlds must rely on insulation from conflicting information if they are to remain stable. To sustain that tidy world of certainties, the tribe must erect a wall between itself and the outside world. Knowledge of other truths—

even absurd ones, much less internally valid ones—is profoundly subversive and eats away at the tribe's security like a cancer. To maintain the stability of the tribe, a certain ignorance must be fostered.

When travelers leave home, they risk discovering a terrible secret: theirs is only one of any number of tribes, each believing its own truth to be paramount. Whether it is Lale going to market or Susan to secretarial school, the result is the same. The walls which both protected and isolated begin to crumble.

Beyond Tribal Gods

Formal education seeks more than mere indoctrination in the given values of a culture. It seeks to enable students to distance themselves from their upbringing, to see their values in a broader context. For only then can the culture remain alive to the possibility of change and develop the consequent capacity to adapt itself to an environment which is inevitably in flux. When it works, good education enables people to construct a coherent and responsive stance from complex information radiating from a rapidly shifting world. Such people are perhaps not as happy as they once were, but they probably do not view happiness as paramount. They have in some sense left the tribe and may suffer for that. Yet, in time they will make themselves at home in a larger tribe—ultimately, we hope, in a recognition of the intrinsic unity of the entire human family. The journey from one home to the next is seldom an easy one, but there is about it a kind of imperative. For some it seems a matter of life or death.

The Outward Journey

Throughout human history, maps of such growth have been handed down in the form of journey tales in which the hero leaves home in quest of some great adventure, usually symbolic of higher consciousness. Travelers in such tales invariably cross several thresholds as they move from one world to another. As the contemporary tale of human development is told, we make one major crossing as we move into conventional adult society. This crossing calls us to move from the security of our immediate family into the conventional adult tribe. We all recognize it as a necessary journey from a smaller to a larger home, and we call it growing up. It involves becoming normal and constitutes the chief task of adolescence. In most societies it is accomplished relatively smoothly and marked by such rituals as confirmation, bar mitzvah, and marriage.

A second crossing, departure from the tribe, is considerably less common and more dangerous. In a tribe like Lale's it is tantamount to death. One simply does not question the rules and remain an acceptable member of the tribe. And until, recently, Lale would have had nowhere else to go. Although Susan's tribe will react with similar disapproval to her rebellion, she can, at least, leave her former psychological home and suffer only a ritual rather than a literal death. With luck, hard work, and good friends, she and Armand will find a way to reconstruct a new home together.

The Second Crossing

Beyond this tightly bound world lies a wider world held together not by external bonds but by the conscious choice of its membership. It is a world in which the rules, formerly invisible, are now seen and chosen. Choice and responsibility are central to entrance. But the passage into this world is difficult. It demands that the pilgrim make a conscious decision to leave home, and the password is a question: Why? With the answer to that question, the world becomes visible in a new way.

Out of the gap between old givens and new discoveries, an inner voice is born, resonates with other voices in the market or at school, and grows stronger. Over time, Susan learns that it may be more important to receive a lesson than an answer. She sees with a crisper clarity that authorities do not always agree and begins to take authority into her own heart, to listen with greater respect to the inner voice even though it may contradict that of her culture. As she repeatedly comes up against conflicting information, she grows more adept at making choices. Nourished by the new light cast by her search for a way to make her own meaning, her inner world grows richer, she acknowledges more complex feelings. And as she does this, she grows increasingly able to understand the complexity of others' feelings as well. Her capacity to see through others' eyes expands, and she discovers that she is more than a reflection in her former tribal mirror. . . . Her horizon no longer stops at the edge of the village.

ACTIVITIES AND QUESTIONS FOR REFLECTION

1. *Can you identify an instance of "tribal thinking" in your own life or that of friends?*

2. *How will your "tribe" or family culture feel about changes that you have already begun to make as a student?*

3. *As you look over the studies you will be expected to complete for your college degree, which ones do you think might help you learn more about your own culture and about other cultures?*

IN THIS READING, Alan Purves, as professor of English and Education at the University of Illinois, explains more fully what is meant by the term culture and the idea of "cultural literacy." He compares the acquisition of cultural literacy to the learning of a language and sees it as having several functions. These functions might be thought of as steps in the development of cultural competence and independence.

AS YOU READ, look for the author's explanation of cultural literacy and the steps toward achieving it.

CULTURAL LITERACY
Alan C. Purves

The idea of culture goes back at least as far as the eighteenth century and was spurred in the nineteenth century by the nationalist impetus. Culture may best be defined as Edward Said [professor of English and Comparative Literature at Columbia University] has defined it:

> Culture is used to designate not merely something to which one belongs but something that one possesses, and along with that proprietary process, culture also designates a boundary by which the concepts of what is extrinsic or intrinsic to the culture comes into forceful play.

Anthropologists tend to see culture somewhat differently from literary people, but this root definition of possession and being possessed seems to apply both to those societies that operate through what might be called natural filiation (a system of intergenerational and familial relationships), and those that operate through affiliation to some arbitrarily instituted set of relationships. Current "American" culture is a culture of affiliation, whether it be the culture of Hawthorne and Harriet Beecher Stowe, the culture of Black Studies, the culture of feminism, or the culture of hard science. Some have argued that the idea of general education came to America in its attempt to define itself as America and to define American culture. Others have seen general education as an attempt by

Excerpt from "General Education and the Search for a Common Culture" in *Cultural Literacy and the Idea of General Education*. National Society for the Study of Education, 87th Yearbook, Part II (Chicago: University of Chicago Press, 1988), pp. 2–3. Reprinted by permission.

American educational institutions to ensure that the European heritage remained part of the American culture.

Any culture serves to isolate its members from other cultures and any culture is elitist in some senses. Cultures are exclusionary by definition; people who have a culture see others as outside or beneath them, and certainly very few people transcend cultures or [they] are full members of several subcultures, such as that of mycologists, joggers, or film aficionados as well as of the broader culture of "generally educated" Americans.

To be a member of a culture, one must possess a fair amount of knowledge, some of it tacit, concerning the culture: its rules, its rituals, its mores, its heroes, gods, and demigods. This knowledge lies at the heart of cultural literacy, and such knowledge is brought into play when people read and respond to a text that comes from the same culture. It is such knowledge that, in fact, enables them to read that text and is brought into play when we read and write as social beings within a particular community. The lack of such knowledge keeps us outside, as witness the problems of visitors to a national or disciplinary culture who often suffer trifling embarrassments or serious misunderstandings.

Cultural literacy may be thought of as language learning, for the study of any discipline or field of knowledge involves the learning of a language which represents a mode of thought culturally appropriate to the discipline. Judith Kadar-Fulop has written that there are three major functions of the language curriculum in school (and by extension the curriculum in any discipline) that accord with the definitions of language functions proposed by Uriel Weinreich [an authority on the Yiddish language]. The first of these functions is the promotion of cultural communication so as to enable the individual to communicate with other members of the culture or discipline. The second function is the promotion of cultural loyalty or the acceptance and valuing of those norms and routines and the inculcation of a desire to have them remain. A culturally loyal literate in physics, for example, would have certain expectations about how texts are to be written or to be read as well as what they should look like, and would expect others in the culture to follow those same norms. The third function of language education may be the development of individuality. Once one has learned to communicate within the culture and developed a loyalty to it, then one is able to become independent of it. Before then, independence of those norms and values is seen as naive, illiterate, or childish. As Lev Vygotsky [an education and language theorist] wrote: "In reality a child's thought progresses from the social to the individual not from the individual to the socialized."

ACTIVITIES AND QUESTIONS FOR REFLECTION

1. *Think about a culture of which you are a part in the sense of a group of people who share a system of values, and often a language, like joggers, musicians, or religious groups. In your own words, describe how you "possess" and are "possessed by" that culture.*

2. *Using that culture as an example, identify aspects that might serve the three functions or characteristics of cultural literacy:*

   a. *Cultural communication*

   b. *Cultural loyalty, the acceptance and valuing of norms and routines*

   c. *Development of individuality within the culture*

3. *If it were a goal of your education to become literate in the culture of Tibet or Haiti, what would you need to learn? What studies would you need to complete?*

⟼

RONALD TAKAKI, professor of ethnic studies at the University of California at Berkeley, grew up in Hawaii. In this reading, he describes his personal experience as a college student and as a professor with a lack of knowledge about the many cultures that compose the larger American culture. He uses the term "multicultural" in his advocacy of studies that will increase Americans' understanding and appreciation of diversity in their own culture.

AS YOU READ, look for the author's specific reasons for advocating multicultural studies in college and for the types of studies he suggests.

⟼

AN EDUCATED AND CULTURALLY LITERATE PERSON MUST STUDY AMERICA'S MULTICULTURAL REALITY
Ronald Takaki

In Palolo Valley, Hawaii, where I lived as a child, my neighbors were Japanese, Chinese, Portuguese, Filipino, and Hawaiian. I heard voices with different accents and I heard different languages. I played with children of different colors. Why, I wondered, were families representing such an array of nationalities living together in one little valley? My teachers and textbooks did not explain our diversity.

After graduation from high school, I attended a college on the mainland where students and even professors would ask me how long I had been in America and where I had learned to speak English. "In this country," I would reply. "I was born in America and my family has been here for three generations."

Today, some 20 years later, Asian and also Afro-American, Chicano/Latino, and Native-American students continue to find themselves perceived as strangers on college campuses. Moreover, they are encountering a new campus racism. The targets of ugly racial slurs and violence, they have begun to ask critical questions about why knowledge of their histories and communities is excluded from the curriculum. White students are also realizing the need to understand the cultural diversity of American society.

Excerpt from "An Educated and Culturally Literate Person Must Study America's Multicultural Reality" in *The Chronicle of Higher Education*, Vol. 35, No. 26 (March 8, 1989), pp. B1–2. Reprinted by permission.

I think [Allan] Bloom [professor at Chicago University, social theorist, and author of *The Closing of the American Mind*] is right when he says: "There are some things one must know about if one is to be educated. . . . The university should try to have a vision of what an educated person is." I also agree with [E. D.] Hirsch [author of *Cultural Literacy: What Every American Needs to Know*] when he insists that there is a body of cultural information that "every American needs to know."

The question is: What should be the content of education and what does cultural literacy mean? The traditional curriculum reflects what Howard Swearer, former president of Brown University, has described as a "certain provincialism," an overly Eurocentric perspective. Concerned about this problem, a Brown University visiting committee recommended that the faculty consider requiring students to take an ethnic-studies course before they graduate. "The contemporary definition of an educated person," the committee said, "must include at least minimal awareness of multicultural reality."

This view now is widely shared. Says Donna Shalala [former Chancellor of the University of Wisconsin at Madison and former U.S. Secretary of Health and Human Services, currently president of University of Miami]: "Every student needs to know much more about the origins and history of the particular cultures which, as Americans, we will encounter during our lives."

But the question often asked is: "What would be the focus and content of such multicultural courses?" Actually there is a wide range of possibilities. For many years I have been teaching a course on "Racial Inequality in America: A Comparative Historical Perspective." Who we are in this society and how we are perceived and treated have been conditioned by America's racial and ethnic diversity. My approach is captured in the phrase "from different shores." By "shores," I intend a double meaning. One is the shores that immigrants left to go to America, those in Europe, Africa, Latin America and Asia. The second is the different and often conflicting shores or perspectives from which scholars have viewed the experiences of racial and ethnic groups.

In my course, students read Thomas Sowell's *Ethnic America: A History* along with my *Iron Cages: Race and Culture in 19th-Century America*. Readings also include Winthrop Jordan on the colonial origins of racism, John Higham on nativism, Mario Barrera on Chicanos, and William J. Wilson on the black underclass. By critically examining the different "shores," students are able to address complex comparative questions: How have the experiences of racial minorities such as blacks and Asians been similar to, and different from, one another? Is "race" the same as "ethnicity?" How have race relations been shaped by economic developments, as well as by culture? What impact have these forces had on moral values about how people should think and behave, beliefs about human nature and society, and images of the past as well as the future?

Other courses could examine racial diversity in relation to gender, immigration, urbanization, technology, or the labor market.

Courses could also study specific topics such as Hollywood's racial images, ethnic music and art, novels by writers of color, the Civil Rights movement, or the Pacific Rim. Regardless of theme or topic, all of the courses should address the major theoretical issues concerning race and should focus on Afro-Americans, Asians, Chicanos/Latinos, and Native Americans.

The need to open the American mind to greater cultural diversity will not go away. We can resist it by ignoring the changing ethnic composition of our student bodies and the larger society, or we can realize how it offers colleges and universities a timely and exciting opportunity to revitalize the social sciences and humanities, giving both a new sense of purpose and a more inclusive definition of knowledge.

If concerted efforts are made, someday students of different racial backgrounds will be able to learn about one another in an informed and systematic way and will not graduate from our institutions of higher learning ignorant about how places like Palolo Valley fit into American society.

—————

ACTIVITIES AND QUESTIONS FOR REFLECTION

1. *How many different cultures can you identify in either your home community or your college community?*

2. *In what ways might your college studies and other activities expand your awareness of different cultures to enrich your college experience and prepare you for life in the world of work?*

3. *Does the college in which you are enrolled offer or require any of the studies Takaki suggests to increase your cultural awareness and your ability to learn about new cultures you will encounter there and in your life?*

↠

IN THIS READING, James Banks, director of the Center of Multicultural Education at the University of Washington, begins by identifying what he believes are the limitations of "community cultures" in a pluralistic society. He goes on to say why he believes multicultural education is needed in American schools and colleges. He contrasts the traditional curriculum of Western European–oriented schools with one that is multicultural in content and argues that a multicultural curriculum will achieve the American democratic ideals more fully than the traditional Western European model does.

AS YOU READ, look for the characteristics of multicultural education that the author is convinced make it the best "education for freedom."

↠

MULTICULTURAL EDUCATION FOR FREEDOM'S SAKE
James A. Banks

An important factor that limits human freedom in a pluralistic society is the cultural encapsulation into which all individuals are socialized. People learn the values, beliefs, and stereotypes of their community cultures. Although these community cultures enable individuals to survive, they also restrict their freedom and ability to make critical choices and to take actions to help reform society.

Education within a pluralistic society should affirm and help students understand their home and community cultures. However, it should also help free them from their cultural boundaries. To create and maintain a civic community that works for the common good, education in a democratic society should help students acquire the knowledge, attitudes, and skills they will need to participate in civic action to make society more equitable and just.

Multicultural education is an education for freedom that is essential in today's ethnically polarized and troubled world. It has evoked a divisive national debate in part because of the divergent views that citizens hold about what constitutes an American

Excerpt from "Multicultural Education for Freedom's Sake." *Educational Leadership*, Vol. 49, No. 4, Dec. '91/Jan. '92, pp. 32–36. Reprinted with permission of the Association for Supervision and Curriculum Development and James A. Banks.

identity and about the roots and nature of American civilization. The debate in turn has sparked a power struggle over who should participate in formulating the canon [or standards] used to shape the curriculum in the nation's schools, colleges, and universities.

Sharing Power

Western traditionalists and multiculturalists must realize that they are entering into debate from different power positions. Western traditionalists hold the balance of power, financial resources, and the top positions in the mass media, in schools, colleges and universities, in government, and in the publishing industry. Genuine discussion between the traditionalists and the multiculturalists can take place only when power is placed on the table, negotiated, and shared.

Despite all of the rhetoric about the extent to which Chaucer, Shakespeare, Milton, and other Western writers are threatened by the onslaught of women and writers of color into the curriculum, the reality is that the curriculum in the nation's schools and universities is largely Western in its concepts, paradigms, and content. Concepts such as the Middle Ages and the Renaissance are still used to organize most units in history, literature, and the arts. When content about African and Asian cultures is incorporated into the curriculum, it is usually viewed within the context of European concepts and paradigms. For example, Asian, African, and American histories are often studied under the topic, "The Age of Discovery," which means the time when Europeans first arrived on these continents.

Facing Realities

If they are to achieve a productive dialogue rather than a polarizing debate, both Western traditionalists and the multiculturalists must face some facts. The growing number of people of color in our society and schools constitutes a demographic imperative that educators must hear and respond to. The 1990 Census indicated that one of every four Americans is a person of color. By the turn of the century, one of every three will be of color. Nearly half of the nation's students will be of color by 2020. Although the school and university curriculums remain Western-oriented, this growing number of people of color will increasingly demand to share power in curriculum decision making and in shaping a curriculum canon that reflects their experiences, histories, struggles, and victories.

People of color, women, and other marginalized groups are demanding that their voices, visions, and perspectives be included in the curriculum. They ask that the debt Western civilization owes to Africa, Asia, and indigenous America be acknowledged. The advocates of the Afrocentric curriculum, in sometimes passionate language that reflects a dream long deferred, are merely asking that the cultures of African and African American people be legitimized in the curriculum and that the African contributions to European civilization be acknowledged. People of color and women are also demanding that the facts about their victimization be told, for truth's sake, but also because they need to better understand their conditions so that they and others can work to reform society.

However, these groups must acknowledge that they do not want to eliminate Aristotle and Shakespeare, or Western civilization, from the school curriculum. To reject the West would be to reject important aspects of their own cultural heritages, experiences, and identities. The most important scholarly and literary works written by African Americans, such as works by W. E. B. Du Bois, Carter G. Woodson, and Zora Neale Thurston, are expressions of Western cultural experiences. African American culture resulted from a blending of African cultural characteristics with those of African peoples in the United States.

Reinterpreting Western Civilization

Rather than excluding Western civilization from the curriculum, multiculturalists want a more truthful, complex, and diverse version of the West taught in the schools. They want the curriculum to describe the ways in which African, Asian, and indigenous American cultures have influenced and interacted with Western civilization. They also want schools to discuss not only the diversity and democratic ideals of Western civilization, but also its failures, tensions, dilemmas, and the struggles by various groups in Western societies to realize their dreams against great odds.

We need to deconstruct the myth that the West is homogenous, that it owes few debts to other world civilizations, and that only privileged and upper status Europeans and European American males have been its key actors.

We should teach students that knowledge is a social construction, that it reflects the perspectives, experiences, and the values of the people and cultures that construct it, and that it is dynamic, changing, and debated among knowledge creators and users. Rather than keep such knowledge debates as the extent to which African civilizations contributed to Western civilization out of the classroom, teachers should make them an integral part of teaching. The classroom should become a forum in which multicultural debates concerning the construction of knowledge take place. The voices of the Western traditionalists, the multiculturalists, textbook authors, and radical writers should be heard and legitimized in the classroom.

Educating for Freedom

Each of us becomes culturally encapsulated during our socialization in childhood. We accept the assumptions of our community culture, internalize its values, views of the universe, misconceptions, and stereotypes. Although this is as true for the child socialized within a mainstream culture as it is for the minority child, minority children are usually forced to examine, confront, and question their cultural assumptions when they enter school.

Students who are born and socialized within the mainstream culture of a society rarely have an opportunity to identify, question, and challenge their cultural assumptions, beliefs, values, and perspectives because the school culture usually reinforces those that they learn at home and in their communities. Consequently, mainstream Americans have few opportunities to become free of cultural assumptions and perspectives that are monocultural, that devalue African and Asian cultures, and that stereotype people of color and people who are poor, or who are victimized in other ways. These mainstream Americans often have an inability to function effectively within other American cultures, and lack the ability and motivation to experience and benefit from cross cultural participation and relationships.

To fully participate in our democratic society, these students and all students need the skills a multicultural education can give them to understand others and to thrive in a rapidly changing, diverse world. Thus, the debate between the Western traditionalists and the multiculturalists fits well within the tradition of a pluralistic democratic society. Its final result will most likely be not exactly what either side wants, but a synthesized and compromised perspective that will provide a new vision for the nation as we enter the 21st century.

ACTIVITIES AND QUESTIONS FOR REFLECTION

1. *How does the author see multicultural education relating to traditional Western education? What changes does he see as necessary?*

2. *What does the author mean by saying that multicultural education is "education for freedom"? How does this relate to concepts of cultural literacy presented by Purves in the second reading in this chapter?*

3. *To what extent, if any, do you think your education has been multicultural? Ask two or three college friends this question. How do you explain the similarities and differences you find?*

4. *Do you see ways in which a broader cultural perspective would help you participate more fully in your culture or the culture around you? Do you see greater understanding of other cultures as a goal of your college education?*

↤

Throughout the history of the university, the concept of what constitutes knowledge worth passing on to the next generation has changed many times—and never without a struggle. In the last half of the twentieth century, the nature of college studies and college students changed radically. In this reading, Joan Wallach Scott, an historian, discusses the diverse interests of students on university campuses today and proposes a new concept of community to address these differences. Most of these changes were made in the 1970s and 1980s and had largely stabilized by 1991, the year from which Scott's statistics are taken.

Scott stresses the importance of the university as a forum of free exchange devoted to learning and reminds us that the function of the university is to question and to find new ways to transmit the knowledge that is fundamental to the definition of culture.

As you read, look for the radical changes in the student body that took place on college campuses between 1960 and the end of the twentieth century and the place these changes have in Scott's definition of the university as a "community of difference."

↤

Diversity, Community, and the University
Joan Wallach Scott

Diversity

Universities have changed dramatically since the 1960s and much of the present controversy has its roots in those changes. In 1960, 94 percent of college students were white; the figure was 96 percent for private universities. Of the remaining 6 percent, 2 percent attended predominantly black institutions. A number of public and private universities did not admit blacks at all, and some of the most highly regarded centers of learning did not

Excerpt from *Change*, 23 (Nov/Dec 1991): 30–43. Reprinted with permission of the Helen Dwight Reid Educational Foundation. Published by Heldref Publications, 1319 Eighteenth Street N.W. Washington, DC 20036-1802. Copyright © 1991.

admit women. Colleges tended to be white male enclaves for students and faculty: 63 percent of college students were men, 90 percent of Ph.D.s were men, and 80 percent of university faculties were men. (When I was a graduate student in this period, the Woodrow Wilson Foundation stated explicitly that no more than one-fourth of their graduate fellowships would be awarded to women.) In 1991, 20 percent of all college students are nonwhite or Hispanic and 55 percent are women. Women make up over one-third of all graduate students and are even more highly represented as Ph.D. candidates in the humanities; they now represent about 30 percent of university faculties.

The new populations in the universities bring with them histories of their own that have not been part of the traditional curriculum; their presence challenges many of the prevailing assumptions about what counts as knowledge and how it is produced. This is so primarily because of the sheer numbers, as well as the new kinds, of students and faculty on campuses. Is critical thinking possible when masses of students are attending college, instead of only the children of elites? Is critical thinking advisable for the masses of students or should they be given a prescribed education that they will passively receive? Can critical thinking take place in communities that are no longer elite and homogeneous?

Is it possible for universities to be centers of intellectual conflict when there are differences that cannot be resolved? I think so, but only if diversity is not conceived in individualistic terms and if our notions of community are redefined.

Community

If universities are to adapt to the new conditions of diversity, the notion of community according to which they operate must change. Some of the extraordinary tensions evident on campuses these days stem from attempts to impose universalist ideas of community that presume homogeneity and that stress consensus and shared values on a situation in which differences seem fundamental and irreducible. The consensual idea assumes that some commonality of interests allows "us" to articulate our common concerns and regulate our disagreements; those who do not accept the consensus are necessarily outside the community.

This is the idea that, in the name of a common culture, is invoked by those who defend the superiority of Shakespeare to, say, Toni Morrison (as if anyone were insisting that contemporary literature entirely replace "the classics"); it is the idea that underlies some disciplinary codes as well as some of the most extreme demands for "political correctness." This vision of consensus ultimately requires, indeed imposes, homogeneity—not of persons, but of point of view. It rests on a set of exclusions of "others."

Something else is needed in these days of diversity and differences, and not only for the university. But the university is the best place from which to search for a different understanding of what a community might be. First of all, universities can be seen to already exemplify an alternative. They are, after all, places where separate and contingent, contradictory and heterogeneous spheres of thought have long coexisted; the grounds for that co-existence are acceptance of difference and an aversion to orthodoxy. (Universities aren't immune to outside influences, but they process them in their own ways.) This doesn't mean there aren't continuing battles for resources, influence, and predominance; indeed, these kinds of politics are the way differences are negotiated. It does mean that there is ultimately no resolution, no final triumph for any particular brand of thought or knowledge.

Second, within the universities, the humanities in particular offer the possibility of thinking about difference and community in new ways. There is one approach within the humanities, to be sure, that would reify a particular canon as the defining mark of our common humanity. But there is another more complicated approach, equally available in the very fact that humanities is "humanity in the plural." Jonathan Culler put it this way:

> A particular virtue of literature, of history, of anthropology is instruction in otherness: vivid, compelling evidence of differences in cultures, mores, assumptions, values. At their best, these subjects make otherness palpable and make it comprehensible without reducing it to an inferior version of the same, as a universalizing humanism threatens to do.

Add to this the fact that interpretation is the name of the game in humanities, that meanings are always contested, reworked, revoked, and redefined, and there is at least a basis for thinking about communities in which consensus cannot prevail. Thought

about in these terms, the humanities become a starting point for discussion of the reconceptualization of community in the age of diversity.

I do not have a blueprint for that idea of community, but I think there are points it must address. Here is a partial list:

> Differences are often irreducible and must be accepted as such.

> Differences are relational, and involve hierarchy and differentials of power that will be constantly contested.

> Conflict and contest are therefore inherent in communities of difference. There must be ground rules for coexistence that do not presume the resolution of conflict and discovery of consensus.

> Communities cannot be based on conformity, but on an acceptance and acknowledgment of difference.

Christopher Fynsk, following Jean-Luc Nancy, suggested that the French word *partage* inform our notion of community. *Partage* means both to divide and to share; this double and contradictory meaning insists on what Fynsk called "openings to the other" as a condition of existence. In contrast, conformity that rules out the other, substituting one set of beliefs for another, brings us the regime of yellow ribbons and American flags as the test of patriotism. It leads students to condemn dissent, as one student did at Princeton last fall, as treasonous and un-American.

Partage is a more difficult concept than consensus, but a much better one, I submit. It accepts difference as a condition of our lives and suggests various ways we might well live with it. It lets us accommodate one another as we strive on a large scale for what is already possible in the classroom, at least in classrooms such as the one described by Elsa Barkley Brown. For her, teaching African-American women's history is not merely an intellectual process. It is not merely a question of whether or not we have learned to analyze in particular kinds of ways, or whether people are able to intellectualize about a variety of experiences. It is also about coming to believe in the possibility of a variety of experiences, a variety of ways of understanding the world, a variety of frameworks of operation, without imposing consciously or unconsciously a notion of the norm.

The University

Can universities become the place where communities of difference—irreducible and irreconcilable difference—are conceptualized and exemplified? This is the challenge we are to face in the coming years. It is a challenge that must be carried on, even in the face of outrageous, threatening, and punitive attacks. It is a challenge that requires the kind of critical intellectual work universities are supposed to encourage. Such critical work is, after all, the university's *raison d'être* and its highest form of achievement.

ACTIVITIES AND QUESTIONS FOR REFLECTION

1. *Did you expect to find that there is disagreement about what knowledge is and about what should be taught in college? Why or why not?*

2. *For many students, attending college also means exposure to people with widely differing backgrounds, personal experiences, and cultural beliefs—social, economic, religious, political, and so on. Which are the most intriguing for you?*

3. *Can you explain how a "community of differences" might contribute to your understanding of yourself and your own culture?*

↦

A SIGNIFICANT CHANGE in our contemporary society is the global nature of economic systems. This economic change, largely a result of advances in technology, has resulted in equally significant social change and will require the ability to understand and communicate with people of many more cultures than was true of previous generations of Americans. This means not only Italian Americans, Japanese Americans, and Muslim Americans but also native Japanese, Kenyans, and Afghani Muslims. In the following reading, Rita Weathersby, professor of management education at the University of New Hampshire, discusses what this will require of workers in the new economy.

AS YOU READ, look for the prerequisites to developing a global perspective.

↦

DEFINING A GLOBAL PERSPECTIVE
Rita Weathersby

To define a global perspective, we must distinguish "global" from "international." An international perspective implies encounters between nations. A global perspective implies a somewhat borderless perspective on the whole. When we look at a photograph of the earth seen from space we see no borders, rather a single, interconnected system. A global perspective implies the consciousness of a world citizen. It also requires an intellectual and emotional understanding of the complex interdependencies among economic, environmental, cultural, and sociopolitical realities affecting all of us. Within these interdependencies, we must manage our affairs with concern for the world system in which our activities are embedded.

Thus there are two prerequisites for developing a global perspective:

a. cultivating the expanded identity of a world citizen, which necessitates moving beyond the parochial and ethnocentric worldviews that characterize most people in most countries of the world; and

b. fostering the development of advanced qualities of thinking that are systematic and integrative, so that complex problems are resolved within increasingly complex intellectual and emotional frameworks.

The crux of a global perspective is an expression of identity past concern for oneself and one's business, and from one's own people or nation, to a concern for fostering the diverse interests and well being of all people in the world system.

At stake is the generation of hope that the world will be a better place, despite our planet's macroproblems of poverty and hunger, the uneven distribution of wealth and resources, environmental decline, and the persistence of war and political conflict. Also, we can increase the potential of our business schools and students being better able to respond positively to world economic and social problems.

Global Thinking Skills

"Complicate yourself!" is good advice to managers whatever the context, but is essential advice in the global arena. "Complicated understanding" is necessary for managerial effectiveness. It is also embedded in advanced progression of human development. The shift to a global perspective necessitates new thinking skills that involve higher-order cognitive, perceptual, and emotional processes in complex combinations.

Systems Thinking

Systems thinking is simultaneously parts-and-whole thinking derived from principles of general systems theory as it has been applied in fields as diverse as the physical and social sciences, engineering, and management. [Peter Senge of the Sloan School of Management at MIT] describes systems thinking as a "discipline for seeing wholes. It is a framework for seeing interrelationships rather than things, for seeing patterns of change rather than static

'snapshots.'" Systems thinking helps people deal with complexity because it organizes a vast amount of detail. Further, focusing on the interrelations and interconnections of a system simplifies complex reality.

The ability to reframe situations because one understands the dynamics of a system (and can therefore find leverage for change) is crucial to global thought. Reframing is a complex intellectual and emotional process, but also a practical one. Ideally, what is needed is a "strategic systems thinking" as opposed to "mechanical systems thinking." Mechanical systems thinking merely leads to a rearrangement of elements in a problem solution, whereas strategic systems thinking leads to a transformation of the problem or a changed configuration of problem elements.

Seeing a Bigger Picture

American business is often criticized because of a short-term focus on profitability that leads to actions that undermine the achievement of an organization's long-term goals. An antidote to short-term decision-making is a "bigger, more complex picture." Developing a broader base of information and developing the ability to shift among multiple contexts and time perspectives are habits of mind associated with the "bigger picture." There are obvious overlaps with systems thinking, but "big picture thinking" is also a distinctive competence.

Resolving Issues from Multiple Perspectives

The ability to resolve issues from more than one perspective is crucial to global thinking. Cognitively, this cluster of skills involves getting beyond dichotomous "either/or" thinking to simultaneous "both/and" thinking. Similar thought processes are involved in "getting to yes" in win-win conflict resolution. Resolving issues from multiple perspectives requires decision logics based in complementarity. The principle of complementarity demonstrates that many phenomena can be understood only if several different perspectives are applied to them. No single theory correctly or completely represents the whole. Originally, complementarity theory reconciled paradoxes in quantum physics. Interdependence, connectedness, and relationship are crucial assumptions. When multiple perspectives coexist, and diverse needs and demands are taken into account, a problem solution can reflect a synergy in which "something new" or "something more" emerges from a thoughtful engagement with difference.

"Thinking Globally and Acting Locally"

A global perspective makes action more complex. It requires people to deal with paradox and contradiction. It expands the number of stakeholders. It requires an expanded commitment to inclusive human values. It also involves generating commitment to a positive vision. The ability to "think globally and act locally" is a useful heuristic for exploring the qualities that enable action in this wider context.

In the face of overwhelming complexity, it is easy to conclude that difficult issues have no resolution, and that individual and organizational actions do not matter. To act, a person must get beyond despair. "Thinking globally and acting locally" requires accepting responsibility for difficult trade-offs and summoning from within oneself qualities such as faith and hope that allow an individual to develop a positive, value-based stance within which to frame actions. Individuals' struggles to develop these qualities create important emotional undercurrents in the classroom that make it essential that the instructional process empower individuals as well as expand their thinking.

ACTIVITIES AND QUESTIONS FOR REFLECTION

1. *What aspects of your daily life have already presented you with the opportunity to think globally? Sports? Music? Weather? Hobbies?*

2. *In what area of your life could you practice systems thinking? For example, an area in which you might see interrelationships and influences, like music or film, a subject in which you see the parts as a function of the whole. Explain.*

3. *What studies does your college offer that would increase your ability to think in systems? Are there any studies that do not teach about systems?*

4. *Is the idea of "complicating" yourself intriguing or anxiety producing? How would you approach this? As you begin your college studies, perhaps you feel that this is what is happening to you now.*

CHAPTER 3

⟿ *Education and the Idea of Culture*

SUMMARY

This chapter has focused on a subject that is of fundamental concern to your future: the ability to acknowledge and respect differences so you can function productively in our increasingly interdependent economies and social systems. All aspects of cultural studies—history, philosophy, languages, literature—will be increasingly relevant and important as you are expected to move beyond your family culture, your national culture, and your religious culture into those of others.

Cultural literacy, comfort with different cultural traditions, and the ability to "get things done" in unfamiliar cultures will predict your success in the future. Both your personal life and your life at work will be increasingly multicultural.

One function your education can serve is to enable you to understand and communicate with those who are different from yourself. In turn, this will bring you greater independence as you understand your own culture more deeply.

Using the Internet

Choose a culture of which you are a member or a subject in which you are interested and imagine how you would "go global" with that culture. For example, if you are a musician or interested in music, you might explore the culture of musicians or the nature of music in Asia, South America, and Iceland. Use InfoTrac College Edition or Google to find five sources that would help you learn about this culture or subject in other countries.

If you don't have a culture or subject you are interested in exploring, try this with medicine, skate boarding, agriculture, psychology, or childcare.

SUMMARIZING ACTIVITIES AND QUESTIONS FOR REFLECTION

1. *In reviewing the readings in this chapter, which most revealed to you questions and assumptions that you would like to study further?*

2. *Have any of these readings challenged your previous assumptions? How? Why?*

3. *For each of the readings in this chapter, describe a way in which the author's ideas and concerns might affect you in your college education.*

4. *Review your goals for your college education and your definition of an educated person and make revisions or additions that capture any new understandings you now have.*

Education and Personal Development

INTRODUCTION: LEARNING AND SELF

The readings and activities in this chapter will help you explore and reflect on your development as a person, appreciate your own complexity, and gain an understanding of your ability to change and grow. With this deeper understanding, you will be able to plan an education that will contribute to your development as a *whole* person, not just in college, but also throughout your life.

Harold Taylor, former president of Sarah Lawrence College, once said, that in education you must involve yourself in discovering the meaning of your own life and the relation between who you are and what you might become. "Without a hard look at the reality of one's own situation the ultimate purpose of education itself—that is to grow, to change, to liberate oneself—is almost impossible to achieve."

These readings will introduce you to the work of psychologists who study various aspects of personal or developmental changes in adulthood, generally defined as beginning between ages sixteen and eighteen. The discovery that we continue to grow and change throughout our lives, not just in childhood, is relatively new. The research has all been done in the last thirty years or so. Thus, some findings are still controversial and not all ages, genders, and cultural group combinations have been studied. A body of knowledge is emerging, however, that provides a sometimes-sketchy pattern of development in adult life.

Laurent Daloz, an educator, makes some useful suggestions for you to keep in mind as you read human development theory. He suggests that you think about it as a kind of map that you can use to study and plan your own life:

> What goes on a map clearly depends on what interests the [map maker], and the map we choose depends on what we wish to know. The same goes for theories of human development. Although developmentalists, like cartographers, may assert at times that their maps are value-free or strictly descriptive, they have made choices in constructing their schemes to highlight some elements and ignore others. Those choices inevitably affect the traveler who is using the map.

Yet good maps offer choices; they are not mere formulas. And although developmental theories do imply direction, none insist that the journey can be taken in only one way or, indeed, that it can be completed at all. Just as a map frames the setting for a journey, developmental theory offers a context for growth. It indicates landmarks, points out dangers, suggests possible routes and destinations, but leaves the walking to us.

Before you begin reading some of the "maps" of adult development, pause for a moment and think about what a map of your own life might look like up to this point. Have you traveled in a straight line over a flat surface? Or have you encountered forks or crossroads along the way? Which direction did you choose and why? Was the road bumpy or smooth? What caused some of the bumps? Perhaps you encountered mountains or rivers that changed your direction. Who did you meet on the way and how did they affect your journey? And where do you expect to go? What do you expect to see?

⤙

SIGMUND FREUD FORMULATED the first theory of human development. He thought what happened between birth and adolescence set a pattern for life, that development stopped at adolescence. He also thought individuals were shaped almost exclusively by their interactions with their parents and their relationships with them. The first theory that development continued into adulthood was formulated by Erik Erikson. Erikson agreed that the roles of the family and childhood experiences were formative, but he saw the later interactions of the individual with the social environment as an important factor. In this reading, David Elkind, a psychologist at Yale University, describes Erikson's work.

AS YOU READ, ask yourself what Erikson means by stages. What new tasks or orientations must one accomplish at each stage? And what does it mean to form an identity?

⤙

ERIKSON'S EIGHT STAGES OF LIFE
David Elkind

At a recent faculty reception I happened to join a small group in which a young mother was talking about her "identity crisis." She and her husband had decided not to have any more children and she was depressed at the thought of being past the childbearing stage. It was as if she had been robbed of some part of herself and now needed to find a new function to replace the old one.

When I remarked that her story sounded like a case history from a book by Erik Erikson, she replied, "Who's Erikson?" Few of the many people who today talk about the "identity crisis" know anything of the man who, two decades ago, pointed out its pervasiveness in contemporary society.

Erikson has, however, contributed more to social science than his delineation of identity problems. His descriptions of the stages of the life cycle have advanced psychoanalytic theory to the point where it can now describe the development of the healthy personality on its own terms and not merely as the opposite of a sick one. Likewise, Erikson's emphasis upon the problems unique to adolescents and adults living in today's society has helped to rectify the one-sided emphasis on childhood as the beginning and end of personality development.

Erikson set forth the implications of his clinical observations in *Childhood and Society*. In that book, the summation and integration of 15 years of research, he made three major contributions:

1. that, side by side with the stages of psychosexual development described by Freud were psychosocial stages of ego development in which the individual had to establish new basic orientations to one's self and one's social world;

2. that personality development continued throughout the whole life cycle; and

3. that each stage had a positive *as well as* a negative component.

Much about these contributions—and about Erikson's way of thinking—can be understood by looking at his scheme of life stages. Erikson identifies eight stages. In each, a new dimension of "social interaction" becomes possible—that is, a new dimension in one's interaction with oneself, and with one's social environment.

Trust vs. Mistrust

The first stage corresponds to the oral stage in classical psychoanalytic theory and usually extends through the first year of life. In Erikson's view, the new dimension of social interaction that emerges during this period involves basic *trust* at the one extreme, and *mistrust* at the

other. The degree to which the child comes to trust the world, other people and him- or herself depends upon the quality of the care that he or she receives. The infant whose needs are met, whose discomforts are quickly removed, who is cuddled, played with, and talked to, develops a sense of the world as a safe place to be and of people as helpful and dependable. When the care is inconsistent, inadequate, and rejecting, it fosters a basic mistrust, an attitude of fear and suspicion toward the world in general and people in particular that will carry through to later stages of development.

The problem of basic trust-versus-mistrust (as is true for all the later stages) is not resolved once and for all during the first year of life; it arises again at each successive stage. There is both hope and danger in this. The child who enters school with a sense of mistrust may come to trust a particular teacher and overcome the early mistrust. On the other hand, the child who comes through infancy with a vital sense of trust can still have mistrust activated at a later stage.

Autonomy vs. Doubt

Stage two spans the second and third years of life, the period which Freudian theory calls the anal stage. Erikson sees here the emergence of *autonomy*. This autonomy dimension builds upon the child's new motor and mental abilities. The child can not only walk but also climb, open and close, drop, hold and let go. The child takes pride in these new accomplishments and wants to do everything him- or herself, whether it be pulling the wrapper off a piece of candy, selecting the vitamin out of the bottle or flushing the toilet. If parents recognize the young child's needs to do what he or she is capable of doing at his or her own pace, then the child develops a sense of being able to control his or her muscles, impulses, and the environment—the sense of autonomy.

When his caretakers are impatient and do what he or she is capable of doing him- or herself, they reinforce a sense of shame and *doubt*. The child who leaves this stage with less autonomy than shame and doubt will be handicapped in attempts to achieve autonomy in adolescence and adulthood. The child who moves through this stage with a sense of autonomy buoyantly outbalancing feelings of shame and doubt is well prepared to be autonomous at later phases in the life cycle. Again, however, the balance can be changed in either positive or negative directions by later events.

Initiative vs. Guilt

In this stage (the genital stage of classical psychoanalysis) the child, age 4 to 5, is pretty much master of his or her body and can ride a tricycle, run, cut and hit, and no longer merely responds to or imitates the actions of other children. The same holds true for language and fantasy activities. Accordingly, Erikson argues, the social dimension that appears at this stage has *initiative* at one of its poles and *guilt* at the other.

Children who are given freedom and opportunity to initiate motor play such as running, bike riding, sliding, skating, tussling and wrestling have their sense of initiative reinforced. Initiative is also reinforced when parents answer their children's questions (intellectual initiative) and do not deride fantasy or play activity. If the child is made to feel that motor activity is bad, that questions are a nuisance and that play is silly and stupid, then he or she may develop a sense of guilt over self-initiated activities that will persist through later stages.

Industry vs. Inferiority

Stage four, ages 6 to 11, the elementary school years (described by classical psychoanalysis as the latency phase), is a time during which the child's love for the parent of the opposite sex and rivalry with the same sexed parent are quiescent (the so-called family romance). It is also a period during which the child becomes capable of deductive reasoning, and of playing and learning by rules. It is not until this period, for example, that children can really play marbles, checkers and other "take turn" games. Erikson argues that the psychosocial dimension that emerges during this period has a sense of *industry* at one extreme and a sense of *inferiority* at the other.

The term *industry* captures a dominant theme of this period—a concern with how things are made, how they work and what they do. When children are encouraged in their efforts to make, do, or build practical things (whether it be to construct creepy crawlers, tree houses, or airplane models—or to cook, bake or sew), are allowed to finish their products, and are praised and rewarded for the results, then the sense of industry is enhanced. But parents who see their children's efforts at making and doing as "mischief," and as simply "making a mess," encourage in children a sense of inferiority.

Now social institutions come to play a central role in the development of the individual.

The child, for example, with an IQ of 80 to 90 has a particularly traumatic school experience that reinforces a sense of inferiority. On the other hand, the child can have his or her sense of industry revitalized at school through a sensitive teacher. How the child develops no longer depends solely on the caretaking of the parents.

Identity vs. Role Confusion

When the child moves into adolescence (Stage five—roughly the ages 12–18), he or she encounters, according to traditional psychoanalytic theory, a reawakening of the family-romance. The means of resolving the problem is to seek and find a romantic partner of one's own generation. Erikson points out that there are other problems as well. The adolescent matures mentally as well as physiologically and, in addition to changes in his or her body, develops new ways of looking at and thinking about the world. Adolescents can wonder what other people think of them. They can also conceive of ideal families, religions and societies which they can then compare with the imperfect families, religions and societies of their own experience. They become capable of constructing theories and philosophies designed to bring the varied and conflicting aspects of society into a working, harmonious, and peaceful whole. The adolescent is an impatient idealist who believes that it is as easy to realize an ideal as it is to imagine it.

Erikson believes that this new interpersonal dimension has to do with a sense of *ego identity* at the positive end and a sense of *role confusion* at the negative end. Given the ado-

lescent's newfound integrative abilities, the task is to bring together all of the things he or she has learned about him- or herself and integrate these different images into a whole that makes sense and that shows continuity with the past while preparing for the future. While the influence of parents during this stage is much more indirect, preparation for a successful adolescence begins in the cradle.

The attainment of a sense of personal identity also depends upon the social milieu in which one grows up. In a society where women are to some extent second-class citizens, it may be harder for females to arrive at a sense of psychosocial identity. When rapid social and technological change breaks down many traditional values, it may be more difficult for young people to find continuity between what they learned and experienced as children and what they learn and experience as adolescents.

The young person who cannot attain a sense of personal identity shows role confusion—a sense of not knowing where he or she belongs or to whom he or she belongs. Such confusion is frequent in delinquent young people who seek a "negative identity," an identity opposite to the one prescribed for them by their family and friends. Having an identity as a "delinquent" may be preferable to having no identity at all.

Failure to establish a clear sense of personal identity at adolescence does not guarantee perpetual failure. Erikson, perhaps more than any other personality theorist, has emphasized that life is constant change and that confronting problems at one stage in life is not a guarantee against the reappearance of these problems at later stages, or against the finding of new solutions to them.

Intimacy vs. Isolation

Stage six in the life cycle is young adulthood; roughly the period of courtship and early family life that extends from late adolescence till early middle age. For this stage, and the stages described hereafter, classical psychoanalysis has nothing new or major to say. For Erikson, however, the previous attainment of a sense of personal identity and the engagement in productive work that marks this period gives rise to a new interpersonal dimension of *intimacy* at the one extreme and *isolation* at the other.

When Erikson speaks of intimacy he means the ability to share with and care about another person without fear of losing oneself in the process. Here, too, as in the case of identity, social conditions may help or hinder the establishment of a sense of intimacy. Intimacy need not involve sexuality; it includes the relationship between friends. Soldiers often develop a sense of commitment to one another that exemplifies intimacy in its broadest sense. If a sense of intimacy is not established with friends or a marriage partner, the result, in Erikson's view, is a sense of isolation—of being alone without anyone to share with or care for.

Generativity vs. Self-Absorption

This stage—middle age—brings with it what Erikson speaks of as either *generativity* or *self-absorption* and stagnation. What Erikson means by generativity is that the person begins to be concerned with future generations and the nature of the society and world in which those generations will live. Generativity can be found in any individual who is actively concerned with the welfare of young people and with making the world a better place for them to live and to work.

Those who fail to establish a sense of generativity fall into a state of self-absorption in which their personal needs and comforts are of predominant concern. But Erikson points out that unhappy solutions to life's crises are not irreversible.

Integrity vs. Despair

Stage eight in the Eriksonian scheme corresponds roughly to the period when the individual's major efforts are nearing completion and when there is time for reflection—and for the enjoyment of grandchildren, if any. The psychosocial dimension that comes into prominence now has *integrity* on one hand and *despair* on the other.

The sense of integrity arises from the individual's ability to look back on life with satisfaction. At the other extreme is the individual who looks back upon life as a series of missed opportunities and realizes that it is too late to start again. The inevitable result is a sense of despair at what might have been.

These, then, are the major stages in the life cycle as described by Erikson. This view of personality growth takes some of the onus off parents and takes account of the role which society and the person play in the formation of an individual personality. Erikson has also demonstrated that each phase of growth has its strengths as well as its weaknesses and that failures at one stage of development can be rectified by successes at later stages.

Figure 4.1   Erikson's Eight Developmental Stages

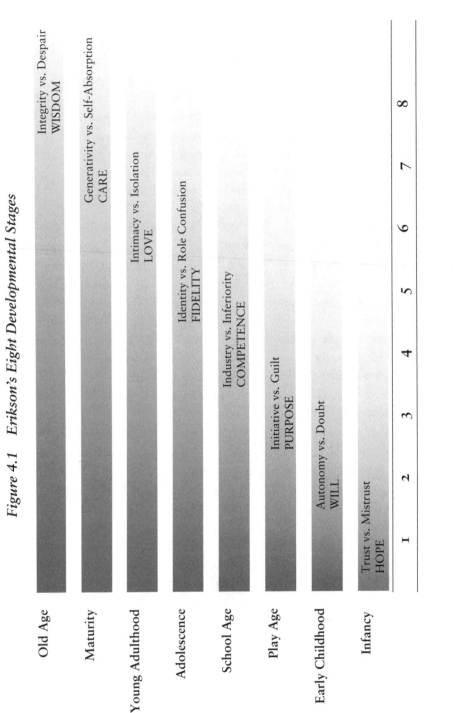

This illustration shows the developmental tasks of each of Erikson's life stages and their possible positive and negative outcomes. It also identifies the virtues that result from a positive resolution of each stage. For example, in infancy the conflict is between trust and mistrust. Establishing trust results in the virtue of hope. The stages are shown overlapping because it is possible to amend or correct the inadequate or partial resolutions of earlier stages.

ACTIVITIES AND QUESTIONS FOR REFLECTION

1. *Where would you place yourself or other members of your family in Erikson's stages?*

2. *What does Erikson mean by overcoming the negative component of a particular stage and finding a more positive solution? Can you give an example from your own experience or that of someone you know?*

3. *Try to capture reflections about your own life either by drawing a map (as discussed in the introduction to this chapter) or writing a narrative that illustrates your life. Try to focus on your life in 5- to 10-year segments. Where do your life events fit in Erikson's stages?*

4. *In reflecting on Erikson's life stages, do you recognize a sense of "development" in your own life?*

WHILE MANY PSYCHIATRISTS with their backgrounds in medical schools were studying the pathologies of personal development, the cases in which something had gone wrong, another group of psychologists was studying what had gone right. Rather than studying what was "normal," they were studying the motivations of persons who were good and caring, and enjoyed life. One of these, Abraham Maslow, studied people who were exceptionally tolerant, spontaneous, creative, autonomous, genuinely caring, and self-confident. From his studies he developed a theory of "self-actualization" and identified the characteristics of self-actualizing individuals. This reading is a summary of Maslow's theory.

AS YOU READ, think about someone you admire who is productive and happy and see if you can identify these characteristics in that person.

MASLOW'S THEORY OF SELF-ACTUALIZATION
Gerald Corey and Marianne Schneider Corey

Maslow postulated a hierarchy of needs as a source of motivation. The most basic are the physiological needs. If we are hungry and thirsty, our attention is riveted on meeting these basic needs. Next are the safety needs, which include a sense of security and stability. Once our physical and safety needs are fulfilled, we become concerned with meeting our needs for belonging and love, followed by working on our need for esteem, both from self and others. We are able to strive toward self-actualization only after these four basic needs are met: physiological, safety, love, and esteem. Maslow emphasized that people are not motivated by all five needs at the same time. The key factor determining which need is dominant at a given time is the degree to which those below it are satisfied. Some people come to the erroneous conclusion that if they are "bright" enough or "good" enough they would be further down the road of self-actualization. The truth may be that in their particular cultural, environmental, and societal circumstances these people are motivated to work toward

Figure 4.2   Maslow's Hierarchy of Needs

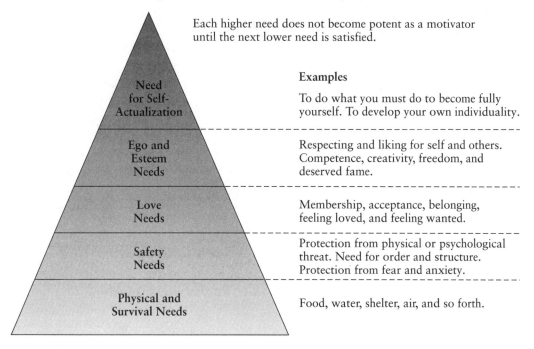

Each higher need does not become potent as a motivator until the next lower need is satisfied.

Need for Self-Actualization

Examples

To do what you must do to become fully yourself. To develop your own individuality.

Ego and Esteem Needs

Respecting and liking for self and others. Competence, creativity, freedom, and deserved fame.

Love Needs

Membership, acceptance, belonging, feeling loved, and feeling wanted.

Safety Needs

Protection from physical or psychological threat. Need for order and structure. Protection from fear and anxiety.

Physical and Survival Needs

Food, water, shelter, air, and so forth.

From *Motivation and Personality* by Abraham H. Maslow. Copyright © 1987. (Upper Saddle River, N.J.: Prentice-Hall, Inc.)

physical and psychological survival, which keeps them functioning at the lower end of the hierarchy. Keep in mind that an individual is not much concerned with actualization, nor is a society focused on the development of culture, if the basic needs are not met.

We can summarize some of the basic ideas of the humanistic approach by means of Maslow's model of the self-actualizing person (Figure 4.2). He describes self-actualization in his book *Motivation and Personality* (1970), and he also treats this concept in his other books (1968, 1971). Some core characteristics of self-actualizing people are self-awareness, freedom, basic honesty and caring, and trust and autonomy.

Self-Awareness

Self-actualizing people are more aware of themselves, of others, and of reality than are nonactualizing people. Specifically, they demonstrate the following behavior and traits:

1. *Efficient perception of reality*
    a. Self-actualizing people see reality as it is.
    b. They have an ability to detect phoniness.
    c. They avoid seeing things in preconceived categories.

2. *Ethical awareness*
   a. Self-actualizing people display a knowledge of what is right and wrong for them.
   b. They have a sense of inner direction.
   c. They avoid being pressured by others and living by others' standards.

3. *Freshness of appreciation.* Like children, self-actualizing people have an ability to perceive life in a fresh way.

4. *Peak moments*
   a. Self-actualizing people experience times of being one with the universe; they experience moments of joy.
   b. They have the ability to be changed by such moments.

Freedom

Self-actualizing people are willing to make choices for themselves, and they are free to reach their potential. This freedom entails a sense of detachment and a need for privacy, creativity and spontaneity, and an ability to accept responsibility for choices.

1. *Detachment*
   a. For self-actualizing people, the need for privacy is crucial.
   b. They have a need for solitude to put things in perspective.

2. *Creativity*
   a. Creativity is a universal characteristic of self-actualizing people.
   b. Creativity may be expressed in any area of life; it shows itself as inventiveness.

3. *Spontaneity*
   a. Self-actualizing people do not need to show off.
   b. They display a naturalness and lack of pretentiousness.
   c. They act with ease and grace.

Basic Honesty and Caring

Self-actualizing people show a deep caring for and honesty with themselves and others. These qualities are reflected in their interest in humankind and in their interpersonal relationships.

1. *Sense of social interest*
   a. Self-actualizing people have a concern for the welfare of others.
   b. They have a sense of communality with all other people.
   c. They have an interest in bettering the world.

2. *Interpersonal relationships*
   a. Self-actualizing people have a capacity for real love and fusion with another.
   b. They are able to love and respect themselves.
   c. They are able to go outside themselves in a mature love.
   d. They are motivated by the urge to grow in their relationships.

3. *Sense of humor*
   a. Self-actualizing people can laugh at themselves.
   b. They can laugh at the human condition.
   c. Their humor is not hostile.

Trust and Autonomy

Self-actualizing people exhibit faith in themselves and others; they are independent; they accept themselves as valuable persons; and their lives have meaning.

1. *Search for purpose and meaning*
   a. Self-actualizing people have a sense of mission, of a calling in which their potential can be fulfilled.
   b. They are engaged in a search for identity, often through work that is a deeply significant part of their lives.

2. *Autonomy and independence*
   a. Self-actualizing people have the ability to be independent.
   b. They resist blind conformity.
   c. They are not tradition-bound in making decisions.

3. *Acceptance of self and others*
   a. Self-actualizing people avoid fighting reality.
   b. They accept nature as it is.
   c. They are comfortable with the world.

This profile is best thought of as an ideal rather than a final state that we reach once and for all. Thus, it is more appropriate to speak about the self-actualizing process rather than becoming a self-actualized person.

ACTIVITIES AND QUESTIONS FOR REFLECTION

1. *Were you able to identify Maslow's characteristics of the self-actualizing person in anyone you know?*

2. *Could this theory be useful in conjunction with Erikson's theory of human development to reestablish or correct levels of trust throughout life? How?*

3. *Remembering that these are characteristics one is striving for, could they be helpful in serving as motivation for a more fulfilling life? How?*

UNLIKE ERIKSON, who looked at human development from birth until death, Daniel Levinson, a psychiatrist at Yale University, studied early and middle adulthood beginning at age seventeen. His perspective focuses on the life structure, *which he defines as "the underlying pattern or design of a person's life at a given time." The life structure is made up of relationships not only to people but to work, groups, organizations, objects, places, and cultures.*

AS YOU READ, ask yourself what Levinson means by life structure? *What might you expect to happen in your life during structure-building* and *structure-changing* periods?

THE LIFE STRUCTURE AND ITS DEVELOPMENT IN ADULTHOOD
Daniel Levinson

The key concept to emerge from my research is the *life structure:* the underlying pattern or design of a person's life at a given time. It is the pillar of my conception of adult development.

The meaning of this term can be clarified by a comparison of life structure and personality structure. A theory of personality structure is a way of conceptualizing answers to a concrete question: "What kind of person am I?" Different theories offer numerous ways of thinking about this question and of characterizing oneself or others; for example, in terms of traits, skills, wishes, conflicts, defenses, or values.

A theory of life structure is a way of conceptualizing answers to a different question:

"What is my life like now?" As we begin reflecting on this question, many others come to mind. What are the most important parts of my life, and how are they interrelated? Where do I invest most of my time and energy? Are there some relationships—to spouse, lover, family, occupation, religion, leisure, or whatever—that I would like to make more satisfying or meaningful? Are there some things not in my life that I would like to include? Are there interests and relationships, which now occupy a minor place, that I would like to make more central?

The primary components of a life structure are the person's *relationships* with various

---

others in the external world. The other may be a person, a group, institution or culture, or a particular object or place. A significant relationship involves an investment of self (desires, values, commitment, energy, skill), a reciprocal investment by the other person or entity, and one or more social contexts that contain the relationship, shaping it and becoming part of it. Every relationship shows both stability and change as it evolves over time, and it has different functions in the person's life as the life structure itself changes.

An individual may have significant relationships with many kinds of others. A significant other might be an actual person in the individual's current life. We need to study interpersonal relationships between friends, lovers, and spouses; between parents and their adult offspring at different ages; between bosses and subordinates, teachers and students, and mentors and protégés. A significant other might be a person from the past or a symbolic or imagined figure from religion, myth, fiction, or private fantasy. The other might not be an individual but might be a collective entity such as a group, institution, or social movement; nature as a whole, or a part of nature such as the ocean, mountains, wildlife, whales in general, or Moby Dick in particular, or an object or place such as a farm, a city or country, "a room of one's own," or a book or painting. . . .

At any given time, a life structure may have many and diverse components. We found, however, that only one or two components —rarely as many as three—occupy a central place in the structure. Most often, marriage-family and occupation are the central compo-

nents of a person's life, although wide variations occur in their relative weight and in the importance of other components. The central components are those that have the greatest significance for the self and the evolving life course. They receive the largest share of the individual's time and energy, and they strongly influence the character of the other components. The peripheral components are easier to change or detach; they involve less investment of self and can be modified with less effect on the fabric of the person's life.

Developmental Periods in Early and Middle Adulthood

The life structure develops through a relatively orderly sequence of age-linked periods during the adult years. I want to emphasize that this is a finding, not an a priori hypothesis. It was as surprising to me as to others that the life structure should show such regularity in its adult development, given the absence of similar regularity in ego development, moral development, career development, and other specific aspects of the life.

The sequence consists of an alternating series of *structure-building* and *structure-changing* (transitional) periods. Our primary task in a structure-building period is to form a life structure and enhance our life within it: We must make certain key choices, form a structure around them, and pursue our values and goals within this structure. Even when we succeed in creating a structure, life is not necessarily tranquil. The task of building a structure is often stressful indeed, and we may discover that it is not as satisfactory as we had hoped. A structure-building period ordinarily

Figure 4.3   Developmental Periods in the Eras of Early and Middle Adulthood

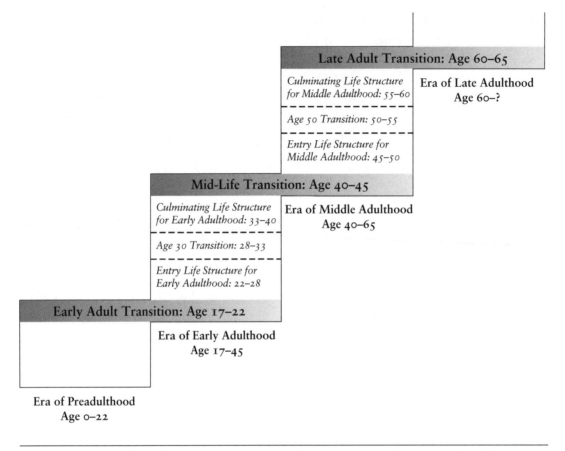

From Original: Note. This is an expanded adaptation of an earlier version that appeared in *The Seasons of a Man's Life* (p. 57) by D.J. Levinson with C.N. Darrow, E.B. Klein, M.H. Levinson, and B. McKee, 1978, New York: Alfred A. Knopf, Inc. Adapted by permission.

lasts 5 to 7 years, 10 at the most. Then the life structure that has formed the basis for stability comes into question and must be modified.

A *transitional* period terminates the existing life structure and creates the possibility for a new one. The primary tasks of every transitional period are to reappraise the existing structure, to explore possibilities for change in the self and the world, and to move toward commitment to the crucial choices that form the basis for a new structure in the ensuing period. Transitional periods ordinarily last about five years. Almost half our adult life is spent in developmental transitions. No life structure is permanent—periodic change is given in the nature of our existence.

As a transition comes to an end, one starts making crucial choices, giving them meaning and commitment, and building a life structure around them. The choices are, in a sense, the major product of the transition. When all efforts of the transition are done—the struggles to improve work or marriage, to explore alternative possibilities of living, to come more to terms with the self—choices must be made and bets must be placed. One must decide "This I will settle for," and start creating a life structure that will serve as a vehicle for the next step in the journey.

Within early and middle adulthood, the developmental periods unfold as follows. We have found that each period begins and ends at a well-defined average age; there is a variation of plus or minus two years around the mean.

The first three periods of early adulthood, from roughly 17 to 33, constitute its "novice phase." They provide an opportunity to move beyond adolescence, to build a provisional but necessarily flawed entry life structure, and to learn the limitations of that structure. The two final periods, from 33 to 45, form the "culminating phase," which brings to fruition the efforts of this era.

A similar sequence exists in middle adulthood. It, too, begins with a novice phase of three periods, from 40 to 55. The Mid-Life Transition is both an ending and a beginning. In our early 40s we are in the full maturity of early adulthood and are completing its final chapter; we are also in the infancy of middle adulthood, just beginning to learn about its promise and its dangers.

This sequence of periods holds for men and women of different cultures, classes, and historical epochs. There are, of course, wide variations in the kinds of life structures people build, the developmental work they do in transitional periods, and the concrete sequence of social roles, events, and personality change. The theory thus provides a general framework of human development within which we can study the profound differences that often exist between classes, genders, and cultures.

ACTIVITIES AND QUESTIONS FOR REFLECTION

1. *Consider your relationships in the sense Levinson uses the term. Can you identify those most important to you?*

2. *In thinking about your goals for your education and possible careers, how would you prepare for or use Levinson's theories to think about structure-building and structure-changing periods?*

3. *According to Levinson's scheme, what are the implications of your present life stage for planning your education?*

↤

RITA WEATHERSBY, now professor of management at the University of New Hampshire, has combined an interest in theories of adult development with research on adults' learning interests. She has found that there are "significant learning interests associated with each life stage" and the challenges adults encounter during their lives can be useful in planning your education. This reading provides an opportunity to review Erikson's and Levinson's theories as well as to learn how the stages of adult development and one's attitudes toward education may be linked.

AS YOU READ, think about why adults seek further education throughout their lives. How do adults use education in periods of transition? In periods of stability?

↤

LIFE STAGES AND LEARNING INTERESTS
Rita Weathersby

At any stage, the choice to enroll [in college] is an act of faith which, whether large or small, is a reaching out for something beyond one's grasp, a declaration that action will have a hoped-for result.

My purpose here is to describe some general principles underlying this imperative for growth, and to relate it to research on adult life stages. We need to know more about adults as learners, and about the processes of transition and development, crisis and opportunity, which are embedded in the life cycle. It's like designing and producing a car

without having an intimate knowledge of the characteristics of the driver, the roads, the roadway conditions, the amount and quality of fuel, and the inner workings of the engine. A car is a vehicle for motion, and so is an education. We can produce better vehicles if we understand the personal and developmental meanings of education in adults' lives.

First, we need a definition of life stages and some agreement about what they are. A life stage is a time period in which certain concerns are salient (such as setting long-range goals and accomplishing them), and

Excerpt from "Life Stages and Learning Interests," a paper presented at the annual conference of the American Association for Higher Education, Chicago, March 20, 1978. Reprinted by permission of Rita Weathersby.

certain adaptive tasks (such as leaving one's parental home, taking on adult roles in work, marriage and parenthood, facing old age and death) provide us with opportunities to become stronger persons, and to become new and different persons if we choose. There is what Carl Rogers calls "significant learning" associated with each life stage. Learning which is self-initiated, which involves us both cognitively and affectively, which influences our behavior and attitudes, which is self-evaluated, and which is inextricably intertwined with the meaning of our lives. Some of the content of this adaptive learning is quite practical (how do I fill out income tax forms, or run a community meeting or achieve excellence in my specialty). Some of it deals with our capacities for caring, thinking and working with our identities as growing persons, and our visions of who we are in the world.

This brings me to my first general point. People's learning interests are inextricably embedded in their personal stories, in their visions of who they are in the world and what they can do and want to do. For many, especially those in life transitions, education involves taking risks not only with one's sense of self-esteem, but with one's sense of self. A 38-year-old woman explained it this way:

> The one thing about adult learning is there are tremendous risks in it because you're always going beyond what you need. You're taking risks with decisions, you're starting to formulate patterns, you're trying to pull together. . . . It's just like walking on eggs with information—new information that you're just processing, just drinking in,

always. And then you're not sure of the validity of your own conclusions, so you've got to take another tiptoe step because *that's part of yourself, you know, that you never looked at.*

This woman was a corporate executive who enrolled [in college] because she grew tired of the insecurity of being a lady vice president without a degree in a corporation increasingly peopled by MBAs. Along with enrolling she made a major change in her career and in her life style—so much so that she described herself as a juggler: "You know it's almost like being a good three-ball juggler with five balls. There's a lot of stuff up in the air for me right now, and I think that has to do with growth." There are many adults who are jugglers, at mid-life and mid-career, with changing personal priorities and worldviews. Some of them enroll in college, and both the process of getting a degree and the results of a degree in terms of new career opportunities, world views, and identities, are changing in themselves and create potential for more change. My impression is that the timing of enrollment differs idiosyncratically. Some people enroll in the middle of a life transition—others enroll in anticipation of changed life circumstances.

Bernice Neugarten, a sociologist at the University of Chicago, has identified age norms related to adult activities. There seems to be a widespread cultural consensus on the proper time to leave home, go to college, marry, have children, stop having children, move to a retirement home, and so on. Adult students are sometimes spurred on by these norms, and sometimes self-consciously breaking them. For many people in their mid to late twenties, there's a culturally induced pressure to get one's life and career together. A 29-year-old man explained why he enrolled at this period of his life in terms of time running out. He said, "I wanted the benefits of a B.A. while I still had the time to use it." What's interesting is that people at many stages say "now is the time for this," and what they have in common is an internal readiness for a particular educational experience. A 52-year-old woman who was starting the same degree program that her daughter had just completed said, "I am perhaps late, but there are things I would like to do in the last half of my life—and I need to know so much more." Our internal clocks often run counter to our cultural clocks. Changing our cultural expectations about what adults are "supposed to be doing" seems to me to be incredibly powerful as an idea which gives adults permission to pursue education without undue self-consciousness.

Continuing the focus on internal and external timing is Erik Erikson's notion that within the life cycle are embedded tasks of personality development. He assigns to adolescence the issue of identity versus role diffusion, but I have found that identity is a key question in any transition. Resolving these critical issues becomes the developmental task of adulthood. A "developmental crisis" occurs when the events of life thrust one of these issues forcefully upon us, and offers us the opportunity for reshaping our intra-psychic balance. These are learning tasks of major proportions. They often appear as the impetus for further education and influence adult's choices of topics for study. A 35-year-old

woman who had studied the biographies of adventurous women such as Margaret Mead and Helen Keller concluded, "*I am that adventurous woman I was searching for.*"

The questions are basic, and profound —who am I? Who am I close to? How can I be productive in the world? Can I look back on my life choices, and the events of my life, and value them as mine? At each life stage we fashion new answers, though one issue may become more developmentally salient. The impetus for learning springs from a combination of growth and necessity and from wrestling with events and choices in relation to work, self, and others.

Daniel Levinson has created the concept of the *life structure,* and it is useful here because adult students are often making changes in their life structures. A life structure is the patterning or design of an individual's life at any given time. One interesting result of Levinson's research is his conclusion that any stabilization is temporary; no life structure seems to last more than 8 to 10 years. The purpose of a transition is to terminate a life structure that has become inadequate and to initiate a new one. To negotiate a transition, we must reassess our lives and either make changes or recommit to old roles and patterns, although they perhaps assume new meanings. An adult student at 41 says,

> After years of being wife, mother, department head, I awoke to the fact, "who the hell am I?" . . . I am concerned about having been in the same job so long. I want to explore new fields, need desperately intellectual stimulation. Perhaps this field is where I can function best, but I need

refreshment or change. [This program] can help me decide . . . My last child is away at school and I am deciding whether I want to be married, not legally or physically, but emotionally. That is a commitment I have never made. [This program] is helping me become a person, not a role—hopefully, a mature person.

This woman is wrestling with a process of personal renewal in almost all aspects of her life, and has turned to an educational setting for a legitimized learning that supports decision and redirection.

Another of Levinson's conclusions is that in creating an integrated life structure we can only use parts of ourselves, which means that important parts are left out. When we restructure our lives we have the opportunity to create a new "goodness of fit" between our daily roles and activities and our inner selves, particularly aspects of self that were neglected or left out of previous life structures. My favorite example of this phenomenon is an 81-year-old student who titled the period of her life she had just left as "The Awakening" and her next life period, "To Be a Successful Poet." The major point, however, is that people *use* an education differently in periods of transition than they do in periods of stability. In transitional periods, people seek redirection; in periods of stability, people seek the same tools for working and building, and also for stimulation and enjoyment, but with less emotional urgency.

The chart accompanying this reading includes a brief characterization of life stages, including the marker events which are common reference points in each life period, and

the major psychic tasks of each stage. Let me briefly identify the uses of education appropriate to different stages.

In the "Leaving the Family" period (16–18 to 20–24) colleges and universities (and maybe the army) are major social institutions that help adolescents break away from their families and establish separate identities. A young adult in his or her twenties—focused on "Getting into the Adult World"—is more likely to be interested in job-related education, whereas someone undergoing an "age 30 transition" is frequently seeking redefinition of life aims or new career directions. A woman in her "age 30 transition" characterizes the life period she just left as, "Faced with Disappointment and Disillusionment, I ask, Who Am I and Where Am I Going?" and says she is "Preparing to Meet New Goals." At the "Settling Down/Becoming One's Own Person" period in one's thirties, people's motives for education are active investments of energy in a life structure experienced as stable. They may be upgrading professional skills or pursuing interests. But there is often more going on underneath. For example, intellectual curiosity is the chief reason impelling a 35-year-old suburban housewife to study for a liberal arts bachelor's degree. But enrolling in college at this point in her life is also part of giving herself permission to develop her capabilities and autonomy.

At Mid-Life, in a transitional period, education can provide a setting for redefining one's work in conjunction with a deeper understanding of self or changed family circumstances. For those seeking professional work roles after homemaking and volunteer or

Figure 4.4 Descriptions of Life Stages

Adapted and updated from a chart by Rita Weathersby "Life Stages and Learning Interests"

Phase and Age	Marker Events	Psychic Tasks	Characteristic Stance
Leaving Home 18-22	Leave home Establish new living arrangements Enter college Start first full-time job Select mate	Establish autonomy and independence from the family Define identity Define sex role Establish new peer alliances	A balance between "being in" and "moving out" of the family
Moving into the Adult World 23-28	Marriage or stable relationship Establish home Become parent Get hired/fired/quit job Enter into community activities	Regard self as an adult Develop capacity for intimacy Fashion initial life structure Build the dream Find a mentor	"Doing what one should" Living and building for the future Launched as an adult
Search for Stability 29-34	Establish children in school Progress in career or consider change Possible separation, divorce, remarriage Possible return to school	Reappraise relationships Reexamine life structure and present commitments Strive for success Search for stability, security, and control Set long-range goals Accept growing children	"What is life all about now that I am doing what I am supposed to do?" Concern for order and stability and with "making it" Desire to set long-range goals and meet them
Becoming One's Own Person 35-44	Crucial Promotion Break with mentor Responsibility for three-generation family (children and parents) For some women: empty nest, enter career	Face reality Confront mortality; sense of aging Prune dependent ties to boss, spouse, and/or mentor Reassess marriage Reassess personal priorities and values	"Have I done the right thing? Is there time to change?" For men: More nurturing stance For women: More aggressive stance Suspended animation
Settling Down 45-56	Cap career Become mentor Launch children; become grandparent New interests and hobbies Physical limitations Active participation in community events	Increase feelings of self-awareness and competence Reestablish family relationships Enjoy one's choices and life style Reexamine the fit between life structure and self	"It is perhaps too late, but there are things I would like to do in the last half of my life" Best time of life
Mellowing 57-64	Possible loss of mate Health problems Preparation for retirement	Accomplish goals in the time left to live Accept and adjust to aging process	Mellowing of feelings and relationships Spouse increasingly important Greater comfort with self
Life Review 65+	Retirement Physical decline Change in finances New living arrangements Death of friends/spouse Major shift in daily routine	Search for integrity versus despair Acceptance of self Disengagement Rehearsal for death of spouse	Review of accomplishments Eagerness to share everyday human joys and sorrows Family is important Death is a new presence

community work, education provides a setting for gaining self-confidence and credentials for legitimized entry. Forty seems an age that for many is a watershed of consciousness. At 40 they feel a new self-acceptance: personality is set, it's too late to change, and they feel free to pursue activities of their own choosing rather than to please others. For those who have been working all their lives, there is sometimes the necessity to revise career ambitions downward, change careers, or find ways to allocate time and energy satisfactorily across the roles of worker, parent, spouse, and citizen.

At 50 there is a "coming of age" quality to students' goals, as if a lifetime's experience were being recast into new, more serviceable molds for action. With retirement there are greater opportunities for recreation and leisure. Aging brings needs for social contact and personal support.

The point is this: each life stage offers opportunities for learning. Each life transition places a person somewhat at risk.

ACTIVITIES AND QUESTIONS FOR REFLECTION

1. *How does Weathersby see a "developmental crisis" leading to a desire to learn more or something new?*

2. *In what ways does Weathersby's thinking contribute to your understanding of the ways education can contribute to personal development?*

3. *What new learning does your present life stage suggest? What about that of your family members? If they were to return to school, why might they do so?*

4. *Refer to your life map/narrative again and note Weathersby's description of life stages and learning interests. Where would you place yourself in Weathersby's scheme? Add your prior and/or current learning interests to your map/narrative.*

ONE OF THE DEVELOPMENTAL TASKS directly affected by being in college is identity or self-definition. Who am I?

In any stage of adulthood, not just the traditional college years of 18–21, the impact of learning can cause an implosion of personal confusion and reevaluation. New information, changes in patterns of daily life, exposure to new people, and heightened expectations combine to make the college experience one of identity definition.

Because this topic is so fundamental to the process of becoming educated, this reading is longer and more detailed than many of the others. This selection is from a comprehensive textbook on human development by two professors at the University of Rhode Island. Although they discuss identity formation as a crisis—and it certainly feels like a crisis when you are wondering who you are, or who you want to be next—identity definition and redefinition is a normal developmental event. As a confrontation with the unknown it can be a crisis, but it is also a time of great opportunity and adventure.

AS YOU READ, note the tasks related to identity formation.

INDIVIDUAL IDENTITY VERSUS IDENTITY CONFUSION

Barbara M. Newman and Philip R. Newman

Later adolescents are preoccupied with questions about their essential character in much the same way that early-school-age children are preoccupied with questions about their origins. In their efforts to define themselves, later adolescents must take into account the bonds that have been built between them and others in the past as well as the direction they hope to take in the future. Identity serves as an anchor point, providing the person an essential experience of continuity in social relationships.

> The young individual must learn to be most himself where he means the most to others—those others, to be sure, who have come to

---

Excerpt from *Development Through Life: A Psychosocial Approach* by Barbara M. Newman and Philip R. Newman, Eighth Edition (Belmont, CA: Wadsworth, 2003), pp. 352–356. Reprinted by permission.

mean most to him. The term identity expresses such a mutual relation in that it connotes both a persistent sameness within oneself (self-sameness) and a persistent sharing of some kind of essential character with others. . . .

The Content Component of Identity

The structure of identity has two components: content and evaluation. . . . The content, what one thinks about, values, and believes in and the traits or characteristics by which one is recognized and known by others, may be further divided into the inner or private self and the public self. The private self, often described as a sense of self, refers to one's inner uniqueness and unity, a subjective experience of being the originator of one's thoughts and actions and of being self-reflective. Through the private self, one recognizes the range of values and beliefs to which one is committed, and one can assess the extent to which certain thoughts and actions are consistent with those beliefs. The private, subjective sense of self, which develops over the course of the life span, includes four basic elements. . . .

A sense of agency—being the originator of thoughts and actions.

A sense of unity—sensing that one is the same basic self from one moment or one situation to the next.

A sense of otherness—recognizing the boundaries between the self and others.

A sense of decentering or distancing—reflecting on oneself so that one can recognize and own one's thoughts and actions

The elements of the public self include the many roles one plays and the expectations of others. As young people move through the stage of later adolescence, they find that social reference groups, including family members, neighbors, teachers, friends, religious groups, ethnic groups, and even national leaders, have expectations of their behavior. A young person may be expected to work, attend college, marry, serve the country in the military, attend religious services, vote, and provide economic support for family members. Persistent demands by meaningful others result in decisions that might have been made differently or not made at all if the individual were surrounded by a different configuration of social reference groups. In the process of achieving personal identity, one must synthesize the private sense of self with the public self derived from the many roles and relationships in which one is embedded.

The Evaluation Component of Identity

The second structural component of identity, evaluation, refers to the significance one places on various aspects of the identity content. Even though most people play many of the same roles, their identities differ, in part because they place different values on some of these roles. Some people are single-minded, placing great value on success in one domain, such as their vocational goals, and little value in the others. Other people strive to maintain a balance in the roles they play; they consider themselves successful if they can find enjoyment in a variety of relationships and activities.

This assessment of the importance of certain content areas in relation to others influences the use of resources, the direction of certain decisions, and the kinds of experiences that may be perceived as most personally rewarding or threatening. College students, for example, may differ in whether their academic success or interpersonal success is most central to their sense of identity. Students who are more concerned about academic success take a different approach to the college environment, become involved in different kinds of activities, and have a different reaction to academic failure than do students who are more concerned about interpersonal success . . .

Both the content and evaluation components of identity may change over the life course. In later adolescence, the focus is on integrating the various sources of content and determining which elements have the greatest salience. This is a major accomplishment that requires self-awareness, introspection, and the active exploration of a variety of roles and relationships . . .

Identity Status

The basic conflict of the psychological crisis of later adolescence is individual identity formation versus identity confusion. It results from the enormous difficulty of pulling together the many components of the self, including changing perspectives on one's inner sense of beliefs and values as well as new and changing social demands, into a unified image that can propel the person toward positive, meaningful action. As part of this process, a young person struggles to formulate a worldview, an outlook on those goals and values that are personally important and to which

the person is willing to make a commitment. Over this period, whether in the context of college, or in other work and community settings, young people begin to examine the beliefs and goals they may have internalized from childhood. Through self-reflection, role experimentation, and feedback from significant others, later adolescents make decisions about whether these beliefs and goals are still meaningful as they look ahead to the future . . .

The process of identity formation is confounded by distractions of all sorts. Many young people find it difficult to sort out what they want to be from what their parents have urged them to become. Others have received little encouragement to become a separate person with independent feelings and views. Still others are so beleaguered by feelings of inferiority and alienation that they do not have the optimism necessary to create a positive vision of their future. Some later adolescents find many paths appealing and have difficulty making a commitment to only one.

Identity formation is a dynamic process that unfolds as young people assess their competencies and aspirations within a changing social context of expectations, demands, and resources. A variety of potential resolutions of the psychosocial crisis of individual identity versus identity confusion have been described. At the positive pole is identity achievement, at the negative pole is identity confusion. Also included are a premature resolution, identity foreclosure, a postponement of resolution, psychosocial moratorium, and a negative identity . . .

One of the most widely used conceptual frameworks for assessing identity status was devised by James Marcia . . . Using Erikson's concepts, Marcia assessed identity status on the basis of two criteria: crisis and commitment. **Crisis** consists of a period of role experimentation and active decision-making among alternative choices. **Commitment** consists of a demonstration of personal involvement in the areas of occupational choice, religion, and political ideology. On the basis of Marcia's interview, the status of subjects' identity development is assessed . . . People who are classified as **identity-achieved** have already experienced a crisis time and have made occupational and ideological commitments. On the other hand, people who are classified as **identity-foreclosed** have not experienced a crisis but demonstrate strong occupational and ideological commitments. Their occupational and ideological beliefs appear to be close to those of their parents. The foreclosed identity is deceptive. A young person of 18 or 19 who can say exactly what he or she wants in life and who has selected an occupational goal may appear to be mature. This kind of clarity of vision may impress peers and adult as evidence of a high level of self-insight. However, if this solution has been formulated through the wholesale adoption of a script that was devised by the young person's family, it may not actually reflect much depth of self-understanding.

People who are classified as being in a state of **psychosocial moratorium** are involved in an ongoing crisis. Their commitments are diffuse. Finally, people who are classified as identity-confused may or may not have experienced a crisis, and they demonstrate a complete lack of commitment. Marcia described the identity-confused group as having a rather cavalier, "party" attitude that allows members to cope with the college environment. He suggested that the more seriously confused persons . . . may not appear in his sample because they are unable to cope with college.

Sometimes, cultural expectations and demands provide the young person with a clearly defined self-image that is completely contrary to the cultural values of the community. This is called a **negative identity** . . . Failure, good-for-nothing, juvenile delinquent, hood, gangster, and loser are some of the labels that the adult society commonly applies to certain adolescents. In the absence of any indication of the possibilities of success or contribution to the society, the young person accepts such negative labels as a self-definition and proceeds to validate this identity by continuing to behave in ways that will strengthen it. Some young people grow up admiring people who have become very successful by following antisocial or criminal paths. Drug lords; gang leaders; leaders of groups that advocate hate, violence, and vengeance; and people who use elected political positions for personal gain are all examples of possible role models around which a negative identity may be formed.

A negative identity may also emerge as a result of a strong identification with someone who is devalued by the family or the community. A loving uncle who is an alcoholic or a clever, creative parent who commits suicide may stimulate a crystallization within the adolescent as one who may share these undesirable characteristics. Linda, for example, established the negative identity of a person going crazy:

Her father was an alcoholic, physically abusive man, who terrified her when she was a child. . . . Linda, herself a bright child, became by turns the standard bearer for her father's proud aspirations and the target of his jealousy. Midway through grade school she began flunking all her courses and retreating to a private world of daydreams. . . . "I always expected hallucinations, being locked up, down the road coming toward me. . . . I always resisted seeing myself as an adult. I was afraid that at the point I stopped the tape [the years of wild experimentation] I'd become my parents. . . . My father was the closest person I knew to crazy." . . .

Identity Confusion

The foreclosed identity and the negative identity both resolve the identity crisis in ways that fall short of the goal of a positive personal identity. Yet both provide the person with a concrete identity. The more maladaptive resolution of the crisis is **identity confusion.** Young people in this state are unable to make a commitment to any single view of themselves. They may be unable to integrate the various roles they play. In addition, they may be confronted by opposing value systems or by a lack of confidence in their ability to make meaningful decisions. Within the private, subjective self, some young people may reach later adolescence having difficulty accepting or establishing clear go boundaries, or they may not experience feelings of agency. At an unconscious level, they may have incorporated two or more conflicting ideas about the self— for example, an abusive, harsh, rejecting powerful father and a wise, loving, nurturant,

powerful grandmother—that stand in opposition to each other. Under any of these conditions, the demands for integration and synthesis of a personal identity arouse anxiety, apathy, and hostility toward the existing roles, none of which they can successfully adopt.

In comparison to the moratorium group, young people in the confused status are less conscientious, more likely to experience negative emotions, and more disagreeable . . . They are generally not outgoing; rather, they describe themselves as self-conscious and likely to feel depressed. Several studies have found that young people who are characterized as identity-confused have had a history of early and frequent involvement with drug use and abuse . . . Difficulties in resolving earlier psychosocial crises, especially conflicts related to autonomy versus shame and doubt and initiative versus guilt, leave some young people with deficits in ego formation that interfere with the kind of energy and playful self-assertiveness that are necessary in the process of identity achievement.

Dolores, an unemployed college dropout, describes the feeling of meaningless drifting that is associated with identity confusion:

> I have two sisters, and my father always told me I was the smartest of all, that I was smarter than he was, and that I could do anything I wanted to do . . . but somehow, I don't really know why, everything I turned to came to nothing. . . . I had every opportunity to find out what I really wanted to do. But . . . nothing I did satisfied me, and I would just stop. . . . Or turn away. . . . Or go on a trip. I worked for a big company for a while. . . . Then my parents went to Paris and I just went

with them. . . . I came back . . . went to school . . . was a researcher at Time-Life . . . drifted . . . got married . . . divorced . . . drifted. [Her voice grew more halting.] I feel my life is such a waste. I'd like to write, I really would; but I don't know. I just can't get going . . .

The theoretical construct of identity status assumes a developmental progression. Identity confusion reflects the least defined status. Movement from confusion to foreclosure, moratorium, or achievement reflects a developmental progression. Movement from any other status to confusion suggests regression. A person who has achieved identity at one period may conceivably return to a crisis period of moratorium. However, those who are in a moratorium or achieved status can never be accurately described as foreclosed, since by definition they have already experienced some degree of crisis . . .

In the process of evolving an individual identity, everyone experiences temporary periods of confusion and depression. The task of bringing together the many elements of one's experience into a coordinated, clear self-definition is difficult and time consuming. Adolescents are likely to experience moments of self-preoccupation, isolation, and discouragement as the diverse pieces of the puzzle are shifted and reordered into the total picture. Thus, even the eventual positive identity formation will be the result of some degree of identity confusion. The negative outcome of identity confusion, however, suggests that the person is never able to formulate a satisfying identity that will provide for the convergence of multiple identifications, aspirations, and roles. Such individuals have the persistent fear that they are losing their hold on themselves and on their future.

ACTIVITIES AND QUESTIONS FOR REFLECTION

1. *Of the elements of the private, subjective self, which do you think may be most well developed in yourself and other students?*

2. *In what ways do you think a college education might help in developing the* evaluation *component of identity? What aspects of identity might it reinforce or neglect?*

3. *Identity confusion is common for college students of all ages and backgrounds. In what ways could you see your college studies supporting you through this experience? Is recognition that questioning is an essential part of growth enough? Why or why not?*

4. *How could a strong sense of self be a part of your definition of an educated person? For your goals for your education?*

CHAPTER 4

⤙ *Education and Personal Development*

SUMMARY

You have had an opportunity through the readings and questions in this chapter to reflect on your life in relation to several theories of personal development. This research reveals life and living as a series of tasks, adjustments, and changes, each one leading to new tasks, adjustments, and changes. In turn, the effect of these changes is determined by our sense of identity. Learning and experience can either reinforce or destabilize our sense of self and who we are in the world. They can also reinforce or cause us to question our world altogether.

Understanding the nature of these changes and the triggers that bring a need for adjustments can help you anticipate the personal development tasks you will need to address now and in the future. You need now to find a way to hold on to the information about yourself that you have gained from the readings and exercises in this chapter.

Using the Internet

Using InfoTrac College Edition: Look up a subject related to one of the readings in this chapter using both a subject guide and a keyword search, for example: identity formation, adult development, Maslow's hierarchy.

1. What did you discover about the differences between using a subject guide search compared with a keyword search?

2. What did you discover about the range of articles that related to your subject? Was there new information that was interesting to you? Any articles that suggested further studies?

SUMMARIZING ACTIVITIES AND QUESTIONS FOR REFLECTION

1. *What further studies would you undertake in college to understand the developmental tasks of life that interest you most?*

2. *How would you locate yourself or someone your know on Maslow's hierarchy of needs? Use the model of human development suggested by Erikson or Levinson in explaining your thoughts.*

3. *Using the Weathersby chart, how do you see your college education influencing your life in each of her life stages? Which stages or aspects of stages have you thought about?*

4. *What do the readings suggest in terms of planning your education? What goals can you identify for your development as a whole person?*

5. *After reflecting on the readings and activities in this chapter, review your goals for your college education and your definition of an educated person and make revisions or additions that capture any new understandings you now have.*

⟜ CHAPTER 5

Thinking and Learning

INTRODUCTION: THE DISCOVERY OF MEANING

How do we know?
Why do we believe?
What is the evidence?

These questions are at the heart of the process of thinking, the process by which we establish a fact, a truth, put two or more of them together, and come to a conclusion about their meaning. This is the kind of questioning and discovery, of meaning making, that is at the heart of the college experience.

But what makes it possible? How do we learn to establish and understand meaningful facts and concepts?

The Association of American Colleges and Universities, a leading professional organization in higher education, has identified as our most important thinking skill our ability to understand "why a question or argument is significant and for whom; what the difference is between developing and justifying a position and merely asserting one; and how to develop and provide justification or reasonable grounds for [our] own interpretations of judgments."

Thinking is not about the ability to memorize information: it is about being able to analyze information and explain it, to be able to generalize what we know about one subject to another subject, and to present our conclusions in original, meaningful ways.

The readings in this chapter discuss ways of developing this approach. They will help you understand how to be more reflective, to think in more critical and complex ways, to use your experience as a source of learning, and to increase your effectiveness as a learner. Knowing it is possible to expand your ability to think more effectively and understanding the stages or steps in that development will enable you to set new goals for your growth as a learner and for becoming an educated person.

Learning is a process of *development*. Just as psychologists have examined the way we develop and change personally, cognitive psychologists have studied the ways we develop and change in our ability to think.

One of the most significant *findings about learning comes from brain research and explains why learning can be exhausting. As we learn, we develop our brain's capacity to learn more. Learning changes our brains structurally and chemically. When we learn, we literally change the way we think and are able to think.*

This reading from the National Research Council, a nonprofit society of scholars administered by the National Academy of Sciences and the National Academy of Engineering, explains implications for learning of these latest findings. Some of these findings are based on animal studies and may not be directly analogous to human learning.

As you read, *look for the distinction between learning and activity.*

LEARNING AND BRAIN DEVELOPMENT
National Research Council

Making Rats Smarter

How do rats learn? Can rats be "educated?" In classic studies, rats are placed in a complex communal environment filled with objects that provide ample opportunities for exploration and play . . . The objects are changed and rearranged each day, and during the changing time, the animals are put in yet another environment with another set of objects. So, like their real-world counterparts in the sewers of New York or the fields of Kansas, these rats have a relatively rich set of experiences from which to draw information. A contrasting group of rats is placed in a more typical laboratory environment, living alone or with one or two others in a barren cage—which is obviously a poor model of a rat's real world. These two settings can help determine how experience affects the development of the normal brain and normal cognitive structures, and one can also see what happens when animals are deprived of critical experiences.

After living in the complex or impoverished environments for a period from weaning to rat adolescence, the two groups of animals were subjected to a learning experience. The rats that had grown up in the complex environment made fewer errors at the outset than the other rats; they also learned more quickly not to make any errors at all. In this sense, they were smarter than their more deprived counterparts. And with positive rewards, they performed better on complex tasks than the animals raised in individual cages. Most significant, learning altered the rats' brains: the animals from the complex environment had 20–25 percent more synapses per nerve cell in the visual cortex than the animals from the standard cages . . . It is clear that when animals learn, they add new connections to the wiring of their brains—a phenomenon not limited to early development . . .

Experiences and Environments for Brain Development

Alterations in the brain that occur during learning seem to make the nerve cells more efficient or powerful. Animals raised in complex environments have a greater volume of capillaries per nerve cell—and therefore a greater supply of blood to the brain—than the caged animals, regardless of whether the caged animal lived alone or with companions . . . (Capillaries are the tiny blood vessels that supply oxygen and other nutrients to the brain.) In this way experience increases the overall quality of functioning of the brain. Using astrocytes (cells that support neuron functioning by providing nutrients and removing waste) as the index, there are higher amounts of astrocyte per neuron in the complex-environment animals than in the caged groups. Overall, these studies depict an orchestrated pattern of increased capacity in the brain that depends on experience.

Other studies of animals show other changes in the brain through learning; . . . The weight and thickness of the cerebral cortex can be measurably altered in rats that are reared from weaning, or placed as adults, in a large cage enriched by the presence both of a changing set of objects for play and exploration and of other rats to induce play and exploration . . . These animals also perform better on a variety of problem-solving tasks than rats reared in standard laboratory cages. Interestingly, both the interactive presence of a social group and direct physical contact with the environment are important factors: animals placed in the enriched environment alone showed relatively little benefit; neither did animals placed in small cages within the larger environment . . . Thus, the gross structure of the cerebral cortex was altered both by exposure to opportunities for learning and by learning in a social context.

Does Mere Neural Activity Change the Brain or Is Learning Required?

Are the changes in the brain due to actual learning or to variations in aggregate levels of neural activity? Animals in a complex environment not only learn from experiences, but they also run, play and exercise, which activates the brain. The question is whether activation alone can produce brain changes without the subjects actually learning anything, just as activation of muscles by exercise can cause them to grow. To answer this question, a group of animals that learned challenging motor skills but had relatively little brain activity was compared with groups that had high levels of brain activity but did relatively little learning . . . There were four groups in all. One group of rats was taught to traverse an elevated obstacle course; these "acrobats" became very good at the task over a month or so of practice. A second group of "mandatory exercisers" was put on a treadmill once a day, where they ran for 30 minutes, rested for 10 minutes, then ran another 30 minutes. A third group of "voluntary exercisers" had free access to an activity wheel attached directly to their cage, which they used often. A control group of "cage potato" rats had no exercise.

What happened to the volume of blood vessels and number of synapses per neuron in the rats? Both the mandatory exercisers and the voluntary exercisers showed higher densities of blood vessels than either the cage potato rats or the acrobats, who learned skills that did not involve significant amounts of activity. But when the number of synapses per nerve cell was measured, the acrobats were the standout group. Learning adds synapses; exercise does not. Thus, different kinds of experience condition the brain in different ways. Synapse formation and blood vessel formation (vascularization) are two important forms of brain adaptation, but they are driven by different physiological mechanisms and by different behavioral events.

ACTIVITIES AND QUESTIONS FOR REFLECTION

1. *What daily activities do you think might increase the complexity of your brain?*

2. *Looking back, what activities in your childhood may have been the most important in increasing your brain's definition and ability to learn more?*

3. *How does the example of the smart rat in the sewer contrasted with the safe and comfortable rat in a cage affect your understanding of learning?*

⟶

A SOURCE OF LEARNING we often overlook is our own rich background of nonschool experience in youth groups, hobbies, community activities, and work. Experience has great value in learning not only because it broadens our store of information but also because it grounds information in experience and provides a context for converting experience to knowledge. The next two readings explain ways your experience can be converted into knowledge. These readings place a special emphasis on the role of reflection in learning, on reviewing our experiences, seeing connections between them, and deriving principles or concepts from them.

In the following reading, Robert Smith, professor at Northern Illinois University at DeKalb, makes a distinction between "examined" or "digested" experience and "unexamined" or "undigested" experience.

AS YOU READ, look for suggestions about how to convert "unexamined experience" into "examined experience."

⟶

LEARNING FROM EVERYDAY EXPERIENCE
Robert M. Smith

In *Rules for Radicals,* [community organizer and political activist] Saul Alinsky calls attention to the tendency of most people to react to life as "a series of happenings which pass through their systems undigested." His efforts to train community organizers led Alinsky to the conclusion that "happenings become experiences when they are digested, when they are reflected on, related to general patterns, and synthesized."

Poets and novelists have also called attention to the possibilities of learning from life experience. Dag Hammarskjöld [Secretary General of the United Nations] said, "Let me read with open eyes the book . . . my days are writing—and learn." In *Mountolive,* the English writer Lawrence Durrell describes the heady experience of becoming immersed in another culture, saying of one of his characters, a European living in Egypt:

Excerpt from *Learning How to Learn: Applied Theory for Adults* (Prentice-Hall Inc., 1988), pp. 127–130. Reprinted by permission of Prentice-Hall, Inc., Englewood Cliffs, NJ.

Mountolive . . . suddenly began to feel himself really penetrating a foreign country, foreign *moeurs,* for the first time. He felt as one always feels in such a case, namely the vertiginous pleasure of losing an old self and growing a new one to replace it. He felt he was slipping, losing so to speak the contours of himself. Is this the real meaning of education? He had begun transplanting a whole huge intact world from his imagination into the soil of his new life.

And the title of one of the great autobiographies, *The Education of Henry Adams,* reveals [historian] Adams's purpose to have been to draw educational implications from his life experience.

Adult educators enjoin us to learn from living and to help others do so. Malcolm Knowles speaks of the possibility of exploiting every experience as a learning experience. Virginia Griffin assigns high potential to personal experience, saying that principles derived by reflecting and conceptualizing from one's own experience are legitimate knowledge if they are thoughtfully and responsibly developed and tested.

It is evident that people do not necessarily place great value on their life experience. ("I've just been a housewife and mother.") Paulo Freire [a Brazilian educational theorist and political activist] found Brazilian peasants ready to assume that literacy was not an appropriate goal for them because they believed that it went with "high culture" and being an important person. The peasants' lack of respect for their own life experience and resulting negative self-image had to be changed before they could be motivated to learn to read and write. Helping them to focus on that experience and on their world became the outside facilitator's central task.

Saul Alinsky is not alone in pointing out that everyday experience does not necessarily accrue to the individual in a desirable way: "Experience may lead to wisdom or it may lead to dogmatism." The renowned psychologist B. F. Skinner calls experience "no school at all, not because no one learns in it, but because no one teaches."

It seems likely that, as people grow older, one obstacle to learning systematically from experience is the tendency to confuse what one has learned with what one has experienced. Harry Miller in his book *Teaching and Learning in Adult Education* identifies several others: the tendency to prejudge, an inability to attain the necessary objectivity to learn (when engaged in conversation, for example), the tendency to approach experience too passively, and the tendency of an individual to focus on differing and limited aspects of what is attended to (resulting in "differential interpretation of experience").

> All of us learn poorly, lopsidedly, and wrongly from some experiences and not at all from others, because we do not know how to compensate for human frailties, how to frame the kinds of questions which can be asked about an experience to make it more meaningful, or how to look for connections and interrelationships which might be relevant to interpret experience.

Learning to make relevant connections between experience and principles or concepts might be approached through a process of guided analysis of a local environment.

People can participate in an election or walk through a neighborhood, for example, and then draw back and reflect about what they have learned. The role of the guide, or trainer, is to make the experiences focuses for learning about learning from experience.

> The objective is not that they learn something [in particular] about [say] a political campaign but that they discover what questions need to be asked, how one overcomes one's own preconceptions, what kinds of inferences may be safely made in a given situation, and the habit of thoughtful reflection.

Lacking a guide, one might approach the development of improved skills in learning from experience by preplanning for an upcoming episode or period. Faced with a month of active military service, a stint as a volunteer, jury duty, or caring for an invalid, one can mull over the potential opportunities for learning—learning about organizations, justice, or human relationships. It should be useful to ask and write down such questions as, What personal assumptions can be tested? and What biases do I bring to the endeavor? Later the products of such planning can serve as a basis for analyzing what has transpired, and perhaps mean the difference between piling up experience and learning from it. One may come to digest the happenings that pass through the system.

Many persons use diaries or journals as a means for learning from experience. In addition to specific events, they record thoughts, questions, insights, quotations, and shifts in interests, points of view, or values. Workshops concerning journal keeping as a tool for personal growth appear to be proliferating.

Reminiscing is an almost universal technique for extracting meaning from experience. At least this constitutes one of its functions; others include coping and providing a means of self-expression. For the elderly, reminiscing has been found to be associated with more positive attitudes toward their pasts and deriving a sense of integrity and purpose in life.

Old age obviously presents a vantage point from which to derive meaning from the environment, to create perspectives, and to sum up. Exploring one's past and the events in which it is imbedded can lead to understanding through the discovery of some things that are timeless: "Each single human life can become a microcosm for all generations." Thus people often search for their roots as a means of interpreting their own lives; when this occurs, reminiscing becomes interwoven with learning new material.

ACTIVITIES AND QUESTIONS FOR REFLECTION

1. *What are some of the ways Smith suggests you can use to "examine" or "digest" an experience?*

2. *Most of Smith's suggestions involve looking back at experience. One involves "pre-planning." How could you "pre-plan" a learning experience?*

3. *Identify a recent experience, perhaps a book you read, an argument or misunderstanding, or volunteer project. Have you examined it? If not, do so now using Smith's suggestions. Can you connect this experience to other experiences? What did you learn?*

↗

THE FOLLOWING ARTICLE BY JOANNE KURFISS, of Metropolitan University in Denver, presents a model that shows how we develop the ability to think critically. It is based on research from two sources: a study by William Perry and his associates of male students at Harvard College, and a study by Mary Field Belenky and her associates of female students from a variety of colleges as well as of some women who were not students.

An intellectual development model, like a theory or model of human development, describes a progression of steps from simple to complex that we take as we increase our abilities to think critically. In this model, the steps of progression are called "levels." Each level describes a shift or change in beliefs, assumptions, or perspectives about what knowledge is and how to acquire it. Here are some typical comments of students that reflect different levels of this model:

Why does the teacher present us with all these different approaches?

Why doesn't the teacher teach us the right one?

One opinion is as good as another.

Opinions have to have good reasons.

What is this poem trying to say to me? How do I analyze it?

Do any of these comments sound familiar to you?

AS YOU READ, look for changes in the way students think about the nature of knowledge, and what they believe knowledge to be in each of the four levels of the model.

↗

DEVELOPMENTAL FOUNDATIONS OF CRITICAL THINKING

Joanne Gainen Kurfiss

Discrepancies between students' and professors' assumptions about knowledge probably account for a major share of the frustration both groups experience when critical thinking is required in a course. Models of college students' intellectual development provide a

---

Excerpt from *Critical Thinking: Theory, Research, Practice, and Possibilities.* ASHE-ERIC Higher Education Report No. 2 (Washington, DC: Association for the Study of Higher Education, 1988), pp. 51–56. Reprinted by permission.

framework for understanding how students come to terms with this discrepancy.

Background of the Research

The first studies of intellectual and ethical development in college were conducted at Harvard by William Perry and his associates. They interviewed over 100 students, nearly all male, in two separate four-year studies at Harvard and Radcliffe in the late 1950s and early 1960s.

Research on women's intellectual and ethical development by Belenky and associates has shown that while the broad categories of the scheme are similar to those identified by Perry, contemporary women frequently differ from the men and women interviewed by Perry in their view of authority, truth, and knowledge.

"Stages" of Intellectual Development

The following summary of intellectual development in college integrates Belenky and associates' extensive research on women's perspectives with the earlier findings reported by Perry. The summary is organized into four major categories or levels and suggests how students at each developmental level will respond to tasks that require critical thinking.

Level 1: Dualism or Received Knowledge

Many students believe that knowledge is a collection of discrete facts; therefore, learning is simply a matter of acquiring information delivered by the professor in concert with the text. Information is either correct or it is not; hence, Perry's label for this belief system is "dualism." Dualistic thinkers do not realize the degree to which the information presented

in a course or textbook is selected, interpreted, and systematized. They view the professor as the authority, presenting factual knowledge known to all experts in the discipline. Their dependence on authority as the source of all knowledge led Belenky and her associates to refer to this belief system as "received knowledge." Professors are always more or less right in this view, because, as one student says, "They have books to look at. Things that you look up in a book, you normally get the right answer."

For these students, the concept of interpretation, essential to critical thinking, is puzzling. Doesn't the text mean what it says? Why can't the author just say what he or she means? They may become confused or indignant when professors ask them to reason independently. Here is one student's response to a general education course that emphasizes thinking:

> It's supposed to teach you to—ah, reason better. That seems to be the, the excuse that natural science people give for these courses—they're supposed to teach you to arrive at more logical conclusions and look at things in a more scientific manner. Actually, what you get out of that course is you, you get an idea that science is a terrifically confused thing in which nobody knows what's coming off anyway.

In the face of "so many conflicting doctrines and opinions," many students in this first level opt "just to keep quiet until [they] really know just what the answer is." Rather than reflecting a personality characteristic like "passivity" or "vocationalism," their resistance to critical thinking reflects a legitimate developmental quandary as they encounter a world far more complex than they have realized.

Level 2: Multiplicity or Subjective Knowledge

Before students can accept the challenges and responsibilities of independent thinking, they must recognize that "conflicting doctrines and opinions" are an inevitable and legitimate feature of knowledge. And they must begin to develop trust in their "inner voices" as a source of knowledge. This is the work of the second level of intellectual development as described by Perry and by Belenky and associates.

In some courses, particularly those in the humanities and social sciences, students encounter numerous conflicts of interpretation and theory. Most students gradually acknowledge the existence of unknowns, doubts, and uncertainties, at least in some areas of knowledge. When the facts are not known, knowledge is a matter of "mere opinion." When no absolute truth exists, one "opinion" is as good as another, and teachers "have no right to call [the student] wrong" on matters of opinion. Many conflicts over grades probably arise from students' failure to understand, or professors' failure to communicate, the criteria used to judge "opinion" papers.

Perry's term "multiplicity" emphasizes his position's departure from dichotomous thinking. Belenky and associates' term "subjective knowledge" highlights women's tendency to turn inward, away from external authorities as their primary source of knowledge. The majority of college students subscribe to this category of epistemological beliefs.

Multiplicity/subjective knowledge is a crucial turning point in the development of critical thinking. Students at this level recognize complexity but have not yet learned how to navigate its waters. They perceive no basis other than intuition, feeling, or "common sense" on which to judge the merits of the opinions they now accept as reflections of legitimate differences.

Level 3: Relativism or Procedural Knowledge

Insistent pressure from peers (for example, in arguments in the residence hall or coffee shop) and from faculty (to give reasons for opinions offered in class discussion, on examinations, or in term papers) leads some students to realize that "opinions" differ in quality. Good opinions are supported with *reasons*. Students learn that they must examine an issue "in complex terms, weighing more than one factor in trying to develop your own opinion." In the arts, students learn that they must substitute analysis using "objective" criteria based on factors in the work for personal responses to its mood and character. Belenky and associates' term "procedural knowledge" captures this emphasis on using disciplinary methods of reasoning. Perry labels this belief system "relativism," because it assumes that what counts as true depends on (is relative to) the frame of reference used to evaluate the phenomenon in question. Many writers use the term "contextualism" or "contextual relativism" to describe this way of thinking.

Level 3 beliefs reflect the traditional academic view of reasoning as objective analysis and argument. Belenky and associates noticed, however, that some women employed an alternative procedure for developing opinions, which they called "connected knowledge." Connected knowledge attempts to understand the reasons for another's way of thinking. The student undertakes a "deliberate, imaginative extension of one's understanding into positions that initially feel wrong or remote." Connected knowledge differs from the objective analytical model of thinking, which they called "separate knowledge." Confronting a poem, separate knowers ask, "What techniques can I use to analyze it?" In contrast, connected knowers ask, "What is this poet trying to say to me?" Connected knowledge does not preclude analysis or criticism; it does, however, begin with a more empathic treatment of divergent views.

In Perry's study, most students came to realize that the "academic" method of deciding issues is generally applicable, because knowledge is inherently indeterminate. Subsequent studies have found fewer than half of college seniors subscribing to this perspective.

Level 4: Commitment in Relativism or Constructed Knowledge

The reasoning procedures of level 3 illuminate a situation, but they do not provide definitive answers. Ultimately, individuals must take a position and make commitments, even though they can have no external assurances of the "correctness" of what they choose to do or believe. Hence, Perry labels this perspective "commitment in relativism."

"Constructed knowledge," as described by Belenky and associates, integrates knowledge learned from others with the "inner truth" of experience and personal reflection. At this level, students understand that knower and known are intimately intertwined and exist in a particular historical and cultural context. Even in the sciences, this realization is possible, as one senior honors student observes:

> In science you don't really want to say that something's true. You realize that you're dealing with a model. Our models are always simpler than the real world. The real world is more complex than anything we can create. We're simplifying everything so that we can work with it, but the thing is really more complex. When you try to describe things, you're leaving the truth because you're oversimplifying.

Constructed knowledge as described in [Belenky's] *Women's Ways of Knowing* captures the interplay of rationality, caring, and commitment that is the ultimate goal of education. Constructed knowers are able to take "a position outside a particular context or frame of reference and look back on 'who' is asking the question, 'why' the question is asked at all, and 'how' answers are arrived at." They include the *self* in their knowing process, no longer executing a procedure but now becoming passionately engaged in the search for understanding. They are committed to nurturing rather than criticizing ideas; they may withdraw into silence if they believe the other person is not really listening, be it spouse, acquaintance, professor, or colleague. They seek integrated, authentic lives that contribute to "empowerment and improvement in the quality of life of others."

ACTIVITIES AND QUESTIONS FOR REFLECTION

1. *With which of the following comments do you identify most strongly or which would you be most likely to make:*

    "Why does the teacher present us with all these different approaches?

    Why doesn't the teacher teach us the right one?"

    "One opinion is as good as another."

    "Opinions have to have good reasons."

    "What is this poem trying to say to me? How do I analyze it?"

2. *Place each of these comments at the appropriate level of Kurfiss' model.*

3. *Why is one opinion* not *as good as another?*

4. *In terms of Kurfiss' model, describe yourself as a learner when you entered college. Usually our thinking will span several of the levels, perhaps in different areas of our lives.*

⌐─↙

IN THE PRECEDING READING, Kurfiss described the development of critical thinking in changing assumptions about what constitutes knowledge and what knowing is. The reflective judgment model presented here by Patricia King, of Bowling Green University in Ohio, examines a similar process. This research studied the kind of thinking necessary in resolving ill-structured problems and the way this kind of thinking, reflective judgment, develops.

Ill-structured problems are those for which there may be no correct answer or solution. Examples of ill-structured problems would include identifying the causes of violence in our society, creating more jobs, or protecting the survival of a species. The solutions and ways of reaching them are widely argued. No one could tell you how to resolve these problems. Therefore, in working with ill-structured problems you must ultimately make a judgment based on the strongest evidence and the most logical reasoning.

A well-structured problem does have a correct solution. Examples of well-structured problems include navigating an aircraft from Chicago to Beijing, calculating the distance from earth to Mars, and balancing a checkbook.

In the reflective judgment model, King describes the steps or stages in a progression from simple to complex thinking about ill-structured problems. The following comments represent different stages of the reflective judgment model:

> I figure if it's on the news, it's got to be true or they wouldn't put it on.

> Art can be anything you want it to be. My judgment is as good as yours.

> One judges arguments by looking at such things as how well thought-out the positions are, what kinds of reasoning and evidence one would use to support them.

AS YOU READ, look for the characteristics of responses to "ill-structured" problems at each stage in our ability to make reflective judgments.

⟞⟶

LEARNING TO MAKE REFLECTIVE JUDGMENTS
Patricia King

The term "reflective thinking" was used by John Dewey [a leading American philosopher in the early twentieth century] to describe the thinking process people use when faced with questions of controversy or doubt for which their current understanding or solution, for whatever reason, no longer is satisfactory. According to Dewey, a "reflective judgment" is the end goal of good thinking: the judgment or solution that brings closure to the problem (if only temporarily).

While reflective and critical thinking can (and should!) be directed toward a variety of types of problems, the reflective judgment model specifically focuses on controversial problems where real doubt exists about correct solutions (or best resolutions). Evaluating the merits of alternative proposals to stimulate the economy, weighing competing interpretations of national or international political events, and deciding how to reduce pollution while respecting economic interests are examples of what [systems philosopher] C.W. Churchman refers to as "ill-structured" problems. Questions such as these are full of the kinds of doubts to which Dewey referred because they can be neither described with a

high degree of completeness nor solved with a high degree of certainty. Other types of intellectual problems—such as calculating interest payments on a loan, converting units of measure between metric and English standards, and balancing a checkbook—can be described more completely and solved with higher certainty; these are called "well-structured" problems. The reflective judgment model describes a sequence of changes in thinking that affects the ways students justify their beliefs and make judgments about ill-structured problems.

The Reflective Judgment Model

For the last fifteen years, several colleagues and I have studied the ways people explain and justify their interpretations and judgments about controversial topics. We have found that individuals' answers to questions of what and how they know are related to their fundamental assumptions about knowledge itself and that these assumptions change during people's college years.

The reflective judgment model describes a developmental sequence of increasingly complex and adequate ways of understanding

Excerpt from "How Do We Know? Why do We Believe? Learning to Make Reflective Judgments," *Liberal Education*, Vol. 78, No. 1, January/February 1992, pp. 2–5. Reprinted by permission of Patricia M. King.

and resolving ill-structured problems. It demonstrates how a person's basis of judgment (the way a belief is justified) is rooted in his or her assumptions about knowledge itself. These assumptions are implicit in individuals' decisions to look for or ignore the facts of a situation, in the strategies they use to gain information about a problem, in their attempts to understand divergent interpretations, and in the degree of certainty they feel about whether a problem has been solved. This model attempts to make these assumptions explicit and to show how they evolve over time.

In the steps toward reflective thinking described by the model, people become better able to evaluate knowledge claims and to explain and defend a point of view on a controversial issue. This developmental progression in reasoning is described by seven distinct sets of assumptions about knowledge and how it is acquired; each set of assumptions, called a "stage," is associated with a different strategy for solving ill-structured problems. Following each of the descriptions below, a verbatim quotation is given to illustrate the type of reasoning associated with these assumptions.

Pre-Reflective Thinking

The early stages, 1 and 2, are characterized by the assumption that knowledge is gained through direct, personal observation or through the word of an authority figure and is therefore assumed to be absolutely correct and certain:

> I figure if it's on the news, it's got to be true or they wouldn't put it on.

Thinking consistent with these assumptions is considered "pre-reflective."

This level of assumed correctness and certainty is less apparent in subsequent stages, but some vestiges remain. In Stage 3, for example, absolute answers are assumed to exist but to be temporarily inaccessible.

> Right now, they are finding things about the pyramids that can't be explained. Right now they are just guessing. . . . Until there is evidence that people can give to convince everybody one way or another, it's just a guess. Then it will be knowledge.

People who use these assumptions to guide their reasoning tend to view all problems as though they were defined with a high degree of certainty and completeness; as a result, they are unable to differentiate between well- and ill-structured problems. Moreover, until this absolutely convincing evidence is in, no one can claim to "know" beyond his or her own personal impressions:

> It doesn't matter what you believe or what I believe because until one of them finds an answer, then I'm just going to believe what I want to believe.

Quasi-Reflective Thinking

Stage 4 reasoning is less whimsical: Evidence emerges as an important ingredient in the construction of knowledge claims, along with the acknowledgment that the evidence itself cannot be known with absolute certainty. Pragmatic reasons such as incorrect calibration of measurement tools, the loss of data over time, or the lack of a first person account are used to explain this lack of certainty:

I'd be more inclined to believe evolution if they had proof. It's just like the pyramids. I don't think we'll ever know [how they were built]. People will come up with different interpretations because people will differ. Who are you going to ask? No one was there.

At this level, differences between well- and ill-structured problems are acknowledged (a developmental advance over the earlier stages), but individuals often are at a loss when asked to make judgments about ill-structured problems because they do not know how to deal with the inherent ambiguity of such problems. Since there are many possible answers to these questions, evidence that can be used to support each answer, and no certain way to adjudicate between or among answers, knowledge claims are viewed as being idiosyncratic to the individual. Reasoning illustrated by these assumptions is considered "quasi-reflective."

Stage 5 reasoning is characterized by a more complete, more balanced, more detached analysis of the factors that contribute to a controversial issue. Knowledge is seen to be strongly contextual, and any given perspective is assumed to reflect its guiding principles, values, or accepted rules of inquiry. Evidence and clear reasoning are assumed to be necessary but not sufficient for constructing or evaluating an argument, since it is further acknowledged at this stage that evidence is not self-explanatory but must be interpreted.

Since no two people are alike, they're thinking differently and so they attack their problem differently. When they do that, they throw out different material and so come from two different positions since their intellectual curiosity is geared to different things.

While these assumptions are useful for evaluating the adequacy of arguments within a given perspective, individuals at this stage are at a loss when asked to evaluate competing explanations or proposals—tasks often associated with resolving ill-structured problems.

There are other theories [of how the pyramids were built] that could be as true as my own theory [but based on different evidence]. Everyone has their own idea of what truth is but for myself, this is my explanation. But other people have their own ideas on it and that's okay.

Reflective Thinking

Stages 6 and 7 represent the most advanced sets of assumptions in the reflective judgment model. At this level, knowledge is understood in relationship to context and evidence, and some interpretations may be judged as being in some way better than others. These stages reflect the assumption that one's understanding of the world is not "given" but must be actively constructed and interpreted and that knowledge must be understood in relationship to the context in which it was generated. An additional assumption made at this level is that some interpretations or knowledge claims may be judged more plausible than others. Criteria that might be used in making such evaluations include conceptual soundness, coherence, degree of fit with the data, meaningfulness, usefulness, and parsimony.

[One judges arguments by looking at such things as] how well thought out the positions are, at what level one chooses to argue the position, what kinds of reasoning and evidence one would use to support it, how it fits into the rest of one's world view or rational explanation, how consistently one argues on this topic compared with other topics.

Individuals who make judgments this way are exhibiting good "reflective thinking."

ACTIVITIES AND QUESTIONS FOR REFLECTION

1. *Which of the following statements is most representative of reflective thinking? What makes this statement reflective?*

   "If the news anchor can say it on television, it must be true or he or she couldn't say it."

   "Art can be anything you want it to be. My judgment is as good as yours."

   "One judges arguments by looking at such things as how well thought-out the positions are, what kinds of reasoning and evidence one would use to support them."

2. *When you are asked to make a judgment on an issue where there may be conflicting data or information, how do you sort through the data to determine the best answer? How do you decide what to believe or what evidence is most important when solving a problem where there is no one right answer?*

   Do you depend on what the experts say? How important is your own opinion in making a judgment? How important is it to obtain evidence (opinions) from multiple sources?

3. *As you reflect on the ways students develop their thinking processes in college as described by Kurfiss and King, do you have any new ideas for your development as a thinker during your college years? Record your reflections in writing.*

IN "DEVELOPMENTAL FOUNDATIONS OF CRITICAL THINKING," Kurfiss explored the steps students take in answering the question "What is the nature of knowledge?" In "Learning to Make Reflective Judgments," King presented her model of students' stages of development in justifying particular beliefs and making reflective judgments. Both readings concluded that developing complex levels of thought requires questioning our assumptions about the nature of knowledge.

In the following reading, Graham Gibbs of the British Open University describes how students change their conceptions of learning while in college. He found that approaches to studying are based on conceptions of learning. As conceptions of learning change, approaches to studying change. In other words, how students study is related more to the assumptions they make about learning than to study skills.

The studies Gibbs reports on were done in several different cultures and educational systems. In all of them, Gibbs found a strong relationship between success in college and a student's concept of learning and how it affected their study skills. When asked about their approach to their reading assignments, students responded:

The whole time I was thinking, "I must remember this."

I made connections with my own experience.

I thought over the logic of the argument.

AS YOU READ, look for descriptions of "course focused" versus "interest focused" and "surface" versus "deep" approaches to studying.

CHANGING CONCEPTS OF LEARNING

Graham Gibbs

Students do not study in the way they do simply because they know how to use certain study techniques and not others, or because they have been taught to study in certain

---

Adapted from "In What Ways Do Students Develop as Learners" by Graham Gibbs in *Teaching Students to Learn: A Student-Centered Approach* (Buckingham, UK: Open University Press, 1981), pp. 72–86. Reprinted by permission.

ways. Nor do they study in particular ways because of fixed personal characteristics or learning styles. Students actively *choose* to study the way they do.

Students have given vivid descriptions in various investigations of how and why they study and how their study habits change during their college career. In one study, their descriptions reveal two "types" of approaches to learning: "course-focus" and "interest-focus." Students using a course-focused approach stick close to the syllabus or reading list: "If you do things which are not on the syllabus they're not going to come up in the exams. The only thing you really come to University for is the degree." In contrast, a student using an interest-focused approach would say, "If I were really interested I would try to read more about it and possibly go and see the tutor again depending on how deeply interested I was."

Most students change from one focus to the other, by choice, depending on the situation. Students who enter college with an interest-focus but find their studies lacking in the level of intellectual stimulation expected, for example, will switch to course-focus. Their study methods are adapted and used in ways which are intended to achieve particular goals.

A strong course focus is chosen on the basis of *what* is studied and *how,* not just the *amount* of work students do or their *degree* of commitment. How students study is determined by the way they interpret the demands of the particular task. It is not study skills, but the conception of learning which determines the approach toward learning which a student will adopt.

In another study as many as half of the students were found to be "cue deaf." They were oblivious to cues about exactly what was to be learned and gained exceptionally poor understanding from reading articles and taking courses. These students' understanding of fundamental economic principles, for example, was no better after completing an economics course than it was before and in some cases was actually worse.

To understand why, researchers asked students to describe their approach to reading a text. Their responses fell into only two types. This basic division has been confirmed by researchers in other studies. In one type of description, the students said:

> Well, I just concentrated on trying to remember as much as possible.

> I remembered . . . but, I'd sort of memorized everything I'd read . . . no, not everything, but more or less.

> It would have been more interesting if I'd known that I wasn't going to be tested on it afterwards, 'cos in that case I'd've more, you know, thought about what it said instead of all the time trying to think now I must remember this and now I must remember that.

In the other type of description, students said:

> . . . I tried to look for . . . you know, the principal ideas . . .

> . . . and what you think about then, well it's you know, what was the point of the article, you know . . .

> No, I . . . tried to think what it was all about . . .

. . . I thought about how he had built up the whole thing.

There is a *qualitative* difference in these two approaches. In the first, the text itself is the focus. In the second, the focus is on what the text is about. These two categories of approach have been named "surface-approach" and "deep-approach." Other researchers have called them "atomistic" (a focus on parts) and "holistic" (a focus on the overall relationships).

There is a very strong relationship between the level of success in academic studies and the approach taken toward studying. This is in contrast to the weak relationship found between study skills and performance. To demonstrate this point, L. Svensson in a large study at Göteborg University in Sweden, set up an experiment in which he accurately predicted the exam scores of 29 of 30 students based on his study of the relative diligence and study techniques of students *in relation to their approach*. Svensson knew that variations in study techniques produce very little difference in learning outcomes while the use of surface/atomistic or deep/holistic approaches would be the greater deciding factor. The deep or holistic approach produced consistently better results.

In addition, students who use surface or atomistic approaches spend less time studying. The focus on detail, the memorizing, and the lack of focus on the larger relevance of the text produces boredom and fatigue.

It has been assumed that students adopt an approach to studying which is in accordance with their specific learning style or some particular personality characteristic. But it has

been found that while some students will rigidly adopt a surface approach, many students will take a surface or deep approach *depending on the nature of the task*. They will adopt a surface approach to one task and a deep approach to others.

Why would students choose a less effective—and less pleasant—approach to learning in any instance?

It appears to be related to the ways students conceptualize learning. Roger Saljö of the Göteborg University study found that for some students, the phenomenon of learning in itself had become an object of reflection where as for others, it had not. For some, learning was something that could be explicitly talked about, discussed, planned, and analyzed. For others, it was taken for granted. He found that students take three main "steps" in the development of their reflection about learning. These steps are:

1. Students become conscious of "cues" about learning in the school context. They may or may not respond to the cues but they become aware that expectations are being set for what you should learn for school and how you should go about it.

2. Students become aware of a distinction between "life" learning and "school" learning. School learning is perceived as stereotyped and routine and related to the needs of the school itself. As negative as this stage is, however, it is a positive step since the student is now able to analyze learning.

3. Students begin thinking about the nature of what is learned. They distinguish be-

tween learning and *real* learning—between remembering and understanding. The focus is on point of view, interpretation, principle, etc. "Facts" become subordinate to meaning.

Beyond these stages of learning awareness, Saljö discovered in a further study five rather distinct conceptions of learning:

1. Learning as the increase of knowledge.

   The responses at this stage are rather vague and generally focus on a set of synonyms for the word learning. "It's to increase your knowledge."

2. Learning as memorizing.

   Learning is seen as the acquiring of pieces of knowledge, facts, from a teacher or book. ". . . sort of to learn, to get things in one's head so they stay there."

3. Learning as the acquisition of facts, procedures, etc., which can be retained and/or utilized in practice.

   Facts, principles, etc. are understood to have a practical application. ". . . to learn so that you know it and so that you can make use of it."

4. Learning as the abstraction of meaning.

   Learning is no longer conceived of as an activity of reproduction or acquisition, but is a process of understanding or interpreting meaning.

   ". . . It means learning about a course of events and how things have developed, and reasoning within my subject but it does not mean sitting and memorizing trifles such as dates and such things as people do . . ."

5. Learning as an interpretative process aimed at understanding reality.

   What you learn should help you understand the world in which you live.

   ". . . learning means to get a sort of insight into your subject so that you can use it in your everyday life. In some ways I think I've found out that you learn things twice somehow. The first time could have been at school really, the second time is the connection, I mean it becomes conscious in some way . . . I mean it should be related to some kind of practice. That's when you have learnt it, I think, terribly much. Then you can live . . . I mean you can sort of *be* your knowledge in some way. Then, the really important thing has happened."

The movement is from the idea of knowledge as external and something which is transferred verbatim, item by item, to an emphasis on the learner as an active part of the process of extracting meaning and relating that meaning to reality. It is similar to the distortion between surface and deep level approaches to learning.

Perry, in his work at the Bureau of Study Counsel at Harvard University on how students develop intellectually, began with developing skill courses. He found that skill training worked better if he understood the student's level of development. Perry discovered that until students revise their sense of purpose, an increase in effort is likely to produce only an increase in bad results. And in order to revise their sense of purpose students need to develop a more sophisticated concept of the nature of knowledge—and what it means to learn.

The movement from surface to deep approaches to learning is facilitated by the student's developing understanding of learning as related to a search for meaning and an understanding of the world. Teaching study skills—taking notes, reading, writing, revising—are much less effective without an accompanying reconceptualization of learning. When this reconceptualization takes place, the implementation of new techniques and the resulting increase in performance is significant.

Activities and Questions for Reflection

1. *How would you compare your present approach to studying your favorite course with studying your least favorite course using Gibbs' terms?*

2. *According to Gibbs, why are students who use a "deep" approach to studying and learning more successful?*

3. *Interview three college students about their approach to reading a textbook for one of their courses. What do they think about while they are reading? Can you relate their answers to Gibbs' categories?*

    Do they try to make a connection with their own experience?

    Do they think about remembering everything they read?

    Do they hurry through the reading just to finish it?

    Do they reflect on their reading?

    Do they consider whether the argument is logical?

4. *How do study techniques relate to Gibbs' findings about success in study?*

5. *Does this reading and your reflection on it suggest some ideas for your development as a learner? If so, how would you describe them?*

↦

THE LAST READING IN THIS CHAPTER is about a state called "flow." Mihaly Csikszentmihalyi, professor of psychology at the University of Chicago, has done the major research on the psychology of optimal experience. He chose the word flow *for the state of pleasure or enjoyment that you reach when you have mastered a particular ability and are performing it with maximum concentration and ease. His research has shown that a balance of mastery and challenge and having a goal are the vital elements of this experience. In the following reading, Ronald Gross, leader of the Seminar on Innovation at Columbia University, describes the features of the flow state, applies them to learning, and gives some illustrations of how flow is achieved when learning.*

AS YOU READ, look for the characteristics of the flow state and the examples of how it is achieved.

↦

PEAK LEARNING: THE FLOW STATE
Ronald Gross

"What do we mean by being happy?" Professor Csikszentmihalyi asks. "Is it just pleasure and the absence of pain? These are rewarding conditions, indispensable to maintain psychic processes on an even keel. But happiness also depends on something else: the feeling that one is growing, improving. That process is, by definition, a process of learning, broadly defined. One might conclude that learning is necessary for happiness, that learning *is* the pursuit of happiness."

Flow is the state in which learning and happiness are most completely merged. An article in the *New York Times Magazine* described it as "a state of concentration that amounts to absolute absorption in an activity. In this state, action flows effortlessly from thought and you feel strong, alert and unselfconscious. Flow is that marvelous feeling that you are in command of the present and performing at the peak of your ability. . . . Research suggests that flow may be a common aspect of human experience."

Flow happens in every activity. In sports, it's that moment of reaching the *zone* where your ability and performance excel. In music,

---

it takes place when you know your instrument and the piece so well that you just *do* it, as if you have *become* the instrument and the music. In dancing, painting, surgery, and even writing, there's a sense of control, a profound focus on what you're doing that leaves no room to worry about what anyone will think of your work. There are a number of features which characterize the flow state:

Flow can occur when perceived challenges match perceived skills.

Perhaps the most crucial feature is the delicate balance between what you *perceive* to be the challenges in the situation you face and how you *perceive* your own abilities to meet those challenges. Perception is important here, because, as has been seen, the mind *actively constructs* the situations it faces. *Any* activity can be turned into a flow experience if viewed in the right way.

The first step in recognizing the conditions for flow is to *have something to do,* an opportunity for action, a challenge. The next step is to recognize that you have some skills you can use to decide what to do next. The balance between these two will start the ball rolling for flow.

Flow states involve a sense of control in the situation.

With that perceived balance comes another characteristic of the flow experience: a sense of control. Imagine sitting down to play a game of chess for the first time. You have some idea of how the pieces are supposed to move, but as the game develops, it may be hard to figure out what you should do next. Yet as you play more, and learn more, you start to recognize certain kinds of situations that repeat. You don't fall for the same traps again. You have a better idea of what to do, and so you have an increased sense of control instead of feeling as if you're helplessly floundering.

Flow happens in situations in which one has clearly defined goals and feedback.

Games provide a good model for describing other features of the flow experience. According to Csikszentmihalyi, it is important in learning to have a clear sense of the goals in a situation and clear feedback about the results of your actions. This knowledge of what you're aiming for and what difference your actions make encourages you to concentrate on what is relevant to the situation, to become immersed in it.

In flow experiences, intense concentration on what is relevant develops the ability to merge unself-conscious action with awareness and to alter the experience of time.

Think of kids who get involved in computer games, even the arcade shoot-'em-ups. What needs to be done to find the treasure or destroy the alien invaders is totally clear in each moment. And so it becomes easy to lose track of time, forget your hunger, and even ignore pain until you stop playing. Thus in a clearly defined situation in which challenge is balanced by skill and there is a sense of control, it becomes possible to focus concentration intensely on the relevant cues, to merge action and awareness in a way that stops any self-consciousness and may even change how the passage of time is experienced. This feature is our next essential in the flow experience.

Flow experiences arise from intrinsic motivation, not from concern with external rewards or goals.

Csikszentmihalyi has found that this feature is as important as the balance of skills and challenge.

Feeding back information for the sake of a good grade can rob learning of its joy and make it torture. Sure, you can be pleased by a good grade, but it is not likely to make the process of cramming for exams any more pleasant.

On the other hand, if you're jamming on a guitar with friends or perfecting your jump shot on a basketball court, what makes those things fun, according to Csikszentmihalyi, is that you're doing them for their own sake. You may wind up with a good riff for a song or the ability to sink a basket from midcourt, but while you're getting there you are just having fun. That is, the experience of learning is enjoyable in itself, not for what you will eventually get out of it.

Csikszentmihalyi believes that people who use flow actually use *less* mental energy than those who are struggling to concentrate because they're bored or anxious. He sees the flow experience as something that's a built-in part of being human, of having a mind that processes information. In his view, new challenges are enjoyable because they prepare human beings to be involved with their environment and to succeed. For Csikszentmihalyi, the joys of learning are as natural as the pleasures of sex, and both serve evolutionary goals for the human species.

ACTIVITIES AND QUESTIONS FOR REFLECTION

1. *Can you describe an experience in which you felt this state of flow? Perhaps as a child playing games or working on a hobby? Or in sports?*

2. *How does Gross say the experience of flow contributes to an athlete's or a musician's ability to study for many hours a day? Is there a similar activity that you would pursue simply to achieve flow?*

3. *Does flow learning suggest any further goals, perhaps a final goal, for you as a learner?*

CHAPTER 5

↜ *Thinking and Learning*

SUMMARY

Through the readings and exercises on thinking and learning, you have had an opportunity to examine some of the ways it is possible to develop intellectually and become a more effective learner including the following:

- How learning itself makes new learning easier by increasing the capacity of the brain to learn more.

- How we make assumptions about knowledge, its origins, its nature, and what can be defined as knowledge.

- How these assumptions change or evolve from simple to complex.

- How reflective judgment develops and how this development is necessary to approach controversial questions or problems that have no "correct" answer.

- How success in college is related to the way you *think* about *learning*, and that there are more and less productive ways of thinking about learning.

- How maximum satisfaction and enjoyment come when we achieve a balance of challenge and mastery, when new information is balanced with prior learning to create a state of maximum involvement, or *flow*.

Using the Internet

Using InfoTrac College Edition, look up the most recent research on learning and the brain. Keywords you might use are *brain* and *learning*. Read a few of the most recent articles.

1. How does the most recent research support or challenge the information presented in this chapter?

2. Given the information available to you, what do you think the impact of this information could be in education? What changes would you suggest for your own education?

SUMMARIZING ACTIVITIES AND QUESTIONS FOR REFLECTION

1. *How have your ideas about learning and what learning is been changed by the readings in this chapter? Review each reading and be specific about the information presented and its impact on your thinking.*

2. *Think about your educational experiences, including life experience, not just classroom experience. Which have been least important to you and how would you have changed them given what you now understand about learning?*

3. *Reflecting on the statement, "Collecting information is not enough. I need to be able to do something with the information—I need to use it, explain it, reflect on it, connect it. . . .," how would you approach studying differently? What approach to study might help you integrate your knowledge better when you study?*

4. *What studies in college might be more interesting to you now that you had not considered seriously before these readings?*

5. *After reflecting on the readings and activities in this chapter, review your goals for your college education and your definition of an educated person and make revisions or additions that capture any new understandings you now have.*

Learning How to Learn

INTRODUCTION: WAYS OF LEARNING

One of the most common misconceptions about learning is that it involves working harder: "You just work harder and it happens." A second is that if you aren't learning it is because you aren't paying enough attention. Although attention is often a problem when we are studying something we don't want to study, more often the problem is in paying attention in the wrong ways. If working harder is the wrong way to pay attention, then what is the right way?

We need to learn to learn—or how to learn most effectively. Learning requires knowing how to learn.

This chapter presents several ways of applying theories of learning to actual learning tasks. The first reading discusses learning styles and explains that we all have preferred ways of learning. Other readings treat experiential learning, self-directed learning, and collaborative or cooperative learning. The final reading discusses applying group learning to team learning.

Team learning is the primary method of learning in most corporate business environments. Teams who study, learn, and execute together are increasingly performing both management functions and manufacturing functions. Contrary to most of our expectations, working is not a task in which one is told what to do and simply does it. Work includes determining how to do the job as well as it can be done and evaluating what you as a worker need to do the job. Because most jobs require interaction with other workers or clients, work also requires understanding how to work well with others.

Thus, learning and knowing how to learn are important not only in college but for one's whole life. College is a place to learn how to learn, not just a place to absorb the "right" information or to be credentialed.

Becoming conscious of how you learn and the ways in which others learn will enable you to take greater control of your own learning and to engage with others to create the kind of learning environment that is most productive for success in life.

↤⟶

IN THE FOLLOWING READING, Arthur W. Chickering, now a distinguished professor at Union Institute at Vermont College and Research Professor at the New England Resource Center for Higher Education at the University of Massachusetts, and Nancy K. Schlossberg, professor at the University of Maryland, describe an important use of the experiential learning cycle developed by David A. Kolb for identifying individual "learning styles." The learning styles are based on combinations of four abilities—concrete experience, reflective observation, abstract conceptualization, and active experimentation—that make up experiential learning.

According to Kolb, who is now professor of organizational management at Case Western Reserve University in Ohio, each of us has a preferred learning style, a way of approaching new experience that makes it easier for us to learn. Becoming aware of your own learning style can be a helpful strategy in learning. You can make the most of your strengths and also strive to broaden your style. An ideal learning style would involve using all four abilities equally.

AS YOU READ, look for the primary abilities in each of the learning styles and consider how knowing your own learning style could be helpful in college.

↤⟶

YOUR PREFERRED LEARNING STYLE
Arthur W. Chickering and Nancy K. Schlossberg

Kolb's experiential learning cycle can be used to consider which combination of elements you prefer in your own learning. Most tennis players have some strokes they like better than others: a dynamite serve, a really powerful forehand, strong volleys. They will use those as much as they can. In learning, most of us have our preferred approaches. Our "learning style" preference has developed over the years to suit our needs and the situations we ran into. But different types of learning call for different approaches. Our learning is less effective than it

---

would be if we adapt our approach to the type of learning called for.

Kolb introduces us to four different styles: *Divergers, Assimilators, Convergers,* and *Accommodators.*

- *Divergers* primarily use *concrete experiences* and *reflective observations* for learning. They are imaginative and able to see situations from diverse perspectives. They are good at generating ideas. They tend to be people oriented, tuned into their feelings, and concerned about meaning and values. As college students, they are often the ones who are interested in the arts and humanities.

- *Assimilators* primarily use *reflective observation* and *abstract conceptualization* for learning. They excel at inductive reasoning and integrating different observations. Their strength is in creating theoretical models. They tend to be more interested in sound concepts than in practical applications. As college students, they frequently work in basic sciences and mathematics.

- *Convergers* primarily use *abstract conceptualization* and testing implications through *active experimentation.* Their strength is in applying ideas to practical situations. They excel at problem solving and decision-making. They are often relatively unemotional and like to deal with things. As college students, they tend to have technical interests and specialize in the physical sciences, computer sciences, engineering, and nursing.

- *Accommodators* primarily use testing implications through *active experimentation* and *concrete experiences* for learning.

They are action oriented and good at implementing plans and doing things. They tend to solve problems by intuition and by trial and error. As college students, they are often in business, marketing, and sales.

These categories are not hard and fast. You probably won't fit neatly into any of these boxes. But they are useful as ways to begin thinking about your own preferred approaches to learning. We enjoy most, and learn best, in courses that match our preferred learning styles.

More often than you may like, you will run into courses where the teaching is at odds with your preferred learning style. This happens to all of us, because very few teachers incorporate activities that span all four parts of the experiential learning cycle. [As explained in the interview below] Jessie finds concrete experiences and active application most effective. Her comments vividly illustrate what happens when her learning style is out of step with the way a course is taught.

What kind of learning do you like best?

"I like practicums and working in the field. When I can actually involve myself in the activity I learn more from it than just listening to someone talk about it or lecture on it. I prefer to learn like that. If you put me in a situation then I will get more from it than if you just tell me about the situation."

Why do you think that is?

"It just sticks in my brain more. Because I am actually doing it. Then, just listening to someone is kind of boring. You know, that doesn't have anything really to do with me. But when

I am involved it has something to do with myself. It is something I can learn from."

What about reflective observation?

"It depends on the situation. If I find it interesting, a movie or play or something, then I will learn from it and be able to digest the information. But if it is not something I am particularly interested in, I don't gain much from it."

Another way to learn is from abstract conceptualization, through theories and concepts . . . You're shaking your head.

"I don't deal with those, especially theories and concepts. I am in philosophy right now. It is really giving me a hassle, to tell the truth. Because I don't know, I am not a deep thinker, I guess. Thinking, if I do this, this, and this, or breaking it down to many, many steps."

So what do you prefer?

"Hands-on, getting involved in a situation."

How are you learning in philosophy then?

"I read the book. I just read it over and over until I pretty much understand what each philosopher is saying. That's the only way I can learn because from the lectures I am not getting much. I really can't understand what he is saying. So I am only learning from reading the book."

So what happens in class?

"I just try to take notes on what he is saying. But, most of the time, I am just wandering off looking out the window or something. I am not really paying attention. Even though it's a small class, with only twenty-five students, it's really boring. It's pure lecture. To

tell the truth, I thought that philosophy was going to be pretty interesting. You know, everybody would have their points of view. I thought that it would be more of a discussion class rather than a pure lecture class. But I was disappointed."

Sometimes we are faced with a teaching style that is out of sync with how we like to learn, like you just indicated for philosophy. When that happens what do you do?

"I have to find another way for me to be able to learn. Like I said, with philosophy, I just read the book. Then I just have to figure a different strategy where I will be able to digest the information."

Jessie's philosophy course is a good example of what happens when a clear learning style preference runs into content and a teacher's approach that is very different. She was interested in the subject and looking forward to the course. Because of the way it is taught, it has become boring and hard for her to learn. She even has begun to believe that she is "not a deep thinker." Jessie tries to find a strategy that will help her learn. But her strategy is limited to reading the book "over and over."

There are other strategies she might use that would be more consistent with her learning style. If she had been aware of these, she might have invested the time she spent in repeated reading in a more productive way. For example, she might have asked some of her friends what they thought about different philosophical concepts or orientations. Or she could have created a study group to discuss the strengths and weaknesses of various philosophical perspectives. If she wanted to be more formal, she might have suggested that she and some of her classmates each take a particular viewpoint and defend it in a debate. She could also seek out faculty members and ask them for their views on the validity of different philosophical positions. She could create a diagram or a flow chart showing the relationships among various philosophical orientations. She could also observe the behaviors and attitudes of fellow students to see how particular philosophical perspectives were reflected in action.

Alternatives like these would have been more consistent with her learning style, with her preference for active involvement, than reading the book over and over. They might have helped her learn, and made the course fun instead of boring. She probably would not begin questioning her ability to be a "deep thinker."

Here are some things you can do to strengthen your learning style so you involve the full cycle:

- *Concrete experiences* can be direct or vicarious. Both can be powerful. Films, television programs, audiotapes, live performances, demonstrations, can engage your emotions and connect with your prior experiences. A moving novel, biography, poem, or play can be a powerful experience. Direct observations, active participation, human contacts, interviews—on the campus, in the community, in natural settings—can give life to abstract ideas. Role-plays, simulations, games, debates can get you actively involved.

- *Reflective observations* can be strengthened by reviewing class notes and thinking about how they connect with other ideas or experiences. You can keep a journal where you comment on meanings that experiences, ideas, pieces of information, have for you. Discussion, study groups, computer conferencing, and teleconferencing—with other students and with faculty members who are willing—can help you share understandings, make connections. Creating visual metaphors and analogies can be especially powerful ways to capture complex sets of ideas and their interrelationships. You won't forget a good metaphor or analogy, and often it will enrich your understanding as well. We have used tennis as an analogy for experiential learning. If you have created a good analogy of your own, you won't forget the concept.

- *Abstract concepts* come to us through print, lectures, and computer programs. A picture is worth a thousand words. Graphs, diagrams, tables, figures, cartoons, can supply rich data and clearly illustrate relationships, contrasts, and comparisons. Computer modeling, computer graphics, and flow charts can describe sequences of cause-and-effect and provide visual images of multiple interactions. Many of us have seen by now the double-helix pictures or models of the DNA molecule that carries hereditary characteristics. Or we have seen weather forecasts, on television or in the papers, that show moving cloud patterns reflecting high and low pressure systems or hurricanes in action. These images convey complex information and interactions clearly and economically. We understand

Kolb's Modes of Experience and Learning Styles

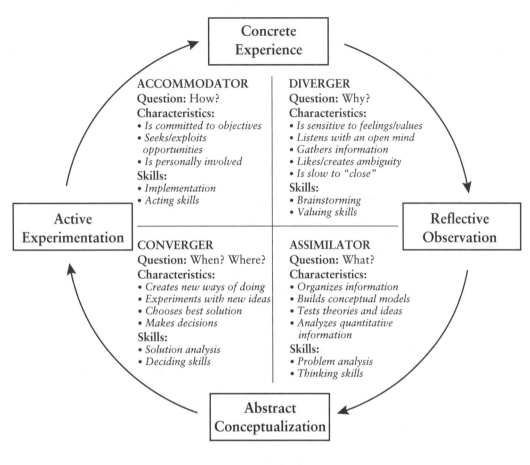

Based on a diagram from Roads to the Learning Society *edited by Barry Sheckley and George Allen (Chicago: Council for Adult and Experiential Learning, 1991), p. 107.*

This diagram is an illustration of the ways in which we attempt to grasp our experiences and perceptions and transform them into understanding. We start with a "concrete experience" that we consider and analyze. This is "reflective observation." From our reflections we form ideas or "abstract concepts." Then we test our ideas in "active experimentation" that takes us back to "concrete experience."

Each of Kolb's learning styles—accommodator, diverger, assimilator, and converger—describes a preferred way of learning. Each learning style is a mixture of two modes of experience—concrete experience, reflective observation, abstract concepts, and active experimentation. For example, a person who prefers to approach problems or questions as abstract concepts and then to test these concepts, is called a "converger."

Although no one would use any one mode or style exclusively, Kolb's model is useful in exploring how we learn and for helping us understand which modes and styles we prefer.

how weather works and what is going on much better than if we simply listened to the words.

- *Testing the implications of concepts* [active experimentation] can occur though systematic experiments in laboratories or elsewhere. Or you can simply try out new behaviors and see what happens. You can put the logic of one concept against the logic of competing concepts and see which seems to make the most sense. You can look for settings where you can observe others trying out particular ideas or actions, and examine the consequences.

ACTIVITIES AND QUESTIONS FOR REFLECTION

1. *Here's the way one student described her learning style in terms of Kolb's model: "I prefer to participate actively in learning rather than observe. I think I learn best by doing, by trial and error, by experiencing things myself rather than listening to abstract ideas."*

   Which of the four styles do you think it most closely represents? Why?

2. *Kolb's model provides a vocabulary to help you express your thoughts about how you learn. Using a successful learning experience, identify which of the learning modes you used most—concrete experience, reflective observation, abstract conceptualization, or active experimentation. Can you identify your primary learning style as a diverger, assimilator, converger, or accommodator?*

3. *Identify another course you are presently taking. Across the top of a piece of paper put the names of the four abilities in Kolb's learning cycle—Concrete Experience, Reflective Observation, and so on. Under each heading list the activities in the course that require or use that ability. For example, you would put "reading a textbook" under "Abstract Conceptualization."*

   Is there one predominant learning style required for the course? Do the activities of the course match your own preferred learning style?

4. *Does this analysis of your learning style and that required in one of your current courses suggest any further goals for your development as a learner in college?*

SELF-DIRECTED LEARNING refers to being proactive, taking the initiative in learning, compared with teacher-directed learning where the learner is told what to do and how to do it, and perhaps coached through the process. This is one of the important differences between the expectations of students in college and those in primary or secondary school. Self-directed learning is also a skill that is transferable to learning outside a school situation. People who are self-directed learners are much less dependent on a structured learning environment.

In this reading, the late Malcolm Knowles, as Professor Emeritus at North Carolina State University, described the skills required for self-directed learning, such as the ability to translate your own needs or interests into learning objectives or purposes.

AS YOU READ, look for Knowles' definition of the principal skills or competencies of self-directed learning.

COMPETENCE IN SELF-DIRECTED LEARNING

Malcolm S. Knowles

Experience has shown that when adults are exposed to a situation in which they are expected to take responsibility for their learning they typically react with confusion, resentment, and resistance. Hence, it is important to provide them with preparatory experiences that will free them from their conditioned dependency and provide them with the attitudes, intellectual understand-ing, and skills necessary to enter into self-directed learning projects with confidence and pleasure.

Although people seem instinctively to engage in self-directed learning in certain situations, relatively few have developed the competencies required to be consistently successful. Among these competencies are the following:

Excerpt from "Fostering Competence in Self-Directed Learning" in *Learning to Learn Over the Life Span,* edited by Robert M. Smith and Associates (San Francisco: Jossey-Bass, 1990), pp. 123–124, 130–132. Copyright © 1990 by Jossey-Bass Inc., Publishers. This material is used by permission of John Wiley & Sons, Inc.

- An understanding of the difference between teacher-directed and self-directed learning and the circumstances under which each is appropriate
- The desire and ability to maintain a sense of curiosity
- The ability to perceive one's self objectively and to accept feedback about one's performance nondefensively
- The ability to diagnose one's own learning needs realistically and to seek the help of peers and experts in this process
- The ability to translate learning needs into learning objectives in a way that makes it possible for the degree of accomplishment of the objectives to be assessed
- The ability to identify resources—human, material, and experimental—for accomplishing various kinds of learning objectives
- The ability to design a plan of strategies for making use of appropriate learning resources effectively
- The ability to carry out a learning plan systematically and proactively
- The ability to collect and validate evidence of the accomplishment of objectives
- The ability to relate to peers collaboratively as resources for helping one's own learning and to make one's resources available to them
- The ability to relate to teachers and other experts as facilitators and resource persons and to take the initiative in making use of these resources

In the broadest sense, "self-directed learning" describes a *process* in which individuals take the initiative, with or without the help of others, in

1. diagnosing their own needs for learning,
2. formulating their own learning objectives,
3. identifying effective human and material resources for accomplishing their objectives,
4. choosing and implementing effective strategies for using these resources, and
5. evaluating the extent to which they have accomplished their objectives.

Of course, self-direction in learning does *not* mean learning alone or in isolation; it usually takes place in association with various kinds of helpers such as teachers, tutors, mentors, resource people and peers.

A number of responsible thinkers who are concerned about the future of our civilization have emphasized that in the world of accelerating change (the knowledge explosion, the technological revolution, the information society) that we are entering, learning must be a lifelong process if we are to avoid the catastrophe of human obsolescence. The single most important competence that people must possess to survive is the ability to learn—with or, more important, without a teacher. Although this ability should begin its development through the schooling of children and youth, all institutions in our society have a responsibility to foster it over a lifetime. And, fortunately, we now know that this is a competence that *can* be fostered.

ACTIVITIES AND QUESTIONS FOR REFLECTION

1. *Identify something you have learned, without a teacher instructing you, because you wanted to learn it. Perhaps it was learning about astronomy or learning to play basketball. Of the competencies identified by Knowles in this reading, which were required?*

2. *What kind of opportunities do you think you might have or might seek in college to acquire and use competencies in self-directed learning? What competencies do you think you need to develop to be successful as an independent learner?*

3. *What benefits do you see for the student who knows how to be a self-directed learner in college? After college?*

IN THIS SECOND READING on self-directed learning, Stephen Brookfield, formerly professor at Teachers College, Columbia University, and currently Distinguished Professor at the University of St. Thomas in St. Paul, Minnesota, adds a further dimension to the meaning of self-directedness. According to Brookfield, the most important factor in becoming a self-directed learner is not techniques or skills but, rather, the internal reflection required in examining the reasons for learning. For example, as a political organizer you could be highly self-directed in learning how to set up a local campaign, but Brookfield would say that if you haven't questioned or reflected on your party's positions on issues, you are not fully self-directed— you are just a follower. Followers are not self-directed because they don't question the assumptions behind their actions. Questioning assumptions is at the root of becoming a self-directed learner.

AS YOU READ, notice why Brookfield places emphasis on examining assumptions in self-directed learning.

EXPLORING SELF-DIRECTEDNESS IN LEARNING
Stephen D. Brookfield

To many practitioners, the term *self-directed learning* conjures up images of isolated individuals busily engaged in determining the form and content of their learning efforts and controlling the execution of these efforts in an autonomous manner. This notion of autonomy centers on the idea that the learner is particularly skilled at setting objectives, locating resources, and designing learning strategies.

If we conceive of self-direction solely in terms of a command of self-instructional techniques, one can become a superb technician of self-directed learning, in command of goal setting, instructional design, or evaluative procedures, and yet be unable to question the validity or worthwhileness of one's intellectual pursuit as compared to competing, alternative possibilities. We might think here of the self-directed party member or religious zealot who is completely unaware of alternative political doctrines or religious creeds but who is skilled in certain technical activities concerned with the design and management of self-instruction.

It is quite possible to exhibit the methodological attributes of self-directed learning in terms of designing and executing learning projects but to do so within a framework of narrow and unchallenged assumptions, expectations, and goals. Learning to be a good disciple, to be an efficient bureaucratic functionary, or to be an exemplary political party member are all examples of projects in which the techniques of self-directed learning may be evident. In none of these projects, however, is there exhibited critical thought concerning other alternatives, options, or possibilities.

Self-directed learning as the mode of learning characteristic of an adult who is in the process of realizing his or her adulthood is concerned as much with an internal change of consciousness as with the external management of instructional events. The most complete form of self-directed learning occurs when process and reflection are married in the adult's pursuit of meaning. As we have said, it is possible to be a technically skilled self-directed learner in one's attempt to be a good party member, employee, or graduate student. The norms or assumptions underlying what it means to be a "good" functionary in any of these settings need never be questioned. All that would be required for an activity to be a technically correct example of self-directed learning would be that the individual concerned was effective in designing a successful learning program with a minimum of external assistance.

The most fully adult form of self-directed learning, however, is one in which critical reflection on the contingent aspects of reality, the exploration of alternative perspectives and meaning systems, and the alteration of personal and social circumstances are all present.

ACTIVITIES AND QUESTIONS FOR REFLECTION

1. *What does Brookfield propose as the most complete form of self-directedness? Does it make room for the competencies listed by Knowles in the previous reading?*

2. *Interview a college graduate about his or her experience with self-directed learning in college. Which competencies as described by Knowles were demonstrated? How was internal reflection as described by Brookfield used?*

3. *Based on your understanding of Knowles and Brookfield, what would you add to your description of an educated person?*

↗

IN ADDITION TO SELF-DIRECTEDNESS as a strategy for learning to learn, as discussed in the two previous readings, another strategy is collaborative learning. Collaborative learning refers to a situation in which small groups of four to six students within a class work together on learning projects. Though you might immediately think that self-directed and collaborative learning are opposites, they actually share some characteristics.

In this reading, Robert Smith, professor at Northern Illinois University at DeKalb, discusses the necessary conditions and the means for making collaborative learning experiences successful. He stresses the importance of the commitment of all participants to the success of the group, rather than only to their individual accomplishments.

AS YOU READ, look for the specific qualities of an effective participant in collaborative learning.

↗

THE LEARNING GROUP
Robert M. Smith

Probably no greater need exists than to learn how to participate effectively. Many studies have shown that humans are, and always have been, social animals.

James W. Botkin, *No Limits to Learning*

A frequently used figure of speech to describe the effective learning group is a "learning team." The members work well together, seek to compensate for one another's shortcomings, utilize the contributions of all to achieve common goals, and try to improve performance as they go along. Achieving learning goals and accomplishing learning-related tasks depend on such matters as coordination (or leadership), communication, appropriateness of resources and procedures, and resolving together of the conflicts that almost inevitably arise. Somewhere along the way, the members must establish a degree of mutual trust.

Excerpt from *Learning How to Learn: Applied Theory for Adults.* (Englewood Cliffs, NJ: Prentice-Hall, 1988), pp. 106–107, 111, 117. Reprinted by permission of Prentice-Hall, Inc., Englewood Cliffs, NJ.

Optimum Conditions

A learning group differs from a task group (for example, a board of review or an infantry platoon) by virtue of the relatively greater importance of meeting individual needs for change and growth en route to common goals and purposes. The group is not primarily concerned with achieving the purposes of one individual or of a larger organization. Individuals tend to realize the most personal benefit from learning in groups to the extent that the following four conditions are present.

1. *Everyone shares in the program development and evaluation.* All members accept responsibility for identifying what is to be learned, why it is to be learned (goals), how it is to be learned (resources and procedures), and for the evaluative criteria employed. Designated or temporarily empowered leaders do a minimum of planning for other members and a maximum of planning with them. Leadership tends to be either shared (group centered) or rotated.

2. *Freedom of expression is allowed.* A climate exists in which learners can disagree, ask for help, and try out new ideas and behavior. People are not volunteered for responsibilities. There is little need to be defensive. One can express feelings that relate to facilitating change and achieving group purposes. And the members seldom abuse this freedom, knowing that responsibility goes with liberty.

3. *Group members possess the skills of joint inquiry and problem solving.* They talk and they also listen actively. They hear one another. They know how to lead discussion, reach consensus, and use one another as resources for learning. They know how to ask for, give, and receive feedback.

4. *A diagnostic attitude toward processes is encouraged.* The group members attend to group functions and problems—how the group is doing as well as what is being done and learned. Opportunities are provided for analysis of progress and possible changes in goals or procedures. People are encouraged to apply their learning, to develop process skills, to examine their experiences in the group, and to get training for members roles as needed.

When people share in program development, they acquire a stake in an educational venture (a discussion is shared, a goal becomes something each learner wishes to help achieve because he or she helped to set it). Freedom of expression is a necessary condition for the sharing process to take place. The skills of joint inquiry enable learners to participate meaningfully in planning and evaluative processes and to learn from the resources and procedures used to explore ideas and problems. If a diagnostic attitude toward all of these matters is maintained, the chances are best of achieving group goals while meeting personal needs.

Responsible Participation

Collaborative learning requires more than skilled leadership. Each person in the boat pulls an oar. The responsible group member takes the following kinds of actions:

- *Communication*
  - Listens actively
  - Helps others understand what is said
  - Keeps remarks related to the task at hand
- *Climate*
  - Helps to arrange for appropriate physical environment
  - Demonstrates support of others
  - Expresses feelings in constructive ways
  - Lets people be themselves
- *Openness*
  - Reveals what he or she wants to learn
  - Tries out new ideas and ways of doing things
  - Requests personal feedback
- *Other Behavior*
  - Shares in program development and evaluation

- Volunteers for special tasks or roles
- Taps the knowledge and experience present in the group and outside resources used
- Shares the responsibility when things go less than well
- Diagnoses learning processes and seeks opportunities to improve process skills

The person skilled in collaborative learning knows how to share in program development and possesses a diagnostic attitude toward group processes. He or she can lead and participate responsibly in group discussions and problem-solving activities and knows how to plan learning activities that meet members' needs and interests while achieving group goals.

ACTIVITIES AND QUESTIONS FOR REFLECTION

1. *Have you ever had a collaborative learning experience in school, as defined by Smith? If so, were the outcomes different from your achievement in traditional classroom activities? In what ways? If you have not had such an experience, in what type of learning situations do you think it might be effective?*

2. *Some students are reluctant to participate in collaborative learning projects because they fear not all members will share equally in the responsibilities of small group learning. How do you think Smith would respond to this concern?*

3. *Can you identify any similarities in self-directed and collaborative learning? If so, what are they?*

In this reading, Kenneth Bruffee, as professor of English at Brooklyn College City University of New York, discusses the techniques of group or collaborative learning and the understanding of knowledge on which it is based. He supports the view that knowledge is "something people construct by talking together and reaching agreement." Knowledge is not simply the transfer of ideas from teacher to student.

As you read, look for the author's reasons for supporting collaborative learning in college classrooms and how he sees it being effectively implemented.

COLLABORATIVE LEARNING

Kenneth A. Bruffee

In collaborative learning students work on focused but open-ended tasks. They discuss issues in small consensus groups, plan and carry out long-term projects in research teams, tutor one another, analyze and work problems together, puzzle out difficult lab instructions together, read aloud to one another what they have written, and help one another edit and revise research reports and term papers.

Collaborative learning gives students practice in working together when the stakes are relatively low, so that they can work effectively together later when the stakes are high. They learn to depend on one another rather than depending exclusively on the authority of the teacher. They learn to construct knowledge as it is constructed in the academic disciplines and professions—the knowledge communities that students aspire to join when they attend colleges and universities. And they learn the craft of interdependence.

The craft of interdependence is not new to most college and university students. Many of them already know they will need it when they go to work in the "real" world of government, industry, business, finance, and the professions, where collaboration, consultation, and teamwork are increasingly the norm, not the exception. So some students prepare themselves for collaborating productively after they graduate by organizing themselves whenever they can to collaborate at school. They play ball; they plan dances, parties, and protest marches; they publish

Excerpt from *Collaborative Learning* (Baltimore: The Johns Hopkins University Press, 1993), pp. 1–3, 28, 49–51. Reprinted by permission.

newspapers, run charitable programs, and organize self-help groups.

Most of us assume a foundational (or cognitive) understanding of knowledge. Knowledge is an entity that we transfer from one head to another—for example, from a teacher's head to a student's or from a staff member's head to the head of the boss. Collaborative learning assumes instead that knowledge is a consensus among the members of a community of knowledgeable peers—something people construct by talking together and reaching agreement.

This is the understanding of knowledge that Thomas Kuhn describes on the final page of his seminal book *The Structure of Scientific Revolutions,* when he says that knowledge is "intrinsically the common property of a group or else nothing at all."

Consensus Groups: A Basic Model of Classroom Collaboration

One model of collaborative learning, although by no means the only one, is classroom consensus groups. In consensus groups people work collaboratively on a limited but open-ended task, negotiating among themselves what they think and know in order to arrive at some kind of consensus or agreement, including, sometimes, agreement to disagree. In organizing these groups, teachers typically do four things:

- They divide a large group—the class—into small groups.

- They provide a task, usually designed (and, preferably, tested) ahead of time, for the small groups to work on.

- They reconvene the larger group into plenary session to hear reports from the small groups and negotiate agreement among the group as a whole.

- They evaluate the quality of student work, first as referee, then as judge.

In a class organized for collaborative learning, authority of knowledge varies according to the size and complexity of the groups of students that, with the teacher's guidance, construct it. The knowledge constructed by small consensus groups has less authority than the knowledge that, based on the reports of those groups, the class as a whole constructs. The knowledge that the class as a whole constructs has this greater authority not only because the class is larger than the small groups, but also because it contains the small groups nested within it.

The knowledge constructed by each small consensus group has only the authority of a group of five students. Nevertheless, the authority of these small groups is greater than the authority of any individual student in the group before the group reached consensus. Small groups increase the authority of their knowledge when they compare their results with the consensus that other groups have arrived at and negotiate a consensus of the class as a whole (of, say, twenty-five students). In that way they increase the authority of the knowledge they have constructed from that of one student to that of twenty-five.

The final step in constructing knowledge and increasing its authority occurs when the class as a whole compares its consensus on the limited issue addressed in the task with the consensus on that issue of the immeasurably larger and more complex disciplinary or linguistic community (such as chemists, historians, or writers of standard English) that the teacher represents. If the two match, the authority of the knowledge that the students have constructed increases once again. The small knowledge community of the class as a whole, with its still smaller discussion groups nested in it, has itself become centered, on one issue, within that much larger community. The students in the class have joined, with respect to that issue, the community that they aspired to join by taking the course.

An example of the process would be the way a class might analyze the key sentence in the Declaration of Independence. Four or five small groups might arrive at quite different definitions of, say, the term "Inalienable Rights." These definitions would be the knowledge (or "understanding") that each group constructed and would have the authority implicit in a consensus arrived at among five people. The teacher would ask the class as a whole, after hearing reports from each group, to work toward a single consensus, acknowledging differences. That consensus would then be the understanding of the term that the class as a whole has constructed. It might be similar to some of the definitions constructed by the small groups, or, as a result of further discussion, it might be quite different. It would have greater authority than the definition arrived at by any one student or any one small group: it would have the authority implicit in an agreement among twenty-five people as opposed to just one or five.

Finally, the teacher might ask the class, perhaps working again in small groups, to compare the whole-class consensus with relevant passages from Supreme Court decisions that, speaking for a still larger community, define which benefits or privileges American citizens enjoy by "inalienable right" and which ones may be limited or eliminated entirely. The Court's understanding of the term would, of course, have a lot more authority than the class's understanding of it. And if the class's consensus matches the Court's, the knowledge the class constructed would have the authority of the whole community that the Court represents, the community of American citizens, in which the class-community is nested. If its consensus does not match that larger community's consensus, the teacher asks students to return to small-group discussion. Their task now is not to decide why their consensus was "wrong." Their task is to try to reconstruct the reasoning by which the Justices of the Court might have arrived at a different consensus and compare it with the reasoning by which the class arrived at theirs.

Communities of knowledgeable peers construct knowledge in an ongoing negotiation to consensus that involves increasingly larger and more complex communities of knowledgeable peers, a conversation in which, as Richard Rorty says in *Philosophy and the Mirror of Nature,* community members socially justify their beliefs to one another.

Activities and Questions for Reflection

1. *How does this reading affect your view of the role of the teacher and of classmates in a college course?*

2. *Does Bruffee have different assumptions about the nature of knowledge than those who support lecturing as the most important means of learning?*

3. *Do they differ from those who support self-directed learning?*

↗

ONE OF THE MOST INFLUENTIAL BOOKS *on organizational theory was written by Peter Senge, Director of the Center for Organizational Learning, Sloan School of Management at the Massachusetts Institute of Technology. In* The Fifth Discipline, *he asserts that the learning organization is the only one that will prosper in an age of high competition. The ability to learn and to create an environment in which all employees can learn, is the only way an organization can continue to innovate and provide the best quality of service.*

Organizations that can profit from having learning teams and learning environments include colleges, schools, clubs, businesses, religious institutions, and hospitals. In this reading, Senge discusses some examples of groups, or teams, that you may not have associated with learning.

AS YOU READ, *look for the three critical dimensions of learning organizations.*

↗

TEAM LEARNING, DIALOGUE, AND DISCUSSION

Peter Senge

"By design and by talent," wrote basketball player Bill Russell of his team, the Boston Celtics, "[we] were a team of specialists, and like a team of specialists in any field, our performance depended both on individual excellence and on how well we worked together. None of us had to strain to understand that we had to complement each others' specialties; it was simply a fact, and we all tried to figure out ways to make our combination more effective. . . . Off the court, most of us were oddballs by society's standards—not the kind of people who blend in with others or who tailor their personalities to match what's expected of them."

Russell is careful to tell us that it's not friendship, it's a different kind of team relationship that made his team's work special. That relationship, more than any individual triumph, gave him his greatest moments in the sport: "Every so often a Celtic game would heat up so that it became more than a physical or even mental game," he wrote, "and would be magical. The feeling is difficult to describe, and I certainly never talked about it when I was playing. When it happened I could feel

---

my play rise to a new level . . . It would surround not only me and the other Celtics but
also the players on the other team, and even
the referees . . . At that special level, all sorts
of odd things happened. The game would be
in the white heat of competition, and yet I
wouldn't feel competitive, which is a miracle
in itself . . . The game would move so fast that
every fake, cut, and pass would be surprising
and yet nothing could surprise me. It was almost as if we were playing in slow motion.
During those spells, I could almost sense how
the next play would develop and where the
next shot would be taken . . . To me, the key
was that *both* teams had to be playing at their
peaks, and they had to be competitive. . . ."

Team learning is the process of aligning
and developing the capacity of a team to create the results its members truly desire. It
builds on the discipline of developing shared
vision. It also builds on personal mastery, for
talented teams are made up of talented individuals. But shared vision and talent are not
enough. The world is full of teams of talented
individuals who share a vision for a while, yet
fail to learn. The great jazz ensemble has talent and a shared vision (even if they don't discuss it), but what really matters is that the
musicians know how to *play* together.

There has never been a greater need for
mastering team learning in organizations than
there is today. Whether they are management
teams or product development teams or
cross-functional task forces—teams, "people
who need one another to act," in the words
of Arie de Geus, former coordinator of Group
Planning at Royal Dutch/Shell, are becoming
the key learning unit in organizations. This is

so because almost all important decisions are
now made in teams, either directly or through
the need for teams to translate individual decisions into action. Individual learning, at
some level, is irrelevant for organizational
learning. Individuals learn all the time and yet
there is no organizational learning. But if
teams learn, they become a microcosm for
learning throughout the organization. Insights gained are put into action. Skills developed can propagate to other individuals and
to other teams (although there is no guarantee that they will propagate). The team's accomplishments can set the tone and establish
a standard for learning together for the larger
organization.

Within organizations, team learning has
three critical dimensions. First, there is the
need to think insightfully about complex issues. Here, teams must learn how to tap the
potential for many minds to be more intelligent than one mind. While easy to say, there
are powerful forces at work in organizations
that tend to make the intelligence of the team
less than, not greater than, the intelligence of
individual team members. Many of these
forces are within the direct control of the
team members.

Second, there is the need for innovative,
coordinated action. The championship sports
teams and great jazz ensembles provide
metaphors for acting in spontaneous yet coordinated ways. Outstanding teams in organizations develop the same sort of relationship
—an "operational trust," where each team
member remains conscious of other team
members and can be counted on to act in
ways that complement each others' actions.

Third, there is the role of team members on other teams. For example, most of the actions of senior teams are actually carried out through other teams. Thus, a learning team continually fosters other learning teams through inculcating the practices and skills of team learning more broadly.

Though it involves individual skills and areas of understanding, team learning is a collective discipline. Thus, it is meaningless to say that "I," as an individual, am mastering the discipline of team learning, just as it would be meaningless to say that "I am mastering the practice of being a great jazz ensemble."

The discipline of team learning involves mastering the practices of dialogue and discussion, the two distinct ways that teams converse. In dialogue, there is the free and creative exploration of complex and subtle issues, a deep "listening" to one another and suspending of one's own views. By contrast, in discussion different views are presented and defended and there is a search for the best view to support decisions that must be made at this time. Dialogue and discussion are potentially complementary, but most teams lack the ability to distinguish between the two and to move consciously between them.

Team learning also involves learning how to deal creatively with the powerful forces opposing productive dialogue and discussion in working teams. Chief among these are what Chris Argyris calls "defensive routines," habitual ways of interacting that protect us and others from threat or embarrassment, but which also prevent us from learning. For example, faced with conflict, team members frequently either "smooth over" differences or "speak out" in a no-holds-barred, "winner take all" free-for-all of opinion—what my colleague Bill Isaacs calls "the abstraction wars." Yet, the very defensive routines that thwart learning also hold great potential for fostering learning, if we can only learn how to unlock the energy they contain. . . .

Despite its importance, team learning remains poorly understood. Until we can describe the phenomenon better, it will remain mysterious. Until we have some theory of what happens when teams learn (as opposed to individuals in teams learning), we will be unable to distinguish group intelligence from "groupthink," when individuals succumb to group pressures for conformity. Until there are reliable methods for building teams that can learn together, its occurrence will remain a product of happenstance. This is why mastering team learning will be a critical step in building learning organizations.

Activities and Questions for Reflection

1. *Describe in your own words the ways in which athletes or musicians are learning teams. How could you apply these to your learning in college?*

2. *Does team learning match your learning style as discussed by Chickering and Schlossberg in the first reading in this chapter? How can you see yourself functioning in a learning group?*

3. *Do you see areas in your life where you are or have been a member of a learning team outside of college? How could work on a learning team in college transfer or be applied to your learning outside of college?*

4. *What distinctions does Senge make between* dialogue *and* discussion?

CHAPTER 6

⌐→ *Learning How to Learn*

SUMMARY

This chapter has presented several strategies or approaches for becoming an effective learner including

- Identifying and broadening your learning style
- Developing skill as a self-directed learner
- Acquiring ability in collaborative, group, or team learning

Learning how to learn and understanding that there are many ways of learning can be very helpful in considering how you learn best. One approach does not work for everyone or even for all subjects. Matching the style to the subject is as important as understanding your own preferred style and learning to use a less preferred style. Learning to speak a language may not be done exclusively from a book but if reading and analyzing is your preferred style, you may learn more through reading than does a person who prefers a more engaged, interactive language lab.

It is also important to understand that learning is a process. Just like self directed learning requires thought about whether one believes what one is learning and team learning requires alignment and understanding of other members of the team, all learning is interdependent and connected. What you learn in one course has relevance to another. Learning in one area of life contributes to your learning in another. The example given by Peter Senge of the team learning in basketball makes one open to more learning and gives the players the ability to come together. They can make something new and greater than they could individually have imagined.

On the other hand, in *The Brain* Theodore Restak, M.D., who wrote *The Mind* and other works on the functioning of the brain, includes a quote from the famed concert violinist Nadja Salerno-Sonnenberg in which she describes how she studies and how she feels when approaching her work:

> [I spend] months and months and months analyzing a piece of music. This process is intense and never ends because you always feel differently about the musical piece. You reanalyze it and reanalyze it. Where's the theme? Where's

the second theme? Where's the development? How does it fit? In effect, you're breaking the musical piece down to nothing and perfecting each of the little details. And then you put it back together like a model airplane. And then you've built your model airplane and it's ready to go. When you walk out on the stage, that's the finished product.

Salerno-Sonnenberg's mind is concentrated and focused as she attempts to reach what she calls *the zone*. Her thoughts and her emotions come together on stage.

> Playing in the zone is a phrase that I use to describe a certain feeling on stage, a heightened feeling where everything is right," she says. "By that I mean everything comes together. Everything is one. Everybody agrees. Everybody sees what you're saying and everybody is enjoying it. Everybody is with you and you, yourself, are not battling yourself. All the technical work and what you want to say with the piece comes together. It's very, very rare but it's what I have worked for all my life. It's just right. It just makes everything right. Nothing can go wrong with this wonderful feeling.

Using the Internet

Using InfoTrac College Edition, look up a current article on or by one of the authors, subjects, or people presented in this chapter. Explain why you were interested in this choice and what you gained from reading the article about learning.

SUMMARIZING ACTIVITIES AND QUESTIONS FOR REFLECTION

1. Write your own learning autobiography and analyze the learning experiences you included. Some questions to help you in this analysis are the following:

    a. How have you enjoyed learning best?

    b. We are often better learners in one area of our lives than in another. Are you a self-directed learner in any area of your life?

    c. Have you ever been a member of a learning group? What kind?

    d. What ways of learning do you avoid? Teams? Self-directed? Reading? Memorizing?

2. How could you have benefited from these readings earlier in your life? Could they have helped you enjoy learning more when you were younger?

3. After reflecting on the readings and activities in this chapter, review your goals for your college education and your definition of an educated person and make revisions or additions that capture any new understandings you now have.

Education and Work

INTRODUCTION: BECOMING EMPLOYABLE

Understanding the nature of work, the future of work, and the place work may have in your life is fundamental to preparing yourself to become fully employable. The readings in this chapter present a range of ideas and information about what will be expected of you as a college graduate in the world of work.

Work is more than an economic necessity. It is an opportunity for adventure and creativity—a challenge that gives meaning to our lives and connects us with others. Those who enjoy their work and feel that it is valued are also the most productive and well-employed workers. Having a career you enjoy will be fundamental to establishing a productive and meaningful role in your family, in your community, and in the world.

In addition to achieving the level of personal self-confidence required to function well in a work environment and understanding your own abilities and interests so you can apply them well, employability requires being able to interpret and adjust to rapidly changing economic realities. When you graduate from college, you will be facing new opportunities and challenges that can only be imagined today.

These readings were chosen to help you expand your idea of the purposes of a college education in preparing you to be successfully and meaningfully employable throughout your life. Before you start reading, take a moment to reflect on how you view the relationships between yourself, possible careers, becoming employable (or more employable), and your understanding of the meaning of a college education.

↗

THIS FIRST READING is an excerpt from a report commissioned by the Secretary of Labor of the United States to determine the skills people will need to succeed in the new high-performance economy of the twenty-first century. This report represents a consensus of the views of a broad range of leaders in education, government, and business. Its recommendations form the basis of many program recommendations made by colleges and professional associations.

AS YOU READ, look for the commission's conclusions about why the concepts academic *and* vocational *have lost their meaning in defining education and work.*

↗

REPORT OF THE SECRETARY'S COMMISSION ON ACHIEVING NECESSARY SKILLS

U.S. Department of Labor, Employment and Training Administration

Identifying and Describing the Skills Required by Work

Which skills are essential to effective work performance? Although this question has been asked many times, there is no generally accepted statement of the skills required to succeed at a career in the United States. During World War II, the identification of key skills was critical to the design of training programs. After enactment of the Great Society measures of the 1960s, the specification of skills became important to the development of bias-free job testing. Today's concern about our schools' ability to prepare young people effectively for the world of work has prompted several studies of workplace skill requirements. Identification of necessary work skills has challenged psychologists, educators, analysts, employers, and lawyers.

Most attempts to characterize the skills used at work focus either on general human characteristics (e.g., intelligence, reasoning ability, reaction time) or on the characteristics of specific jobs (e.g., ability to assemble items, load ammunition, route packages). The level of detail communicated varies from the very general (e.g., ability to solve problems) to the very discrete (e.g., perform a tack weld in aluminum sheet metal). As a result, the operational implications and meaning of these lists are frequently difficult to determine. In short, they lack context. Thus, they do not provide direct links to the "stuff" of schools or a sense of the work enabled by the skills identified.

The Secretary's Commission on Achieving Necessary Skills (SCANS) has an opportunity to break from this practice and, as a result, to change the nature of both schooling and work. People learn best when they are taught in a context of application—in a functional context. If teachers and students know what performance is required for success in modern work contexts, schools can organize instruction to teach the skills that support such performance—and test developers and businesses can develop reliable assessments of performance.

In recommending the skills required for work readiness, the Commission must identify the skills required for success in a high-performaing environment; its findings must speak to both the world of work and the world of schools. This report suggests a language for this message and presents an initial working inventory of necessary skills.

There are three elements of this language. The functional skills that describe what people actually do at work; the enabling skills, that is the specific knowledge and procedures developed through the traditional teaching and learning activities of schools; and the scenario, a communication device to demon-

strate the way in which work integrates these skills into a productive outcome.

Changes in What Workers Do

One of the most profound implications of computers in the workplace is that they replace learning based on visual observation with learning acquired primarily through symbols, whether verbal or mathematical. For example, in textiles, semiliterate operators used to be able to move into technician jobs because they literally could see how textile machines functioned. Today, many machines have microprocessors and other electronic components that are not observable. To understand, diagnose, and fix the new machines, technicians now have to be able to represent their structures and processes symbolically in their heads by decoding complicated manuals, diagrams, and updates provided by the manufacturers. Literacy requirements have accordingly increased.

One hallmark of successful competition in today's market place is flexibility in service and manufacturing industries. "Total customer service" and "total quality management" are the bywords of high-performance business organizations. The variations in product and service associated with this flexibility multiply the number of workplace decisions that must be made. In more productive companies, these decisions are being made at lower and lower levels in the corporate structure, requiring both higher- and lower-skill workers to think critically and regulate their own performance.

The ability of organizations to compress the time between product design and marketplace delivery has become a major competitive weapon in both manufacturing and service industries. Companies can no longer afford to buck decisions up and down the management ladder; decisions must be made right at the point of production or point of service. As a result, frontline workers have to deal with the unfamiliar, atypical, and irregular. In order to make the decisions that previously were made by others, these workers must understand their firm's market environment and organizational context. To minimize work stoppage by generating initial hypotheses about the source of equipment breakdown for maintenance technicians, frontline workers must stay on top of the latest technologies. As one personnel manager for a plant noted, "Our operations change too fast to be able to spell everything out. Operators have to be better able to figure things out for themselves."

Changes in How They Work

Not only must workers do multiple tasks, they must do them well. As a trainer at Motorola Corporation said, "Now that the new technologies can be easily bought, the real edge is in how well you use them. We are in a situation that is like the International Race of Champions, where everyone has the same cars, and these cars are traded between races. The prize goes to the most skilled driver."

Changes in Those with Whom They Work

Increasingly, workers have to work in teams—within the same function, across functions, across hierarchical levels, and within supplier-producer-customer networks—and in a multicultural environment. These features of the work environment generate the need for skills in both interpersonal communication and conflict resolution.

The workplace will continue to change. In the past decade, shifting international markets and sources of comparative advantage, fickle customers, and rapid innovations in products and processes have forced fundamental changes in corporate strategies. The speed with which new products are being introduced suggests that technologies and markets will not stabilize. Ongoing change generates the need for a continuous adaptation of employee skills.

Implications for Schooling

Changes in the workplace have consequences for the skills that students must learn, for the ways in which they are taught and for the performance standards to which they are held. For example, facing a life of continuous learning, they need to learn how to learn. The emphasis on teamwork in more and more workplaces means that instructional approaches must also emphasize learning collaboratively not just individually. The need for high-quality work performance means that students must be held to, and come to hold themselves to, high standards of careful and best effort performances.

These changes also have consequences for who learns. As job content changes rapidly, narrow, specific skills have become less important, and broader, more generic skills more important. The generic skills required (i.e., meta cognitive skills—the ability to think about what one is doing and its consequences for the work goal) have become more similar across higher- and lower-skill jobs. This blurring of historical skill differences between occupations implies a change in who is taught what. It raises serious questions about our distinct educational traditions of elite education and mass education, as usually embodied in "academic" versus "vocational" tracks.

ACTIVITIES AND QUESTIONS FOR REFLECTION

1. *What does "Our operations change too fast to be able to spell everything out" mean?*

2. *Why will just having the latest technology no longer be an advantage?*

3. *Why will interpersonal communication and conflict resolution be more important?*

IN THIS READING, Joseph Boyett of Boyett & Associates, an international consulting and research firm, reports the results of research on trends in the workplace and predicts their implications for individual workers. Management consulting and research firms conduct research by interviewing executives and employees of corporations about working conditions and at regular intervals obtaining their responses to extensive questionnaires. By compiling and analyzing this data, these firms then identify trends and project future directions. Boyett has been studying changes in the workplace for more than 20 years.

AS YOU READ, look for the trends that could affect your own preparation for careers you are considering.

21ST CENTURY WORKPLACE TRENDS AND THEIR IMPLICATIONS

Joseph H. Boyett

Since the late 1980s, several trends have emerged that are having a profound impact on American workers and educational institutions that prepare workers.

Trend 1: The Growing Contingent Workforce

As American companies continue to downsize, restructure, and lay off workers, work that is not part of the core competency of the corporation is being outsourced or performed by temporary, part-time, or contract workers. The largest employer in the U.S. is Manpower, the temporary staffing firm, and 20 percent of Manpower's growth is in the placement of highly skilled professionals in temporary positions.

Trend 2: Telecommuting

Because of new technology and the changing nature of work, the number of employees who are telecommuting or working at nontraditional work sites has been growing. The geographic same-time-same-place workplace is being replaced by anytime-anywhere-

---

Condensed from an article posted on the Boyett & Associates Web site: http://www.jboyett.com/trends.htm.

workspaces. The phrase "going to work" will become meaningless for most Americans. Work for them will be what they do, not the place they go.

Trend 3: Upskilling of Jobs

Practically all jobs are being "upskilled." Workers with strong technical skills—lab technicians, computer professionals, drafters, paralegals, medical technicians, and engineers—are becoming the front-line workers in most organizations. Even jobs that have not traditionally been considered technical jobs, such as courier, now have a strong technical component and require the use of computers and other sophisticated electronic devices.

Trend 4: Self-Led Teams

We are seeing rapid growth in the use of temporary, cross-functional, multi-disciplinary teams with globally- and ethnically-diverse memberships. Team members take on responsibility for planning, organizing, staffing, scheduling, directing, monitoring, and controlling their own work. These teams are increasingly linked with instantaneous and unrestricted flow of information.

Implications for Individuals

The new workplace will reward the "specialized generalists" who have both a solid basic education plus professional and technical skills in demand across a range of companies and even industries. Everyone will have to be able to do something that adds value in order to be considered for employment in all but the most marginal jobs.

Americans will be responsible for managing their own careers. Temporary staffing services, career counselors, and employment agencies will stress their role as agents.

Most workers will need to build and maintain liquid savings equivalent to a year or more of income as a shield against periods of unemployment or underemployment. Home ownership will become difficult since their incomes will fluctuate and financial institutions will be likely to respond slowly to these changes.

Americans will begin working earlier in life and continue to work longer. Today's concept of retirement will all but disappear.

Housing will change dramatically. Homes will be wired for commerce as well as for recreation. Houses and apartments will become both homes and work sites.

Everyone will be expected to demonstrate strong team skills and to have the ability to function effectively in a new team from the start. Companies will no longer accept or tolerate 6 to 12 months of team building.

As we move increasingly to self-managed teams, everyone will be expected to contribute to the team by performing one or more of the following leadership roles:

Envisioning—facilitating idea generation and innovation in the team and helping the team members think conceptually and creatively;

Organizing—helping the team focus on details, deadlines, efficiency, and structure so the team gets its work done;

Spanning—maintaining relationships with outside groups and people, networking, developing and maintaining a strong team image, intelligence gathering, locating and securing critical team resources; and

Socializing—uncovering the needs and concerns of individuals in the group, ensuring that everyone has the opportunity to present his or her views, injecting humor when it is needed to relieve tensions, taking care of the social and psychological needs of group members.

Since most teams will be cross-functional and international, everyone will require strong language skills (fluency in at least one language other than English) and the ability to appreciate differences and work effectively with diverse cultures.

Implications for Organizations

Every organization, whether public or private, profit or non-profit, will be forced to clarify its core competencies and reason for existence. Those groups which fail to identify and guard what is truly core will risk keeping the wrong things inside the organization while outsourcing those things that make them unique and vital.

Highly skilled contingent workers will be more loyal to their discipline than to their employer. They will demand respect, interesting and challenging work, the chance to develop their skills further, freedom and resources to use their talents and knowledge to do the work they were hired to do and enjoy doing, and an equitable share in the financial rewards that flow from their contribution.

As work is increasingly performed away from the traditional work site, managers and supervisors will have to learn to manage without depending upon face time as an indicator of contribution. Performance goals will become more explicit and measurement will become more sophisticated and objective. Results will count more than activities.

A key role of leaders of the new organization will be to create a shared vision that both permanent and contingent team members can grasp and to which they can commit. Without mission statements that link teams to the overriding vision, there will be perpetual conflict, competition for resources, and misdirected energy.

Organizations will succeed or fail based upon the ability of their leadership to assemble teams with the right mix of talent quickly.

Implications for Society as a Whole

As we move to the new economy, businesses will increasingly resist taking on responsibility for delivering social services, particularly to the 50 percent of the workforce who are non-core employees. Healthcare, childcare, elder care, and education, they will argue, are not business problems, and should be addressed by individuals or governments.

As more workers telecommute or use satellite offices, cities will no longer be the center of commerce. Rural areas will boom as we see a migration back to the countryside.

As Americans increasingly work on cross-functional, diverse, multi-national teams, they will become more global in outlook. This globalization of individuals will make the nation-state irrelevant as people everywhere identify more closely with their professional peers than with their fellow citizens.

Implications for Educational Institutions

As continuous learning becomes the norm, educational institutions will be swamped with demand. The new student will expect quality, speed of delivery, and effectiveness in addition to availability and convenience. Education will be a critical personal investment for which the consumer will demand an exceptionally high return. Technology will play an increasingly important role. Education at all levels will become less labor intensive and more capital intensive. The majority of education budgets will no longer be devoted to salaries but to software, computers, and multi-media.

The majority of students will never set foot on campus. Students will attend classes thousands of miles from their homes. Instruction will become international. Distance learning will increase dramatically. The trend toward hiring part-time and temporary faculty will continue and accelerate.

Students will have access to a limitless variety of courses. Almost every course taught anywhere in the world will be available to anyone who has access to inexpensive hardware and software. Students will be able to construct their own curriculum with courses taught by internationally recognized experts in each field.

Any course, any subject matter, no matter how non-traditional or narrowly focused will find an audience in what will become a vast, global educational marketplace. Educational consumer rating services will review and rate educational offerings much the way they now review and rate movies, books, and music.

National and international education providers will produce and distribute courses directly to students on an international basis. Course selections will no longer be mediated by local or regional policy makers.

New multi-media educational technology will make it possible for a few hundred of the most skilled teachers to provide the instruction of several thousand.

Three quarters of graduate students will work in the private sector, not academia. This migration to business is being driven by sharp reductions in funds for basic research due to government cutbacks, tighter restrictions or the elimination of tenure, and increased demand for applied research in the private sector.

As the demand for employees with graduate level training increases in the private sector, universities and colleges will be under pressure to reduce the time to complete a graduate degree and to supply graduates who can effectively communicate complex ideas to non-specialists and to work well in teams.

These trends foreshadow a quantum shift in our understanding of what it means to work, learn, and live. We are about to experience a wave of change that many will see as frightening. But, it doesn't have to be viewed that way. It also offers unparalleled opportunity.

ACTIVITIES AND QUESTIONS FOR REFLECTION

1. *Which aspects of the new workplace sound interesting to you? Which seem intimidating or would you prefer to avoid?*

2. *Working in teams will be an essential feature of the new workplace, so how can you ensure that you will learn the required skills?*

3. *Have you considered using the new technologies to expand your educational opportunities? Distance learning? Internet accessible sources? Special interest groups via email?*

⟞⟝

MANY COLLEGE GRADUATES plan eventually to move into the ranks of management during their working lives either in corporations or other organizations. The following reading by Michael Useem, a professor at the Wharton School of Management at the University of Pennsylvania, reports the outcomes of a study on the effects of a liberal education on a new generation of managers. It also examines other factors related to a college education that have an impact on "getting ahead" and the kind of corporation or organization the graduate may enter.

AS YOU READ, try to identify the elements that could contribute to success in management.

⟞⟝

LIBERAL EDUCATION AND A NEW GENERATION OF CORPORATE LEADERSHIP
Michael Useem

Liberal Education and the Individual Manager

For individuals intending a career in the private sector, a liberal education or strong exposure to liberal-arts courses may be important for reasons that go well beyond the issue of managerial effectiveness. Liberal education can assist managers in coping with unanticipated limitations they may face in their own career prospects. It is an era in which many companies are no longer able to assure expanding managerial opportunities,

and a growing number of corporations are not able to assure continuing employment to managers who have invested their entire career in the company.

At the same time, employee commitment to the corporation has also sharply declined in recent years, with managers more prepared to move from company to company in search of a suitable position. If managers are thus more likely to face layofffs, periods of unemployment, and jobs with several employers during their career, flexibility and adaptability are all the more essential. So, too, are more generic

---

skills and abilities, capacities that can be readily transferred to other work settings.

Most company managers start relatively well and many are promoted by one or more levels, but the great majority, regardless of educational origin or other factors, experience a rapidly diminishing rate of upward mobility. A large number of managers will reach a plateau of responsibility from which they are likely to raise little further.

For even the most-career-driven student, then, it can be important to prepare for later career periods when company work may not be fully preoccupying, either because further promotions are unlikely or possibly even because there is at least momentarily no employment at all. A liberal education certainly offers no protection against such circumstances, but it can enhance making the most of them. Numerous studies confirm that a college education, and above all a liberal education, increases interest in political activity; heightens awareness of culture and the arts and increases involvement in community and public affairs. This is evident, for instance, in the rates of participation in community and public affairs among the managers surveyed for the present study. In both the officer and non-officer ranks, and especially in the latter, managers with a liberal-arts degree are found to be significantly more likely than those with a business degree to take active part in the local community and to serve in voluntary positions with nonprofit organizations. Exposure to a liberal education can thus better prepare managers for later periods of their lives in which extra-corporate involvements acquire greater significance.

College Education and Corporate Employment

The evidence presented here confirms an originating hypothesis that the degree area of a college education can have lasting effects on white-collar company careers. In thinking about and analyzing the impact of higher education on managerial careers, it is no longer sufficient to know that an individual has completed a college education. The quality and reputation of the institution must be taken into account, as should the academic performance of the student. And so too should the field of study.

The importance of earning a college degree for entry into business is reconfirmed by the educational profile of the 505 surveyed managers. Nearly 9 out of 10 had graduated from college, signifying again that without a college credential one's prospects for advancement in the corporate hierarchy are very limited.

The quality of the college is also important, according to indirect evidence produced in the present study. When the 535 surveyed companies were asked to evaluate the importance of a number of factors in a college graduate's record, the quality of the undergraduate institution was viewed as an important hiring criterion by four out of five corporations. As a result, companies tend to concentrate their recruitment efforts at a limited number of relatively high-quality institutions, a common practice at the major companies studied in more detail here.

The graduate's academic record has also been found to make a difference, corroborating other research findings summarized earlier.

Virtually all—96%—of the surveyed corporations stressed a "strong academic record on campus" in the hiring of a new graduate. This factor was viewed as important by more companies than any of the other nine factors considered. The recruitment practices of the companies examined in more detail confirm the importance of academic performance. In recruiting liberal-arts graduates, the consumer-products company required an undergraduate grade-point average of at least 3.0 and preferably 3.5. The high-technology company and the industrial-products corporation considered a grade-point average of at least 3.0 in the core field of study to be essential. Similarly, the diversified financial company stressed a grade-point average of at least 3.5 in the candidates it sought.

A college education, the reputation of the graduating institution, and the graduate's academic record are thus all found to make a significant difference, and it was hypothesized that the field of the college degree should also make a difference for those who enter the private sector. This expectation has been repeatedly confirmed in the present study, though not always in expected ways.

We have found little difference in the vertical distribution of managers as a function of their general field of college study. Liberal arts, business, and engineering graduates fare about equally well. The aggregate pattern, however, masks significant variation from company to company. In some companies, such as AT&T, liberal-arts graduates are found to have accelerating prospects for further advancement as their career develops. In others, such as the industrial-products company, few liberal-arts graduates are hired, and a dominant engineering culture impedes the advancement of those who are employed. In still other companies, such as the consumer-products corporation, MBA graduates with liberal-arts undergraduate degrees displayed particularly strong staying power: All of the product managers who had been hired by the company 5 or 10 years earlier and were still with the company in 1987 held both an MBA degree and a liberal-arts degree.

Yet overall vertical differentiation among college-degree holders is not prevalent. Liberal arts, business, and engineering graduates are about equally likely to "get ahead" in business at large. Horizontal differentiation, however, is considerable. The field of undergraduate study has a major bearing on the kind of company a graduate is likely to enter and the kind of work performed in the company. Liberal-arts graduates are found to be more prone than other graduates to work for service companies, to acquire responsibilities for consumer rather than industrial goods and services, and to become involved in marketing and sales. Engineering graduates, by contrast, tend to acquire managerial responsibilities for industrial rather than consumer goods and services, and business graduates are far more likely to work on the financial and accounting side of a company.

The field of undergraduate study has also been found to affect the likelihood of a manager's involvement in external affairs. Compared to business graduates, liberal-arts graduates are serving significantly more often as company representatives to the local community and more often as volunteers in nonprofit organizations or advisers to government. The field of the college degree thus also makes a difference in the experiences of managers in representing a company to its external world.

The understanding of white-collar-career paths, then, requires information about more than the level of college completed. To forecast and analyze such paths more fully, it is essential to know the individual's academic performance in college, the selectivity and reputation of the college, and the general field of undergraduate study. While this has been demonstrated here for careers in business management, the proposition probably stands as well for other professional careers, including those in law, health, architecture, and teaching.

It should be noted, however, that majoring in the liberal arts is not necessarily a superior way to acquire a liberal education or to prepare for a career in corporate management. The most generic elements of a liberal-arts program, such as learning how to learn and to lead, are often incorporated into undergraduate business and engineering programs. Many of these programs stress liberal learning as a central part of their curricula. Moreover, some liberal-arts courses are so narrowly conceived that they qualify as part of a liberal-arts curriculum in name only. If we turn to an outcome measure, such as ascent to the higher levels of corporate management, we have also found that liberal-arts graduates on average fare no better than do business and engineering graduates. Liberal-arts graduates gravitate toward companies and functional areas within companies that are somewhat different from those of business and engineering graduates. Yet overall it cannot be said that a liberal-arts degree is necessarily a preferred way to prepare for a career in company management.

ACTIVITIES AND QUESTIONS FOR REFLECTION

1. *What are the elements of a college education that seem to affect employability of the individual other than completion of the degree?*

2. *What impact does a student's field of undergraduate study seem to have on the kind of company the graduate enters?*

3. *What are some of the benefits of a liberal education for the manager of the future?*

4. *What implications do you see for your own educational goals from this reading?*

⟜

THE WORK OF JOHN HOLLAND is similar to studies in learning styles and personality types but differs in that he studied those aspects of personality that are directly related to career choices. As a classification interviewer with the army, Holland realized that many people in particular jobs seemed to share personality characteristics and prefer similar work environments. During the next 25 years, he researched and revised a theory of personality and vocational environmental types. Based on his research, he developed a test that has become one of the most reliable methods of predicting the kind of vocational satisfaction that leads to success. In 1995, Holland received the American Psychological Association award for Distinguished Contributions to Knowledge for his theory of careers that "provided an intellectual tool for integrating our knowledge of vocational intentions, vocational interests, personalities, and work histories."

AS YOU READ, consider the aspects of personality that have been found to predict different vocational interests.

⟜

HOLLAND'S THEORY OF VOCATIONAL PERSONALITIES AND ENVIRONMENTS

Nancy J. Evans, Deanna S. Forney, and Florence Guido-DiBrito

A meeting of the planning committee for the student government orientation is about to begin. The group's agenda is determining how to proceed. Sherry is the first to speak; she suggests that the usual way of doing orientation be scrapped. She wants to try out some new and creative approaches this year. Jeff disagrees; he does not want to change anything. He argues that if the group sticks with what was done last year, the schedule can be followed just as it is outlined in last year's report. Michele suggests that the group look into how other schools organize their orientation programs. She would also like to do a formal survey of new officers' needs and interests to obtain some hard data on which to base the program. Scott indicates that he is will-

ing to try some new ideas, but he is concerned with an issue that he thinks is more
important. He believes that the planning
team members should be paid for the work
they are putting in or at the very least receive academic credit for organizing the orientation program. Susan is not too crazy
about being part of this planning team in
the first place, but when asked what she
thinks they should do, she states that she
would like to see some "action" types of activities added, like a volleyball game or a
"teams challenge course." Bethany suggests
that more social events are needed to allow
people to get to know each other better.
Everyone seems to have a personal agenda,
and as the meeting goes on, people become
frustrated because no one seems willing to
compromise and no progress occurs.

Down the hall, another group is meeting
to plan the orientation for the new student
activities fee allocation board. Kelli isn't
quite sure how she got on this committee because she has no background in accounting,
but she is creative and figures that she can
offer some really innovative and interesting
suggestions for livening up the orientation
program. She suggests to the committee that
they pitch last year's program and start
over. Tammy is appalled; she notes that last
year's group worked hard on the program
and that since it went well, nothing should
be changed. Diane agrees, pointing out that
all the leftover handouts could be used to
save time and paper. Joe offers that following last year's schedule will make assigning
responsibilities easier. Alicia adds that if the
old schedule is followed, all the committee

members will know what they are supposed
to do and deadlines can be set for completing
each assignment. Jennifer chimes in that she
has only so much time to devote to this committee and that sticking to the old plan will
be more efficient. Poor Kelli; she feels like she
is on another planet. No one is listening to
her new ideas. Her enthusiasm and desire to
make a contribution are rapidly disappear-
ing. She can't wait to get out of the room and
is having serious doubts about continuing
her involvement on this committee.

The group dynamics in the two situations
described in the scenario can be explained
using a theory outlined by John Holland.
Holland's theory of vocational personalities
and work environments can be categorized
as both a typology theory and a theory of
person-environment fit. Holland . . . identified six basic personality types and six cor-
responding types of environments. He
hypothesized that satisfaction, achievement,
and persistence can be predicted by the degree of "fit" between persons and the environments in which they find themselves.
Although Holland's main purpose in developing his theory was to explain vocational
behavior, the concepts he introduced are also
useful in explaining behavior in social and
educational settings.

Holland's theory has been identified as the
most popular and influential theory of career
development . . . It has generated extensive research, a number of assessment instruments,
and practical strategies for assisting people
with career decision making. The major
tenets of Holland's theory will be presented in

this chapter, and research and applications related to it will be reviewed. . . .

The Theory

Holland's theory begins with four assumptions. First, Holland . . . proposed that to varying degrees, people resemble each of six personality types. The more similar they are to a particular type, the more they exhibit the behaviors and attitudes associated with it. Similarly, there are six model environments that parallel each of the personality types with regard to qualities and attributes. This parallel structure exists because "environments are characterized by the people who occupy them" . . . Third, Holland suggested that people seek out environments that provide them with opportunities to use their talents and express their values and attitudes. That is, people seek out environments made up of individuals similar to themselves. Finally, Holland restated Lewin's hypothesis . . . that behavior results from the interaction of the person and the environment.

Type Development

Holland has often been criticized for not explaining how individual types develop . . . In the latest iteration of his theory, however, Holland . . . discussed the role of environment in shaping development. In particular, Holland sees the personality types of parents playing an important role in determining the type of opportunities provided for their children and the kinds of activities and attitudes that are reinforced. Holland also believes that children inherit a biological predisposition to certain characteristics.

As children's preferences for certain activities are reinforced, the preferences become more strongly defined interests and skills . . . Children come to value particular activities they are good at and for which they are rewarded, and they build their self-concepts around these activities. Changes in personality are less likely to occur as the person ages because of the cumulative effect of learning and experience. Environments are also less likely to allow people to change the longer persons have been engaging in particular kinds of activities. For example, a woman who has been in one career for an extensive period of time is likely to find that people will have trouble accepting that she wants to change fields.

The Six Types

Holland's six personality types are defined by specific interests, behaviors, and attitudes. The environmental types provide opportunities to engage in the activities and reward behaviors that each type values. The types are defined as follows.

Realistic   Realistic people tend to be interested in and prefer activities that involve working with objects, tools, machines, and animals. They are competent in manual, mechanical, agricultural, and technical areas. They value concrete things like money and personal qualities such as power and status. Realistic people tend to be frank, practical, inflexible, uninsightful, and uninvolved. In the first planning meeting in the opening scenario, Susan could be described as Realistic; she wasn't crazy about being part of a group, and the types of activities she preferred involved physical, outdoor activity.

Investigative   Investigative types prefer activities that call for systematic investigation designed to understand and control physical, biological, or cultural phenomena. They are competent in scientific and mathematical areas. They value science and can be described as analytical, intellectual, precise, reserved, and cautious. Michele was the Investigative type in the first planning meeting. She wanted to investigate what other schools did for orientation, and she favored a survey of students.

Artistic   Artistic people prefer spontaneous, creative, unregulated activities that lead to the creation of various art forms. They are competent in artistic areas such as language, art, music, drama, and writing. They value aesthetic qualities and tend to be emotional, expressive, original, imaginative, and impulsive. In our student government planning group, Sherry would be described as Artistic. She wanted to see some new, creative ideas and was the first to express her opinions.

Social   Social individuals prefer activities that involve working with others in ways that educate, inform, cure, or enlighten. They possess interpersonal and educational competencies. They value helping others and engaging in social activities. Social types can be described as cooperative, friendly, helpful, empathic, and tactful. Bethany was the Social member of the planning committee. She was interested in making sure that social activities were included

in the orientation and that everyone had a chance to get to know each other.

Enterprising   Enterprising types prefer working with other people to achieve organizational goals or material outcomes. They possess skills in leadership and persuasion. They value political and economic achievement and tend to be domineering, extraverted, self-confident, talkative, and adventurous. Scott, the entrepreneur who wanted to be sure he was getting something in return for his involvement, was the Enterprising member of the planning team.

Conventional   Conventional types like activities that involve working with data in systematic, orderly, and explicit ways. They are competent at clerical and computational tasks. They value business and monetary achievement and can be described as conforming, efficient, inflexible, practical, and unimaginative. Jeff represented the Conventional type in the first group. He was interested in doing things efficiently by using existing materials and saw no need for new ideas.

Holland's theory of personality type and vocational environments is one of the best-known theories in the fields of counseling and student affairs. A major reason for the popularity of Holland's is its simplicity. The theory is easy to use and understand. Concepts are clearly defined, and the hypotheses are well-delineated. . . . It has applicability not only to vocational decision making but also to many other areas, such as group interaction, design of programming, and structuring of effective work and living environments. . . . At a time when career decision making is becoming a much more challenging process for many people because of the increasing complexity of society, Holland provides a tool for simplifying and understanding some of the many factors involved. Holland's theory also helps us understand individual behavior and interpersonal interactions in a variety of settings.

ACTIVITIES AND QUESTIONS FOR REFLECTION

1. *Which of the personality types do you identify as most like yourself?*

2. *In the story at the beginning of the reading, which person took the position that you might have taken in this situation? Does the description of the character's type match one of the types you felt reflected your personality? Why or why not?*

3. *What vocational choices do you think might match your personality type? Why?*

4. *If you were able to create the perfect job for yourself, what would it be? Address as many aspects of the work environment as you can. Indoors or outdoors? Physical or sedentary? Office or industrial plant? Solitary or social? What level of responsibility? Reflective or active? Consistent or changing?*

IN THE CONCLUDING READING, Arthur Chickering, now a distinguished professor at Union Institute at Vermont College and Research Professor at the New England Resource Center for Higher Education at the University of Massachusetts, brings together the four major themes in this text: developing as a person, developing as a learner, becoming an educated person, and becoming employable. Chickering argues not only that education, but liberal education, will provide you with the abilities needed for success in the workplace both today and tomorrow. He argues further that your personal development—which he calls ego development—is inextricably linked to your cognitive development—your development as a thinker and learner.

AS YOU READ, look first for the outcomes of a liberal education that are required for successful careers according to Chickering, and second, the links between personal or ego development and liberal education.

LIBERAL EDUCATION, WORK, AND HUMAN DEVELOPMENT
Arthur W. Chickering

Since Cambridge University began 600 years ago, colleges and universities have assumed that liberal education and preparation for work go hand in hand. A college education should lead to a better job as well as a better life. You probably want your education to lead to a good job and a good life also. But can you pursue a rich liberal education and also come out prepared for a successful career? Or do our current social conditions and work requirements mean they must be addressed separately?

Liberal Education

One of the first, and best, definitions of liberal education comes from Cardinal Newman's *The Idea of a University* (1852):

> A University training . . . aims at raising the intellectual tone of society, at cultivating the

Adapted for this book by the author in 1994. Original work was "Integrating Liberal Education, Work and Human Development," *American Association for Higher Education Bulletin*, Vol. 33, No. 7, March 1981, pp. 1, 11–13, 16. Reprinted by permission.

public mind, at purifying the national taste, at supplying true principles to popular enthusiasm, and fixed aims to popular aspiration in facilitating the exercise of political power and refining the intercourse of private life. It gives one a clear conscious view of one's own opinions and judgments, a truth in developing them, an eloquence in expressing them, and a force in urging them. It teaches one to see things as they are, to go right to the point, to disentangle a skein of thought, to detect what is sophisticated, and to discard what is irrelevant. It prepares one to fill any post with credit and to master any subject with facility. It shows one how to accommodate oneself to others, how to influence them, how to come to an understanding with them, how to bear with them. One is at home in any society, one has common ground with every class, one knows when to speak and when to be silent, one is able to converse, one is able to listen, one can ask a question pertinently and gain a lesson seasonably when one has nothing to impart oneself. . . . One is a pleasant companion and a comrade you can depend on. . . . One has a repose of mind which lives in itself, while it lives in the world, and which has resources for its happiness at home when it cannot go abroad.

Take that paragraph apart and you have the key objectives for liberal education:

- Communication skills—"an eloquence in expressing them and a force in urging them."
- Critical thinking skills—"to see things as they are, to go right to the point, to disen-

tangle a skein of thought, to detect what is sophisticated, and to discard what is irrelevant."

- Interpersonal competence, respect for others, empathy—"how to accommodate oneself to others, how to influence them, how to come to an understanding with them, how to bear with them."
- Preparation for work and learning how to learn—"to fill any post with credit and to master any subject with facility."
- Cultural sophistication and cross-cultural understanding—"one is at home in any society, one has a common ground with every class."
- Capacity for intimacy—"a pleasant companion and comrade you can depend on."
- Clarity of values and integrity—"a clear conscious view of one's own opinions and judgments, a truth in developing them."
- A basic sense of identity—"a repose of mind which lives in itself, while it lives in the world."

That's a good list. You probably would like to achieve many of those outcomes yourself. There may be others you might want to add, like computer literacy, computational skills, developing artistic talents. But perhaps this list will serve as we turn to preparation for work.

Preparation for Work

The Bible says that work became necessary because of a divine curse. When Adam ate the apple, he threw away Paradise without toil and turned the world into a workhouse.

Today we view work not as a curse but a blessing. Useful work is an antidote to stagnation. Complex, challenging work is a major stimulus for personal development. Achievement, contribution, and productivity are the cornerstones for self-respect.

Our changing orientation toward work grows out of the changing nature of *work*, away from repetitive, mindless, physically demanding drudgery, toward "service workers" and "knowledge workers." The key to effective service is *quality*, not *quantity*. Achieving high-quality service is more complicated than producing high-quality goods. A television set is a complex instrument, but producing high-quality sets in large numbers is much easier than producing high-quality programming. Designing high-powered automobiles and supersonic airplanes requires high-level technological skills but we are far from designing environments and transportation systems that effectively serve human needs. To work in this kind of "post-industrial" and "post-technological" knowledge and service society, with rapidly changing job structures and a global economy, you need broad-based competence and adaptability.

There is a growing body of research that identifies the skills, abilities, and personal characteristics required for effective careers. One of the early studies by George Klemp [an expert in competency based assessment of job skills] and his colleagues examined a variety of career areas including human services, military services, small businesses, police work, sales, civil service, and industry management among others. What did they find?

Our most consistent—though unexpected—finding is that the amount of knowledge one acquires of a content area is generally unrelated to superior performance in an occupation and is often unrelated even to marginally acceptable performance. Certainly many occupations require a minimum level of knowledge on the part of the individual for the satisfactory discharge of work-related duties, but even more occupations require only that the individual be willing and able to learn new things. . . . In fact, it is neither the acquisition of knowledge nor the use of knowledge that distinguishes the outstanding performer, but rather the *cognitive skills* that are developed and exercised in the process of acquiring and using knowledge. These *cognitive* skills constitute the first factor of occupational success.

What cognitive skills are most important to success at work?

1. Information processing skills related to learning, recall, and forgetting.

2. Conceptualizing skills [which] enable individuals to bring order to the informational chaos that consistently surrounds them. . . . such skills go beyond an ability to analyze. . . . They involve an ability to synthesize information from a prior analysis.

3. The ability to understand many sides of a controversial issue. Persons with this skill can resolve informational conflicts better than persons who can't conceptualize in this way. Persons without such skills typically resolve conflicts by denying the validity of other points of view and are

equipped to mediate disputes or to understand what their positions have in common with the positions of others.

4. The ability to learn from experience . . . , the ability to translate observations from work experience into a theory that can be used to generate behavioral alternatives.

The second major factor linked with success in the world of work involves *interpersonal* skills:

1. Non-verbal Communication—"Fluency and precision in speaking and writing is important of course, but often it is the nonverbal component of communication, both in sending and receiving information, that has the greater impact."

2. "Accurate empathy"—the ability to *diagnose* a human concern and to respond appropriately to the needs of the other. There are three aspects to this skill: (a) positive regard for others, (b) giving another person assistance, whether asked for or not, that enables that other person to be effective, and (c) controlling hostility or anger that, when unleashed on another, make that person feel powerless and ineffective.

But these cognitive and interpersonal skills by themselves do not guarantee superior performance. The third critical factor is *motivation.*

Motivation is, a need state . . . and for a variety of reasons people are often unable to translate their dispositions into effective action . . . This variable describes a person who habitually thinks in terms of cause and outcomes as opposed to one who sees the self as an ineffective victim of events that have an unknown cause. . . . . Our own analysis of complex management jobs . . . has shown that a person who takes a proactive stance, who initiates action and works to dissolve blocks to progress, will, with few exceptions, have the advantage over a person who is reactive, who does not seek new opportunities, but sees the world as a series of insurmountable obstacles.

So effective performance in the world of work involves a clear set of cognitive skills, interpersonal skills, and motivational characteristics. You probably have some of these skills already well-developed. But you can use courses and classes as well as activities outside of the academic program to improve them and work on others which need strengthening. The chart below compares Newman and Klemp. There seems to be a striking agreement. This agreement supports higher education's traditional assumptions about the congruence of a liberal education and preparation for work.

Human Development

How do our desired outcomes for liberal education, and the skills and personal characteristics required for effective careers, correspond with what we know about major dimensions of human development? Jane Loevinger's research and theory concerning ego development provide one of the most comprehensive formulations currently available. "Ego development" is a good way to approach the issue because it is a "master trait" whose different structures heavily influence our perceptions, our thinking, and

Liberal Education and Preparation for Work	
Newman: Liberal education objectives	**Klemp:** Competence and characteristics for work
Clarity of values, integrity	
Communication skills	Communication skills
Critical thinking skills	Information processing skills, conceptualizing skills
Preparation for work	
Learning how to learn	Ability to learn from experience
Cross-cultural understanding	Ability to understand many sides of a complex issue
Empathy, understanding, respect for others	Accurate empathy, positive regard for others
Loyalty and intimacy	Giving assistance, controlling impulsive feelings
Sense of self in social and historical context	Define oneself as actor, cognitive initiative, proactive stance

our behavior. Loevinger posits four structures or areas of ego development, namely, (a) *impulse control* and *character development,* (b) *interpersonal style,* (c) *conscious preoccupations,* and (d) *cognitive style.* There is a sequence of developmental stages in these four structures beginning with the "Pre-social" and "Symbiotic" stages associated with infancy and childhood. The six major stages associated with adolescence and adulthood range from "Impulsive," "Self-protective," "Conformist," "Conscientious," "Autonomous," and "Integrated." The higher stages are conceptually complex and have high tolerance for ambiguity. For example, integrated persons have reconciled their inner conflicts, renounced the unattainable, and cherish individuality.

The higher stages of the four structures integrate areas of development that include

the major kinds of competence and personal characteristics addressed by Newman and found by Klemp, which are associated with liberal education and preparation for work. For example, the structures labeled *conscious preoccupations* and *cognitive style* describe the kinds of changes necessary to achieve high level communication skills, critical thinking ability, information processing and conceptualizing skills, and the ability to understand many sides of a complex issue. The structures labeled impulse control, character development, and interpersonal style describe the changes necessary for cross-cultural understanding; respect, empathy, and positive regard for others; giving assistance; and controlling impulsive feelings.

Ego development theory shows that when you pursue a liberal education and the skills and characteristics required for successful work you are tackling the bedrock task of taking charge of your own development. Can you pursue a liberal education and prepare for successful work at the same time? Certainly. In fact, if you short-change yourself in achieving some of these key outcomes for liberal education, you will lack some of the key characteristics required for a successful career and, more importantly, you will fall short of achieving your own developmental potential for a rich, complex, challenging life.

ACTIVITIES AND QUESTIONS FOR REFLECTION

1. *What is the relationship between liberal education and career success according to Chickering?*

2. *How does your personal, or ego, development affect your overall success in education and your career according to this author?*

3. *As an outcome of this final reading, how do you see your education enabling you to take control of your life?*

CHAPTER 7

↤ *Education and Work*

SUMMARY

As each of these readings has explained in a different way, workers of tomorrow will be expected to assume greater responsibility for the nature of their work than in the past. Preparing for these tasks will be much more like the preparation for leadership that was expected from the college graduates in the early part of the twentieth century. The task of a leader is very different than that of a follower. It requires imagination, planning, goal setting, resource allocation, people skills, and systems thinking, as well as completing assigned tasks. Preparation for leadership means much more than mastering a technical skill or proficiency in job-specific knowledge.

As you begin your college education, this is the ideal time to determine how you will learn the skills necessary to assume the required level of responsibility in the workplace. The college environment is an excellent place to develop these skills, *if* you take this opportunity to research and plan your education well.

Using the Internet

An important factor in career success is finding the right career. Holland, who focused on matching personalities with job requirements and interests, developed the Self-Directed Search, which is now available on the Internet. The Self-Directed Search has been used by more than 22 million people worldwide and translated into 25 different languages. A sample test result with an interpretation by Robert C. Reardon is available for review, and you can also take the test yourself for a small fee. The Web site contains more information on the personality styles, the 750 vocations they correlate with, and the method of determining the three-letter code that is used to link personalities with vocations.

1. Using the Web site, www.self-directed-search.com/, determine what personality type you may be and look at jobs that match that personality type.

2. Using email or other means, identify someone currently working in an occupation in which you might be interested and interview him or her about

the preparation needed for that occupation. To locate this person if you don't know someone, there are Yahoo Groups for every conceivable subject: www.groups.yahoo.com/. Yahoo Groups are special interest email lists that you may join to discuss topics with members. There are thousands and thousands of groups. As always on public lists, guard your personal information.

SUMMARIZING ACTIVITIES AND QUESTIONS FOR REFLECTION

1. *The* Occupational Outlook Handbook *is in your college or public library or online at www.bls.gov/oco/home.htm. Look up the occupations you may be interested in and review the predictions about educational requirements and employment opportunities. How would you fit these jobs and how would the preparation fit your current plans for college?*

2. *Review your statement of goals for college and your educated person statement and modify them based on your readings and activities in this chapter.*

    Take time to think about this. Skim back through the readings. Review your responses to activities and your journal. Identify ideas that seemed important or relevant to you. Writing your ideas will help you clarify and preserve them for future reference as you continue your college studies.

Conclusion

At the end of a study it is important to reflect on your experience and integrate your learning. In the introduction to this text, you were asked to think about why you are going to college, what you hope to achieve in your education. Then readings and activities were presented to broaden your sense of what a college education might mean for you. Now is the time to consider how your ideas have changed since you began this study and how they have affected your goals for your college education. The readings presented information and ideas about

- The nature and purposes of college with an emphasis on the role of the liberal arts and sciences and an understanding of the importance of cultural awareness in education,

- The ways people grow in adulthood and the ways you may want to use your college education to develop as a whole person, not just absorb information and gain skills, and

- Thinking and learning presented ideas you may want to consider in assessing your approach to your college studies so you can become a more curious and thoughtful student.

The final readings presented the realities of the changing workplace and the ways your education can contribute to your employability. Your employability involves not only the subjects studied or the designation of your degree as "business" or "education" but it also means becoming an effective learner who can manage change and confront an unknown future as a healthy person and a productive member of society.

Throughout the text you were asked to write and revise a statement about your goals for college and an educated person statement to help you define your own personal goals for college and to think about how your college education will prepare you for learning throughout your life.

To help you bring together the information you have gathered and the new perspectives you have gained, take time to skim back through the readings, review your responses to activities, your journal entries, and particularly, the changes in your definition of an educated person and your statement of educational purposes. Identify the ideas that seemed important or relevant to you. Then try to write a final statement describing the qualities and goals you want to achieve in your education. These may include studies you want to pursue, understandings you want to achieve, and personal qualities you may want to develop. Writing your ideas will help you clarify them and will preserve them as a guide as you continue your college program.

And finally, as a reflective and critical learner, also consider the ways in which this text might have helped you learn more, understand more, and accomplish more. What was helpful to you and what was not? How could the text have been more useful? What would you include that was not included? Which authors seemed most relevant to you? Which readings triggered new ideas? What other readings or activities would you have included?

If you would like to share your ideas and comments, you may subscribe to a discussion list for students and instructors using the text, orientationtocollege@yahoogroups.com, by sending a blank message to orientationtocollege-subscribe@yahoogroups.com or send your comments to the author of the revised edition at orientationtocollege@sharonvillines.com.

Bibliography

This bibliography includes the primary sources for the readings and other selected publications and references mentioned in the readings.

Association of American Colleges. *Integrity in the College Curriculum: A Report to the Academic Community*. Second edition. Washington, DC: The Association of American Colleges, 1990.

————. *Liberal Learning and the Arts and Sciences Major,* Volume 1: *The Challenge of Connecting Learning*. Project on Liberal Learning, Study in Depth, and the Arts and Science Major. Washington, DC: Association of American Colleges and Universities, 1991.

Atwell, Robert H. "What Does Society Need from Higher Education?" In *An American Imperative: Higher Expectations for Higher Education* by the Wingspread Group on Higher Education. Racine, WI: Johnson Foundation, 1993.

Banks, James A. "Multicultural Education for Freedom's Sake." *Educational Leadership,* 49, No. 4 (December 1991/January 1992): 32–36.

Belenky, Mary F., Blythe M. Clinchy, Nancy R. Goldberger, and Jill M. Tarule. *Women's Ways of Knowing: The Development of Self, Voice and Mind*. New York: Basic Books, 1986.

Bellah, Robert, Richard Madison, William Sullivan, Ann Swindler, and Steven Lipton. *Habits of the Heart: Individualism and Commitment in American Life*. New York: Harper & Row, 1985.

Bloom, Allan. *The Closing of the American Mind*. New York: Simon and Schuster, 1987.

Booth, Wayne C. "What Is an Idea?" In *The Harper & Row Reader: Liberal Education through Reading and Writing* by Gregory, Marshall W., and Wayne C. Booth. Third edition. New York: HarperCollins, 1992.

Bowen, Howard R. "The Baccalaureate Degree: What Does It Mean? What Should It Mean?" *American Association for Higher Education Bulletin,* 34, No. 3 (November 1981): 11–15.

Boyer, Ernest L. *College: The Undergraduate Experience in America.* A Report of the Carnegie Foundation for the Advancement of Teaching. New York: Harper & Row, 1987.

Boyett, Joseph H. "21st Century Workplace Trends and Their Implications." Paper posted at the Joseph H. Boyett and Associates Web site, http://www.jboyett.com/trends.htm. Copyright 2002.

Brookfield, Stephen D. "Exploring Self-Directedness in Learning." In *Understanding and Facilitating Adult Learning: A Comprehensive Analysis of Principles and Effective Practices.* San Francisco: Jossey-Bass, 1986.

———. *Developing Critical Thinkers: Challenging Adults to Explore Alternative Ways of Thinking and Acting.* San Francisco: Jossey-Bass, 1987.

Bruffee, Kenneth A. *Collaborative Learning.* Baltimore, MD: Johns Hopkins University Press, 1993.

Brush, Carey W. "The Liberal Studies and Institutional Excellence." In *The Necessary Learning* edited by Robert Moynihan. Lanham, MD: University Press of America, 1989.

Chickering, Arthur W. "Integrating Liberal Education, Work and Human Development." *American Association for Higher Education Bulletin,* 33, No. 7 (March 1981): 1, 11–13, 16.

_____ and Linda Reisser. *Education and Identity.* Second edition. San Francisco: Jossey-Bass, 1993.

_____ and Nancy K. Schlossberg. "Your Preferred Learning Style." In *Getting the Most Out of College.* Boston: Allyn & Bacon, 1995.

Committee on Policy for Racial Justice. *The Inclusive University.* Washington, DC: Joint Center for Political and Economic Studies, 1993.

Corey, Gerald, and Marianne Schneider Corey. "Maslow's Theory of Self-Actualization." In *I Never Knew I Had a Choice.* Pacific Grove, CA: Brooks/Cole, 2002.

Csikszentmihalyi, Mahaly. *Flow: The Psychology of Optimal Experience.* New York: HarperCollins, 1991.

Daloz, Laurent A. "Beyond Tribalism: Renaming the Good, the True, and the Beautiful." *Adult Education Quarterly,* 38, No. 4 (Summer, 1988): 234–241.

Dewey, John. *Democracy and Education: An Introduction to the Philosophy of Education.* New York: Free Press, 1944.

Elkind, David. "Erickson's Eight Stages of Man." In *Readings in Adult Psychology: Contemporary Perspectives* edited by Lawrence R. Allman and Dennis T. Jaffee. New York: Harper & Row, 1977, pp. 3–11.

Erikson, Erik. *Childhood and Society.* Second edition. New York: Norton, 1963.

Evans, Nancy C., Deanna S. Forney, and Florence Guido-DiBrito. "Holland's Theory of Vocational Personalities and Environments." In *Student Development in College: Theory, Research, and Practice*. San Francisco: Jossey-Bass, 1998.

Friere, Paulo. *The Politics of Education: Culture, Power, and Liberation*. South Hadley, MA: Bergin and Garvin, 1985.

Giamatti, A. Bartlett. *A Free and Ordered Space: The Real World of the University*. New York: Norton, 1988.

Gibbs, Graham. *Teaching Students to Learn: A Student-centered Approach*. Buckingham, UK: Open University Press, 1981.

Gregory, Marshall W., and Wayne C. Booth. *The Harper & Row Reader: Liberal Education through Reading and Writing*. Third edition. New York: HarperCollins, 1992.

Gross, Ronald. *Peak Learning*. New York: Putnam/Tarcher, 1991.

Hirsch, E. D. *Cultural Literacy*. Boston: Houghton Mifflin, 1987.

Jones, Thomas B., Editor. *The Educated Person: A Collection of Contemporary American Essays*. Revised edition. St. Paul, MN: Metropolitan State University, 1989.

King, Patricia M. "How Do We Know? Why Do We Believe? Learning to Make Reflective Judgments." *Liberal Education*, 78, No. 1 (January/February 1992): 2–5.

———. and Karen S. Kitchener. *Developing Reflective Judgment: Understanding and Promoting Intellectual Growth and Critical Thinking in Adolescents and Adults*. San Francisco: Jossey-Bass, 1994.

Knefelkamp, L. Lee. "Seasons of Academic Life: Honoring Our Collective Autobiography." *Liberal Education*, 76, No. 3, May/June 1990.

Knowles, Malcolm S. *The Self-Directed Learner*. New York: Association Press, 1975.

———. "Fostering Competence in Self-Directed Learning." In *Learning to Learn Across the Lifespan* edited by Robert M. Smith and Associates. San Francisco: Jossey-Bass, 1990.

Kolb, David. *Experiential Learning: Experience as a Source of Learning and Development*. Englewood Cliffs, NJ: Prentice Hall, 1984.

Kurfiss, Joanne Gainen. *Critical Thinking: Theory, Research, Practice, and Possibilities*. ASHE-ERIC Higher Education Report No. 2. Washington, DC: Association for the Study of Higher Education, 1988.

Levinson, Daniel S. *Seasons of a Man's Life*. New York: Knopf, 1978.

———. "A Conception of Adult Development." *American Psychologist*, 41, No. 1 (January 1986): 3–13.

Loevinger, Jane. *Ego Development: Conceptions and Theories*. San Francisco: Jossey-Bass, 1976.

Mezirow, Jack, and Associates. *Fostering Critical Reflection in Adulthood: A Guide to Transformative and Emancipatory Learning*. San Francisco: Jossey-Bass, 1990.

Moynihan, Robert, Editor. *The Necessary Learning*. Lanham, MD: University Press of America, 1989.

National Research Council. "Learning and Brain Development." In *How People Learn: Brain, Mind, Experience, and School*. Washington, DC: National Academy Press, 2000.

National Society for the Study of Education. *Cultural Literacy and the Idea of General Education*. 87th Yearbook, Part II. Chicago: University of Chicago Press, 1988.

Newman, Barbara M., and Philip R. Newman. "Individual Identity Versus Identity Confusion." In *Development Through Life: A Psychosocial Approach*. Eighth edition. Belmont, CA: Wadsworth, 2003.

Newman, John Henry Cardinal. *The Idea of a University*. New York: Doubleday, 1959.

Pellegrino, Edmund D. "Having a Degree and Being Educated." In *Foundations: A Reader for New College Students* edited by Virginia N. Gordon and Thomas Minnick. Second edition. Belmont, CA: Wadsworth Learning, 2002.

Perkinson, Henry J. "The Educated Person: A Changing Ideal." *New York University Education Quarterly*, 10, No. 2 (Winter 1979): 17–21.

Perry, William G. *Forms of Intellectual and Ethical Development in the College Years: A Scheme*. New York: Holt, Rinehart and Winston, 1978.

Pierce, David R. "What Does Society Need from Higher Education?" In *An American Imperative: Higher Expectations for Higher Education* by the Wingspread Group on Higher Education. Racine, WI: Johnson Foundation, 1993.

Purves, Alan C. "General Education and the Search for a Common Culture." In *Cultural Literacy and the Idea of General Education* by the National Society for the Study of Education. 87th Yearbook, Part II. Chicago: University of Chicago Press, 1988.

Restak, Theodore. *The Brain*. New York: Bantam, 1988.

Rosovsky, Henry. *The University: An Owners Manual*. New York: Norton, 1990.

Rudolph, Frederick. *The American College and University: A History*. Athens, GA: University of Georgia Press, 1990.

Scott, Joan Wallach. "The Campaign Against Political Correctness: What's Really at Stake." *Change*, 23 (Nov/Dec 1991): 30–43.

Senge, Peter. *The Fifth Discipline: The Art and Practice of the Learning Organization*. New York: Doubleday Dell, 1990.

Smith, Robert M. *Learning How to Learn: Applied Theory for Adults*. Englewood Cliffs, NJ: Prentice-Hall, 1988.

———, and Associates. *Learning to Learn Across the Life Span*. San Francisco: Jossey-Bass, 1990.

Strasser, Bruce E. "Beyond the Machine: Liberal Education for an Information Society." In *The Necessary Learning* edited by Robert Moynihan. Lanham, MD: University Press of America, 1989.

Takaki, Ronald. "An Educated and Culturally Literate Person Must Study America's Multicultural Reality." *Chronicle of Higher Education*, 35, No. 26 (March 8, 1989): B1–2.

————. *From Different Shores: Perspectives on Race and Ethnicity in America.* Second edition. New York: Oxford University Press, 1994.

U.S. Department of Labor. Report of Secretary's Commission on Achieving Necessary Skills (SCANS). *What Work Requires of Schools: A SCANS Report for America 2000.* Washington, DC: U.S. Department of Labor, 1993.

Useem, Michael. *Liberal Education and the Corporation: The Hiring and Advancement of College Graduates.* New York: Aldine de Gruyter, 1989.

Weathersby, Rita. "Life Stages and Learning Interests." Paper presented at the annual conference of the American Association for Higher Education, Chicago, March 20, 1978.

————. "Developing a Global Perspective: A Crucial 'Changing of Our Minds'." *Journal of Management Education,* 16, Special Issue (December 1992): 10–23.

Whitehead, Alfred North. *The Aims of Education and Other Essays.* New York: Macmillan, 1929.

Wingspread Group on Higher Education. *An American Imperative: Higher Expectations for Higher Education.* Racine, WI: Johnson Foundation, 1993.

↢ Index